I0729724

HANS MEMLING

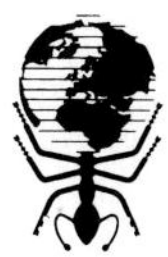

Books in the RENAISSANCE LIVES series explore and illustrate the life histories and achievements of significant artists, rulers, intellectuals and scientists in the early modern world. They delve into literature, philosophy, the history of art, science and natural history and cover narratives of exploration, statecraft and technology.

Series Editor: François Quiviger

Already published

Albrecht Dürer: Art and Autobiography *David Ekserdjian*
Aldus Manutius: The Invention of the Publisher *Oren Margolis*
Andreas Vesalius: Anatomy and the World of Books *Sashiko Kusukawa*
Botticelli: Artist and Designer *Ana Debenedetti*
Artemisia Gentileschi and Feminism in Early Modern Europe *Mary D. Garrard*
Benvenuto Cellini and the Embodiment of the Modern Artist *Andreas Beyer*
Blaise Pascal: Miracles and Reason *Mary Ann Caws*
Botticelli: Artist and Designer *Ana Debenedetti*
Caravaggio and the Creation of Modernity *Troy Thomas*
Descartes: The Renewal of Philosophy *Steven Nadler*
Donatello and the Dawn of Renaissance Art *A. Victor Coonin*
Erasmus of Rotterdam: The Spirit of a Scholar *William Barker*
Filippino Lippi: An Abundance of Invention *Jonathan K. Nelson*
Giorgione's Ambiguity *Tom Nichols*
Hans Holbein: The Artist in a Changing World *Jeanne Nuechterlein*
Hans Memling and the Merchants *Mitzi Kirkland-Ives*
Hieronymus Bosch: Visions and Nightmares *Nils Büttner*
Isaac Newton and Natural Philosophy *Niccolò Guicciardini*
Jan van Eyck within His Art *Alfred Acres*
John Donne: In the Shadow of Religion *Andrew Hadfield*
John Evelyn: A Life of Domesticity *John Dixon Hunt*
Leon Battista Alberti: The Chameleon's Eye *Caspar Pearson*
Leonardo da Vinci: Self, Art and Nature *François Quiviger*
Lucas Cranach: From German Myth to Reformation *Jennifer Nelson*
Machiavelli: From Radical to Reactionary *Robert Black*
Michelangelo and the Viewer in His Time *Bernadine Barnes*
Paracelsus: An Alchemical Life *Bruce T. Moran*
Petrarch: Everywhere a Wanderer *Christopher S. Celenza*
Piero della Francesca and the Invention of the Artist *Machtelt Brüggen Israëls*
Piero di Cosimo: Eccentricity and Delight *Sarah Blake McHam*
Pieter Bruegel and the Idea of Human Nature *Elizabeth Alice Honig*
Raphael and the Antique *Claudia La Malfa*
Rembrandt's Holland *Larry Silver*
Robert Hooke's Experimental Philosophy *Felicity Henderson*
Rubens's Spirit: From Ingenuity to Genius *Alexander Marr*
Rudolf ii: The Life and Legend of the Mad Emperor *Thomas DaCosta Kaufmann*
Salvator Rosa: Paint and Performance *Helen Langdon*
Thomas Nashe and Late Elizabethan Writing *Andrew Hadfield*
Titian's Touch: Art, Magic and Philosophy *Maria H. Loh*
Tycho Brahe and the Measure of the Heavens *John Robert Christianson*
Ulisse Aldrovandi: Naturalist and Collector *Peter Mason*

HANS MEMLING

and the Merchants

MITZI KIRKLAND-IVES

REAKTION BOOKS

Published by Reaktion Books Ltd
Unit 32, Waterside
44–48 Wharf Road
London N1 7UX, UK
www.reaktionbooks.co.uk

First published 2025

Printed and bound in India by Replika Press Pvt. Ltd

A catalogue record for this book is available from the British Library

ISBN 978 1 83639 031 2

COVER: Detail from Hans Memling, *Madonna and Child with Angels*, *c.* 1490, oil on panel. National Gallery of Art, Washington, DC (Andrew W. Mellon Collection, 1937.1.41).

CONTENTS

Introduction 7

1 Memling's Life: A Biographical Sketch 17

2 Memling's Bruges 53

3 Memling's Career in Bruges:
The Painter's Workshop 94

4 Memling and His Clientele 129

Conclusion 192

CHRONOLOGY 203

REFERENCES 207

SELECT BIBLIOGRAPHY 255

PHOTO ACKNOWLEDGEMENTS 259

INDEX 261

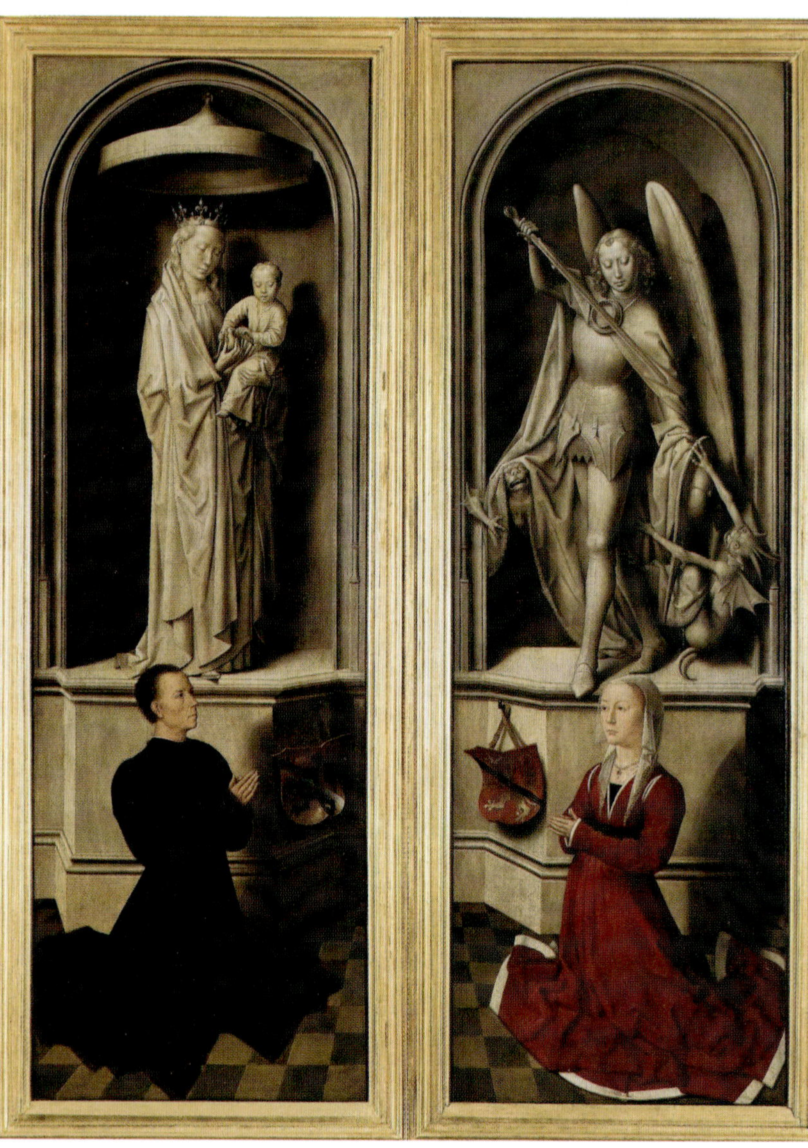

Introduction

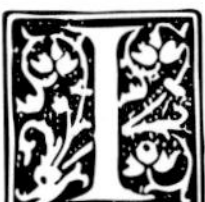In the early years of his career in the Flemish city of Bruges, Hans Memling received a substantial commission from a prominent international client, an indication that already – shortly after the painter's arrival in the city in 1465 as an immigrant from southern Germany – he enjoyed a promising reputation. This imposing triptych, now preserved in the National Museum in Gdansk, presents the theme of the Last Judgement in its opened state, which typically would have been visible on Sundays and feast days (illus. 2). The archangel Michael stands in gleaming gold armour at the centre of the composition, his lush brocade cape secured by a richly bejewelled morse and his wings tipped with peacock feathers. The nude figures he weighs with his scales – one kneeling with his hands clasped reverently, one writhing in agony – serve as representatives of the hosts of figures that emerge from their graves across the landscape, the saved and the damned who are subsequently sorted by angels and demons and directed towards the side panels of the triptych.

To the viewer's right the hills and low mountains visible in the distance across the bleak plain of the landscape rise into jagged rocks that fill the right wing of the triptych. Here the terrified damned – nude bodies depicted in a virtuoso range of foreshortened poses – are herded into flames by demons who carry out their duties with merciless zeal.

1 Hans Memling, *Triptych of the Last Judgement*, exterior: *Agnolo Tani and Caterina di Francesco Tanagli*, c. 1468–71, oil on oak.

To the viewer's left, the grassy groundcover breaks into col-umbines and lilies at the feet of the saved, who are welcomed on to a crystalline stairway by St Peter and an assisting angel with rosy wings; here, instead of flames, the rocky foreground features scattered gemstones and rose coral. Issued with robes by a line of angels, the saved are ushered through a lavishly dec-orated portal into a golden interior. The first figures to enter appear to be clerics, some tonsured and some wearing ecclesi-astical caps and mitres; a bishop and a cardinal are represented, and all that can be seen of the most distant figure is his papal tiara. In the portal's sculpted tympanum sits Christ in majesty, with a lamb at his feet and surrounded by the animal symbols of the four evangelists. The torsos of cherubim and seraphim ornament niches along the archivolts. The buttresses and portal jambs to the sides of the entrance present Old Testament kings, removing their crowns and playing a range of musical instruments, seem-ingly accompanied by the clusters of brightly coloured angels that sing and play from the top of the buttresses; one angel on the balustrade above the entrance drops a shower of assorted flowers upon the new arrivals to this heavenly city.

This sizeable, luxurious triptych was neither an ecclesiastical commission from a wealthy diocese or monastery, nor arranged by a civic government. In common with the vast majority of works in Memling's oeuvre, it was commissioned by a private citizen, who, as is often the case among Memling's clientele, was a member of the emergent bourgeoisie, a relatively new class of patrons of the arts. Neither was the patron a Flemish native; perhaps sur-prisingly, given its current location in Gdansk, this triptych was probably originally destined for the Florentine merchant banker Agnolo Tani's newly endowed family chapel at the Badia Fiesolana monastery outside Florence. Operating largely on behalf of the recently established northern branches representing the famously successful Medici family, Tani had been present in Bruges since

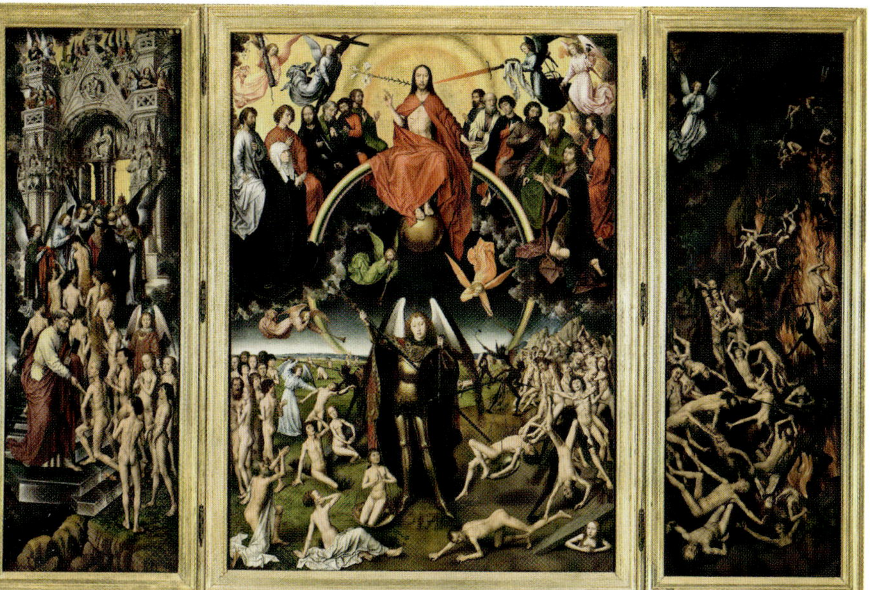

1450, serving as the Medici bank's branch manager there from
1455 until 1465. At this time he was replaced as manager and
returned to Florence, where he married the following year before
returning north, this time to the London branch.

The theme of the altarpiece, the Last Judgement, would have
been appropriate for this chapel, which was dedicated to St Michael,
the archangel who weighs souls at the centre of the composition
of the opened triptych (and who would have been Tani's name
saint).[1] Tani himself appears on the exterior of the triptych, which
would have been visible to viewers most days of the year (illus. 1).
Clad in sumptuous robes – jet-black and edged with grey fur
collar, cuffs and hem – Tani kneels piously with his hands raised in
prayer before a figure of Mary and the Christ Child. Depicted in
grisaille to simulate sculpted stone in an arched niche, the Virgin
stands crowned beneath a canopy, holding the robed Christ, who
reaches for the dove she bears in her right hand. On the opposite

2 Hans Memling, *Triptych of the Last Judgement*, interior, *c.* 1468–71, oil on oak.

wing, a grisaille figure of St Michael in armour twists gracefully while subduing two diminutive demons with his raised sword, similarly set in a niche behind the kneeling figure of Tani's spouse, Caterina di Francesco Tanagli. Like that of Tani, her costume is simultaneously inconspicuous and lavish, as befits her piety and her wealth: a voluminous gown in extravagant scarlet cloth trimmed with white ermine, her pearl pendant necklace complemented by the pearl edging of her otherwise simple white head-covering.

The motivations that led Tani and merchants like him to commission such works would have been varied. On the one hand, doing so served as an act of devotion. The production of religious art that would beautify chapels and inspire reverence was understood as part of a lifetime of pious activity intended to help secure his and his family's salvation. On the other hand, this good work would have been public or semi-public, and that it was a conspicuously expensive and magnificent work would have been immediately apparent to all who encountered it, as would have been the identity of Tani, upon whose wealth and good taste it depended. In this way such a pious act also served his efforts at status-building as a public demonstration of his financial and political achievements, and an implicit statement of his ambitions for the future; to sponsor such a grandiose work makes a claim to a certain social standing.

Such works often marked meaningful personal life events or successes. The date of this commission, for example, has been determined partly on the basis of Tani's biographical details, since he seems to have been preoccupied with his legacy in these years. One occasion that Tani may have wished to commemorate would have been his wedding in 1466, when he would have been in his early fifties and his bride in her early twenties.[2] Although he was no longer managing the Bruges branch, in the service of the Medici he was again sent north in 1467 to sort out the financial difficulties of the London branch, and he drew up a will before leaving for England. The triptych would have made a bold statement of his financial station, the importance of his family and lineage, and his piety at this important juncture in his life.[3]

Tani returned to Bruges as part of Margaret of York's cortège in late 1467 into 1468 and would have been able to check on Memling's progress and sit for additional portrait work.[4] If, as some have suggested, the work was not commissioned until 1469, it may have been arranged on his passage through Bruges en route again to Florence. Then it would have marked a different stage in his tumultuous career as he returned to the city of his birth, where the altarpiece would have been one of the earliest large Flemish works in the Florentine public eye.[5]

The work never reached its intended destination, however, and the fate of the completed altarpiece further testifies to the complex intersections of art, commerce and politics. The triptych was one of two altarpieces carried in a shipment belonging to Tommaso Portinari, Tani's successor as manager of the Bruges branch of the Medici bank (and whose portrait was added to the saved figure in Michael's scale, for reasons that are unclear). The galley in question was built for the Duke of Burgundy on Medici credit and sailed under the neutral Burgundian flag but was leased by Portinari as part of a venture fleet.[6] Destined for Pisa via England, it set off in 1473 from the port of Bruges, at Sluis. It was captured shortly after its departure, however, as it entered the sea just outside the Zwin inlet at Gravelines, by a privateer from Gdansk working for the Germanic Hanseatic League, Paul Beneke, who defended the piracy as a legitimate act of war against England.[7] Portinari reported the piracy in July that year, but despite the attempted intervention of the pope and the Duke of Burgundy, the altarpiece was installed in the chapel of the Confraternity of St George in the Church of Our Lady in Gdansk.[8] After continued protest by the Florentines, the civic government of Bruges eventually stepped in and paid the reparations in an effort to appease both the Italians and the Hanseatic cities, since each party's mercantile activity was considered vital to the economic prosperity of the city.[9]

Such a significant commission indicates that even immediately after Hans Memling's arrival in the city, he had built a reputation sufficient to have drawn the attention of Tani, who would by that time have been only intermittently present in Bruges. That Tani, a Florentine merchant banker, would have commissioned a work destined for a chapel in Tuscany from Memling, a south German painter working in Flanders, is a result of the distinctive environment of fifteenth-century Bruges (illus. 3). When Memling arrived in Bruges, it still boasted a reputation as one of the most active and impressive trading ports of northern Europe; the fourteenth-century *Merchants' Handbook* by Francesco Pegolotti of Florence describes the city as a commercial hub where merchants of different nations met to pursue business and finance, and Venetian handbooks likewise testified that Bruges was the regional centre of commerce.[10]

As foreigners, Memling and Tani were among the many international artists, merchants and courtiers who pursued careers in Bruges. Pero Tafur, a historian and author from Córdoba, Spain, had already experienced Rome, Venice, Cairo and Constantinople on his travels, but by the time he arrived in Flanders late in his journey in 1437 the splendour of the city still made an impression on him:

> This city of Bruges is a large and very wealthy city, and one of the greatest markets of the world . . . In the whole of the West there is no other great mercantile centre except Bruges, although England does some trade, and thither repair all the nations of the world, and they say that at times the number of ships sailing from the harbour

of Bruges exceeds seven hundred a day . . . the products of the whole world are brought here, so that they have everything in abundance, in exchange for the work of their hands. From this place is sent forth the merchandise of the world, woollen cloths and Arras cloths, all kinds of carpets, and many other things necessary to mankind, of which there is here a great abundance . . . Anyone who has money, and wishes to spend it, will find in this town alone everything which the whole world produces. I saw there oranges and lemons from Castile, which seemed only just to have been gathered from the trees, fruits and wine from Greece, as abundant as in that country. I saw also confections and spices from Alexandria, and all the Levant, just as if one were there; furs from the Black Sea, as if they had been produced in the district. Here was all Italy with its brocades, silks and armour, and everything

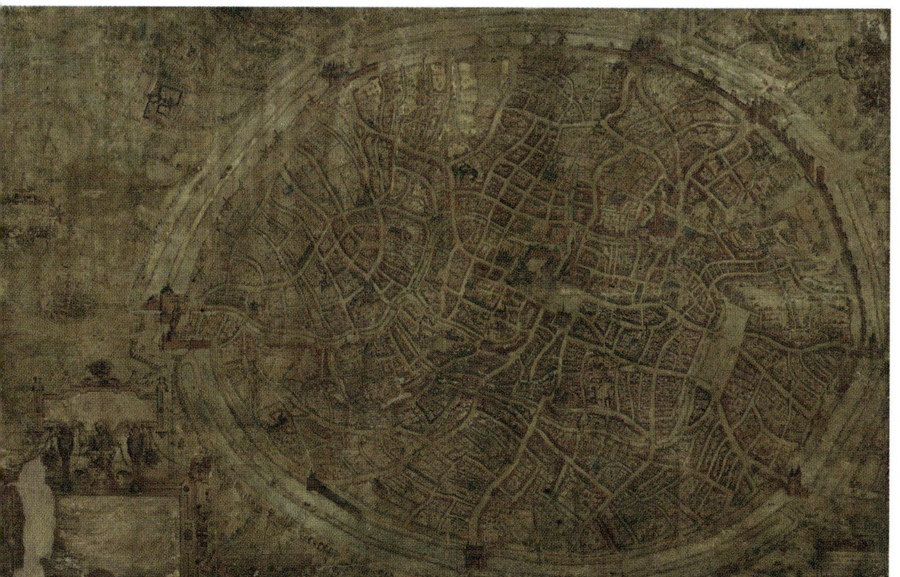

3 Marcus Gheeraerts, *Map of Bruges*, 1562–3, oil on canvas.

which is made there; and, indeed, there is no part of the world whose products are not found here at their best."

The merchants and merchant bankers who thrived in this environment would be Memling's principal clientele. Among his patrons who have been identified with some certainty are counted natives of Bruges and other Flemish merchants and politicians who had made the city their adopted home; numerous merchant bankers and diplomats from the Italian peninsula, from cities including Florence, Bologna and Venice; merchants from the member cities of the north German Hanseatic League, such as Lübeck; and patrons in the Kingdom of Castile, among others.

This book focuses on Memling and the artisanal class that he represented, the community of merchants, commodity bankers and brokers who constituted the core of his clientele, and the economic, social and built environment of the city of Bruges in which they interacted. It does not seek a complete accounting of Memling's oeuvre, but rather aims to focus attention on the manner in which his career intersected with this new commercial and economic milieu. While the earlier Burgundian period was dominated by such prominent artists as Melchior Broederlam, Claus Sluter and Jan van Eyck – each of whom served as *valets de chambre* for the dukes and produced works for major ecclesiastical institutions, city governments and the nobility – Memling's career is characterized above all by work for the local and international community of merchants and the developing bourgeoisie in the precise period in which the city's fortunes appear to have begun to turn as twilight fell on the Burgundian era.

The background setting of Memling's Bruges as a commercial centre reveals the circumstances that affected patterns of trade and economic opportunity in the city, and the factors and events that shaped the character of the artisanal and merchant classes. The latter included, on the one hand, Flemish merchants and other burghers, and, on the other, the various foreign merchant nations – together the emergent urban middle class that formed the vast bulk of Memling's clientele. The origins and life abroad of international merchants – their activity and their place in the built environment of the city (principally the merchant-nation houses and other commercial sites) – are considered in these chapters on a collective level, as are the lives and careers of their local counterparts who had adapted to the distinctive character of the city's economy.

If we continue to consider Memling himself as a burgher and as a professional artisan operating in the city, he was, in common with many others of the era, an immigrant seeking a career in the thriving economy of Bruges. This work investigates his integration within the community, how he adapted successfully to the market and fashions of both his era and his clients' preferences, and standard practices relating to contracts and the commissioning of artworks. Memling's workshop is considered as a typical late fifteenth-century commercial artistic operation, reviewing what is known about the location and character of his home and atelier, the traditions and civic government- and guild-imposed labour regulations that would have controlled that workshop, the training of personnel (apprentices and assistants) and the distribution of labour within the workshop. The 'home economics' of the workshop's expenses and the sourcing of required materials, such as pigments and supports, some of which would have been locally available but some of which would have had to be imported from distant cities or countries, further reveals much about business and trade as they affected the lives of artists in the period.

Finally, this book considers the intended destinations of several of Memling's artworks and the socio-political functions their owners hoped these commissions would serve. The individual identities of many of his clients are known with some confidence, and the general demographic identities of many others can be approximated. The careers and fortunes of the individual commissioners of some of Memling's most prominent works — those of the international community, such as the Florentines Tani and Portinari, and locals, among them Willem Moreel — are considered as case studies of the new class of entrepreneur at the heart of Memling's clientele, and of the aspirations that these artworks were meant to support. Their lives and their motivation for commissioning artworks are some of the many intersections between commerce and craft that shaped Memling's career in this cultural and economic environment and that are discussed in this book. As an international immigrant who succeeded in becoming the most sought-after artisan in late fifteenth-century Bruges, Memling's life is emblematic of this transitional moment as the city enjoyed the last years of its reign as the commercial capital of northern Europe.

ONE

Memling's Life: A Biographical Sketch

Over the last two centuries the contents of Memling's oeuvre have been debated and painstakingly reconstructed by scholars based on the starting point of his two signed and dated works: each dated 1479 in what is accepted as original paint on their frames, and both preserved at the Sint-Janshospitaal in Bruges, then one of the city's hospices and now the home of the Memlingmuseum. One of these, known as the St Johns altarpiece, was of significant size and destined for the high altar of the institution.

The second work was probably intended for a side chapel at the hospital and is a much smaller work at just under 80 centimetres (31½ in.) wide when opened, but it provides an example of the high craftsmanship and appeal of Memling's mid-career production. The individual who commissioned this elegant work is identified as Jan Floreins in the inscription that survives on the original frame; the frame's small lock is still attached. The closed view of the triptych rejects the frequent use in the later fifteenth century of grisaille on exterior panels in favour of vividly coloured figures set in lush landscapes, reserving the monochromatic illusion of painted stone for the decorative architectural surrounds that serve as internal framing devices (illus. 4). Serving as capitals to simulated marble columns, figures of Adam and Eve are set within contemporary Gothic niches on the left panel, and their expulsion from Paradise appears to the right. Seated on a grassy bank in the left panel, John the Baptist – Floreins's patron saint – gestures casually at the lamb that accompanies him; the saint's traditionally ascetic costume is ennobled by the scarlet mantle that envelops his body. In the meticulously rendered landscape, cool-hued hills recede into the distance. The tranquil body of water must represent the River Jordan, since a tiny narrative episode of the Baptism of Jesus appears in the middle ground: an angel clad in white stands on the bank holding Jesus' garments. The same hills and river appear to continue into the scene on the right wing, where Veronica sits humbly on the grassy outcropping of the foreground, clad in voluminous purple with white trim and delicately lifting the corners of the *sudarium* that miraculously bears Christ's features.

The wings and centre panel of the opened altarpiece depict scenes from Christ's infancy: the Holy Family in the Nativity to the left, the Adoration of the Magi at centre, and the Candlemas Presentation of Christ in the temple on the right (illus. 5). The last two scenes appear to be pared-down variations on compositions used in the Flemish master Rogier van der Weyden's Columba altarpiece: one of a number of correspondences throughout Memling's oeuvre that have suggested some connection to the older master, or at least Memling's presence at some point in Cologne, where he would have seen that work. In a derelict structure depicted on the left-hand panel the Virgin attends to the nude child, who rests on the edge of her blue mantle, as two small angels assist. Joseph observes from a discreet distance, standing alongside the curious cow and donkey and shielding the candle he holds from the wind; in the background, the shepherds presently arrive through a gate. On the right-hand panel Mary passes the child to Simeon in a temple interior featuring rounded arches that would have been old-fashioned at the time, perhaps inspired by the actual architecture of Bruges cathedral.[1] Anne watches the ritual closely, while

Joseph reaches into a wicker container, presumably for the occasion's requisite turtle doves.

In the centre panel the richly attired Magi arrive and present their gifts in the same crumbling building; the elder magus – whose offering has already been accepted by Joseph – bends over to kiss the feet of the child, and the middle-aged king kneels and offers a golden vessel. Removing his cap and dressed in a rich blue-and-gold brocade tunic, the youngest magus enters, recognizably of African origin (Memling may have witnessed Africans in Bruges among the retinues of Portuguese traders).[2] In the background the same entourage advances through the carefully rendered city streets on horses and camels. Floreins himself, aged 36 according to the inscription on the wall nearby, appears to the left in a black gown, his eyes cast down towards his prayer book and separated from the main event only by a low, crumbling rock wall. The young man who stands behind him has been tentatively identified as his youngest brother, Jacob, a spice merchant – the family trade in which Jan, too, would have operated before his vocation at Sint-Janshospitaal.[3]

Floreins joined the hospital in 1472, but there his duties were perhaps surprisingly worldly; he served as the wine-gauger and treasurer, and later master, of the institution. In these rather concrete and business-orientated offices he had responsibility for much of the hospital's economic and financial affairs, including the purchase of food, drink and other necessities, the receipt of rent from lands held in the Franc of Bruges and Flemish Zeeland, and the gauging of the imported wine that provided most of the institution's income.[4] With his mercantile background, he was perhaps naturally suited to these tasks; the administrators of such institutions were often recruited from among the city's prosperous semi-elite. Floreins is relatively well documented among Memling's clients, partly owing to a series of surviving account books in which he tracked the finances and

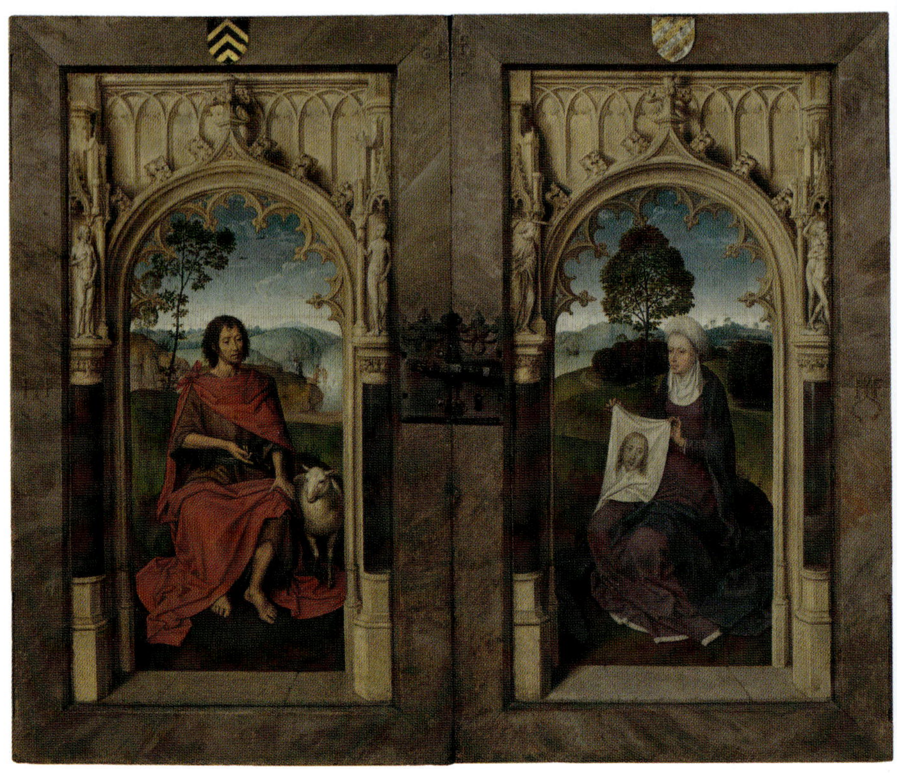

expenditures of the Sint-Janshospitaal during his tenure. Memling's work, on the other hand, while undeniably skilled and clearly holding great appeal to his client, for the large part must speak for itself, since the historical record of Memling's own life remains nearly silent. The dated frame on Floreins's altarpiece is one of the more solid facts to have been preserved.

Tantalizingly little archival evidence survives concerning Hans Memling's life, as is unfortunately the case for many personalities of the late medieval and early modern eras. The few references to him in published works from the sixteenth and seventeenth centuries are vague or contain factual errors or

4 Hans Memling, *Triptych of Jan Floreins*, exterior, 1479, oil on oak.

unsubstantiated assertions. Memling is, for example, described by the Italian merchant and writer Lodovico Guicciardini in his *Description of the Low Countries* of 1567 as a student of Rogier, a fact that is unconfirmed. Their successors cited by Guicciardini include numerous artists, including Petrus Christus and Justus van Ghent (both of whom pre-date Memling), claims that are echoed in Giorgio Vasari's *Lives of the Most Eminent Architects, Artists and Sculptors* (1550).[5] Carel van Mander's *Book of Painters* (1618) mentions 'Hans Memmelinck' among a roster of assorted painters, and specifically praises the *St Ursula Shrine* at the Sint-Janshospitaal (another object produced for that hospice) for its artfully rendered small figures.[6] Other than these terse indications and what is offered by the paintings themselves, precious little evidence has been unearthed. Meticulous research in recent centuries has, however, revealed some traces that clarify the contours of Memling's life.

This archival evidence suggests that Memling was drawn to Bruges as a cosmopolitan place of professional opportunity, an immigrant like so many others of the era seeking a career in the flourishing economy of the city. In his registration in the list of new residents who purchased full burgher status in the city – the so-called *Poortersboek* – Hans Memling is listed as having arrived from outside Flanders, stemming from 'Zaleghenstat'.[7] Additional

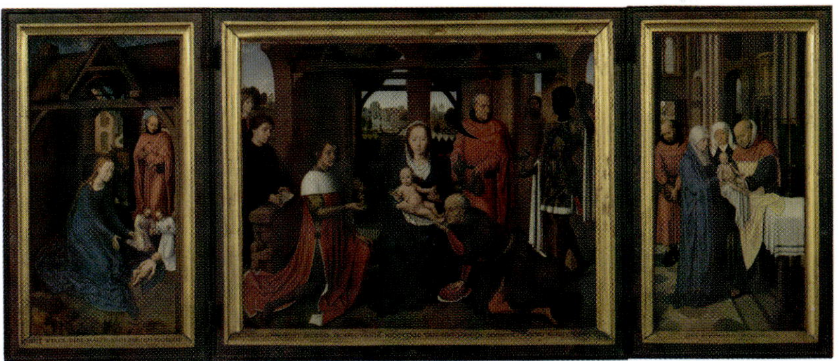

5 Hans Memling, *Triptych of Jan Floreins*, interior, 1479, oil on oak.

documentation confirms that this refers to the southern German town of Seligenstadt, a short distance upriver from Frankfurt am Main.[8] Surviving entries from 1451 and 1454 in the parish church of Seligenstadt record Memling's mother, Luca Styrn, and her second husband, Hamman Mommelingen, both of whom may have died in a plague outbreak recorded in local chronicles.[9] The varied spellings of this surname have suggested an ancestral origin in the town of Mömmlingen, southeast of Seligenstadt. Memling's father's occupation is unknown, but Luca Styrn's first husband, Henricus Appel, seems to have belonged to a prominent local family, some members of which served as mayors in the neighbouring town of Klein-Krotzenburg. Both sides of Memling's family must have been economically secure and respected members of the bourgeoisie.[10]

Confirmation of the essential fact of Hans Memling's birth itself in Seligenstadt appears only, ironically, in accounts of his death. He is listed as 'a citizen of Bruges in Flanders' in the roster of payments for anniversary masses in the family's parish church in the 1540s (it is likely that Memling planned ahead and arranged for these masses himself).[11] Memling's place of birth was likewise reported by his contemporary Rombout (or Romboud) de Doppere, secretary of the Sint-Donaaskerk in Bruges, in a chronicle that recounted the events of De Doppere's time that he deemed most important, and the record was subsequently consulted by the chroniclers Jacobus de Meyere and Nicolaas Despars.[12] The exact date and even year of Memling's birth, however, remain unknown; the death of his father recorded in 1450 firmly sets a latest possible date, while his inscription as a master in the Bruges painter's guild in 1465 suggests the years between 1430 and 1440 as most likely, placing Memling in his late twenties or early thirties on his arrival in the city.[13]

Seligenstadt – the town of Memling's youth – was of modest size, with just over 1,000 inhabitants in the fifteenth century.

While the inevitable tension between town, abbey, archbishopric
and surrounding agrarian countryside would escalate in later years,
in the fifteenth century it was quiet and prosperous and enjoyed
some political representation through the collective power of the
'League of the Nine Towns', of which it was a member.[14] It had
a vibrant cultural and intellectual atmosphere centred on the
nearby Benedictine monastery (its founder and first abbot was
Einhard, the illustrious Carolingian court scholar and biographer
of Charlemagne), an environment that drew foreign artisans.
In Memling's time a painter named Hans Cranich appears several
times in the abbey's tax records, and a handful of master sculptors were also active; in the early sixteenth century the painter
Matthias Grünewald operated a workshop in the town.[15] Various
members of the Appel family – relatives of Memling's mother's
first husband – were tenants of the abbey lands, suggesting close
connections to that institution.[16] The abbey church itself may
be depicted in the background of an appealing panel of the
Madonna and Child now in Berlin, a basilica in the Ottonian
style with two west towers and a squat octagonal crossing tower,
perhaps based on drawings from the artist's youth (illus. 6).[17]
Seligenstadt was on the shipping routes of the Main and Rhine
rivers, which carried the wool trade to Frankfurt, as well as an old
land route linking the imperial cities of southern Germany to
northern Germany and Flanders via Cologne, the same networks
that Memling would have followed north.[18] A merchant population from Nuremberg operated in Bruges, enjoying trading
privileges from the mid-fourteenth century onwards, and in the
fifteenth century merchants from Ravensburg had likewise
opened a branch office in the Flemish city, so the south German
artist would not have been alone as he forged a career abroad.[19]

At some point the young Memling left Seligenstadt to
begin, or perhaps continue, his professional training as an
apprentice and to find work as a journeyman assistant. Where

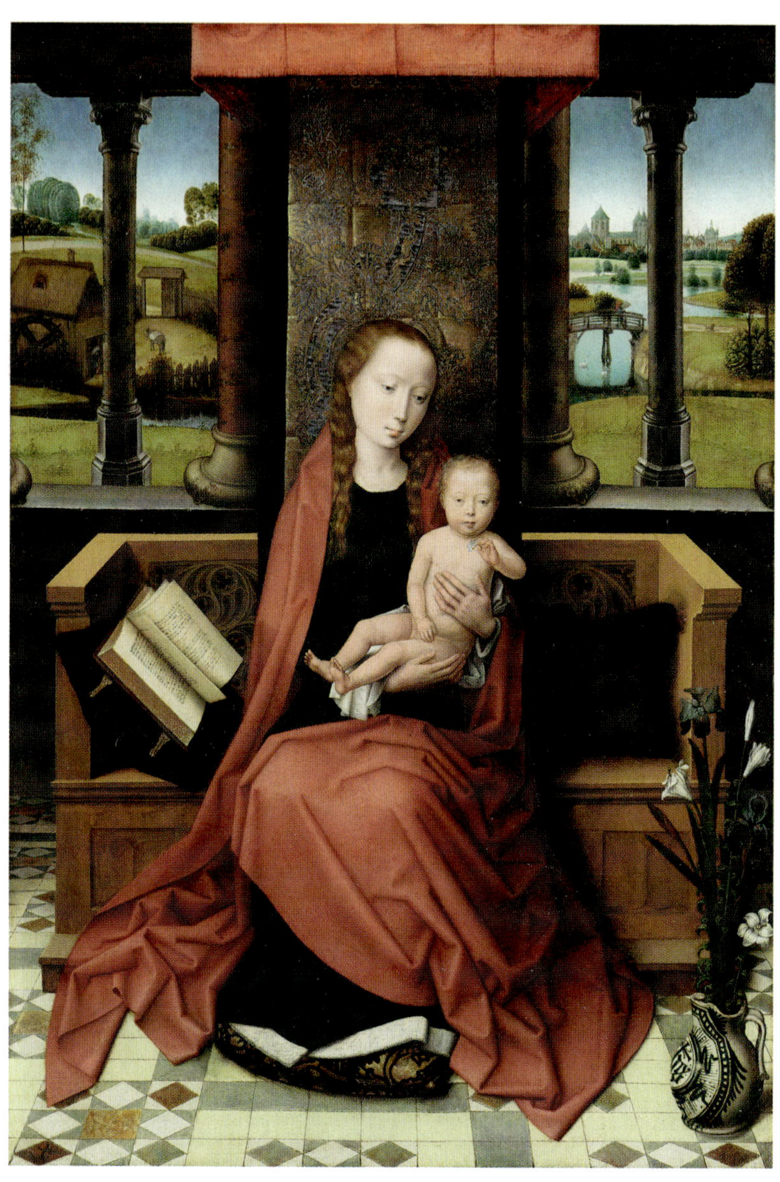

6 Hans Memling, *Virgin and Child Enthroned, c.* 1470–80, oil on oak.

precisely he trained remains undocumented, but this education probably took place in an active artistic environment, such as that of Mainz, Frankfurt or Cologne. The dominant painter in southern Germany in the middle of the century was the Master of the Darmstadt Passion, who may have worked in Mainz or Aschaffenburg and who carried on a strongly southwestern German painting tradition; he must have been familiar to the young artist.[20]

Considering a trajectory from Seligenstadt to Bruges, Memling's training in Cologne – a city of 40,000 inhabitants and one of the principal artistic centres of the Rhine region in the fifteenth century – is a strong possibility. The relationship of Memling's style and approach to the Cologne *Dombild* Master (an artistic identity tied circumstantially to Stephan Lochner, who died in 1451) and other works in Cologne has generated much speculation about a possible apprenticeship and early journey-man training under that master or another in the city (most of whom remain anonymous to us; it has been difficult to connect the names of Cologne painters known from archival documents to specific artworks).[21] The topographically accurate rendering of the buildings of Cologne's cityscape in some of Memling's works – in particular the depiction in *St Ursula Shrine* at the Sint-Janshospitaal of the churches of Groß St Martin, St Kunibert and Cologne cathedral in progress with its construction crane – indicate at least a temporary presence in the city.[22] The similarities in style and approach between Memling and his rough contemporaries in Cologne – such as the so-called Master of the Lyversberg Passion, the Master of the George Legend and the Master of the Life of Mary in particular – are tantalizingly suggestive of a shared artistic upbringing.[23] It is tempting to think that as an apprentice or young journeyman Memling may have encountered Rogier's *Columba Triptych*, probably installed in the 1450s in the Wasserfass family chapel at the church of

St Kolumba in Cologne, and have been lured towards Rogier's Brussels workshop.[24]

While no archival evidence confirms a direct connection, the work of Rogier clearly influenced Memling's compositions. Rogier's death only seven months before Memling registered his citizenship in Bruges supports the possibility that Memling served as a journeyman in Rogier's workshop and perhaps even completed some commissions left unfinished there at the master's death. In recent years information gleaned from infrared reflectography studies has suggested that Memling's working method – in particular the character of his preparatory underdrawings – relates to direct experience of Rogier's workshop operations, while others suggest that Memling's very formal underdrawing method in his early work might have been used for his budding independent career, in order to recommend himself to potential clients as Rogier's successor.[25]

It is possible that some works attributed to Rogier or his workshop are early works by Memling, such as the large *Annunciation* produced for Ferry de Clugny, a bishop and member of the Burgundian court council (illus. 7). Here the winged figure of the archangel Gabriel lands gently within a tidy domestic interior, interrupting Mary's reading. Gabriel is clad elegantly in a burgundy and gold brocade deacon's dalmatic and a green stole, and the cross that crowns his pearl tiara is tipped with gemstones. The blue banner still flutters from the movement of his descent at the end of the delicate cross he holds, even as his body gives the impression of weightlessness. In a vivid red velvet dress that extends beyond the edges of an intensely blue mantle hemmed with gold embroidery, Mary turns slightly at the intrusion and raises her right hand in demure surprise. Grasping a coiled beeswax candle in her left hand, she holds open a prayer book set on a green cloth. Visible on the open pages is a blue initial 'A', perhaps suggesting that she has been in the act of reading the prayer *Ave Maria*, as if the words presently spoken aloud by Gabriel have been predicted on the page. In front of the simple wooden prie-dieu sits an elaborate golden ewer in which a stem of white lilies stands, its petals just beginning to fall. Through an arched window, beyond the canopy bed and carved wooden bench that furnish the simple room, is visible a walled garden in which a woman tends a topiary shrub and a man strolls towards the open gate. The double-key motif of de Clugny's family — a subtle statement of ownership — appears both in the upper portion of the stained-glass window and woven into the thin Eastern carpet that covers the floor upon which Mary kneels, its right edge folded upon itself.

Of monumental scale at almost 2 metres (6½ ft) tall, this *Annunciation* was perhaps destined for a funerary chapel at Saint-Lazare, where de Clugny served as a canon in 1465. The work was conceivably completed at the end of Memling's proposed tenure in Rogier's Brussels studio, and this professional connection may have aided Memling on his arrival in Bruges.[26] The composition is indeed a variation on that found in other works from Rogier's studio, notably the left wing of the Columba altarpiece of the 1450s, and aspects of both the painted and the underdrawn styles can be related to that of Rogier. Memling, however, clearly drew on a range of sources for his compositions. He may have been familiar with Dieric Bouts's Leuven workshop, for example, and, given that Memling's career in Bruges overlapped for several years with that of Petrus Christus, it is possible that Memling spent some time as an assistant in that workshop. He may have been present in the city as an unregistered journeyman before 1465, during which time he would have adapted his style for the Bruges market.[27]

Whatever the circumstances of Memling's training, however, he established a reputation in his adopted city rather quickly and appears to have secured commissions — such as that ordered by

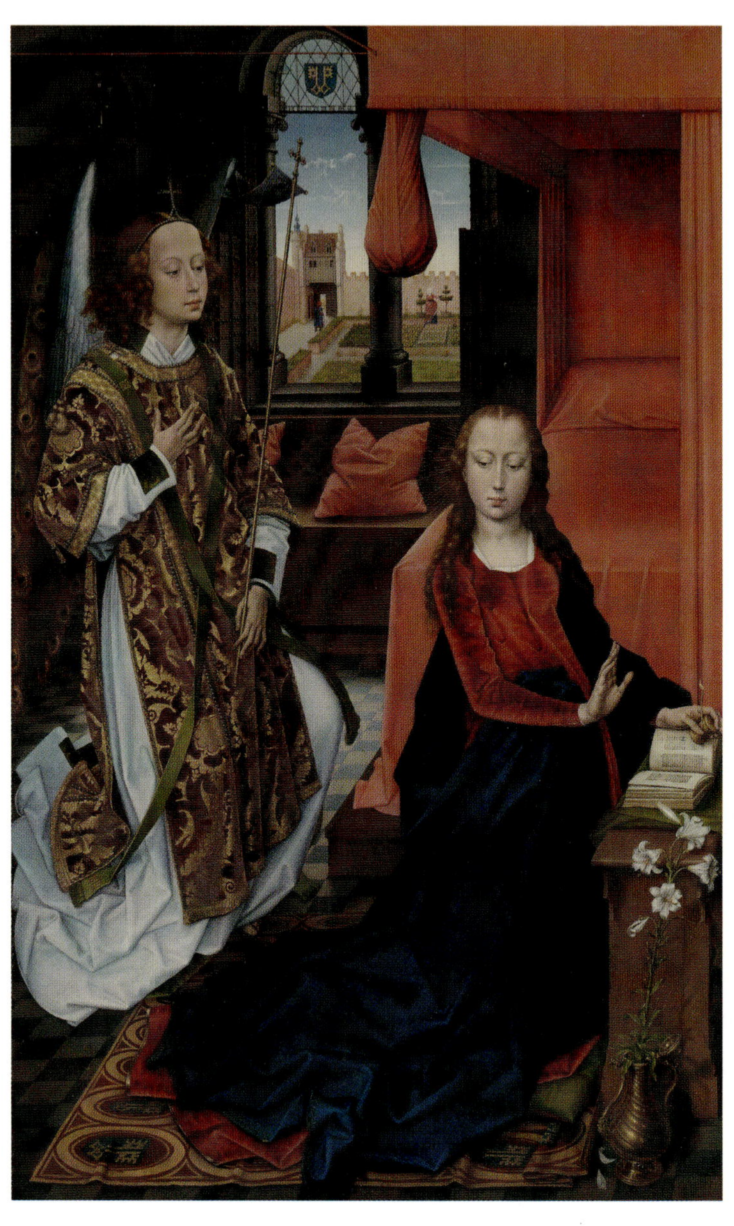

7 Hans Memling or studio of Rogier van der Weyden, *Annunciation*, c. 1465–70, oil on wood.

the Florentine Agnolo Tani – with prominent clients within a short time after his registration as a master. The scanty archival evidence that documents Memling's initial appearance in Bruges has presented some puzzles. It has been accepted by scholars for many years that he arrived at the Poortersloge (civic hall) to register his presence in the city in early 1465, appearing in the *Poortersboek* that recorded these new burghers who paid for full citizenship rights. Curiously, in the record he appears out of order; while noted as registering on 30 January, he appears not with the entries of that day but as a separate entry added to the bottom of the next page, among late February entries.[28]

It also remains unverified that Memling paid the required fee for citizenship (a not inconsiderable amount of money), since he does not appear in the appropriate place in the city accounting records to which these citizenship registrations and their payments were copied.[29] The city archivist of Bruges, Noël Geirnaert, suggests that Memling simply had not registered by September of that year, when citizenship payment records were copied into the accounting books, and that his addition to the *Poortersboek* must post-date that.[30] In some cases, the Bruges *Poortersboek* notes the vocation of a new citizen, to clarify that it was the immigrant's intention to pursue that trade in the city. This was not deemed necessary in Memling's case, and indeed it appears to have been included very infrequently (on the page on which Memling's inscription is included, only two of twenty-five records note an occupation). In accordance with the ordinances, however, his place of origin is included, as was required both for those arriving from the rural territories of the Franc that surrounded Bruges (who needed permission to leave their district) and for those born outside the county of Flanders. After a peak in the middle of the century, perhaps spurred in part by Philip the Good's efforts at economic revitalization, the immigration of foreign craftsmen like Memling remained high for the remainder of the century; in the years between 1466 and 1496 almost a third of the new masters registered in the painters' and saddlers' guild, for example, were from outside the city.[31]

Until recently, another lasting puzzle for historians was Memling's apparent absence from the registration lists of the Guild of Sint-Lucas en Sint-Eloi (St Luke and Eligius), which painters, saddlers and members of several other trades were compelled to join. Only a handful of exceptions exist of persons who are known from records of other activities in the guild – such as taking on apprentices or appearing in legal actions, or in records of obituary masses – but who do not appear in this registration roster. Noting the murky identity of 'Jan Damman, master painter', inscribed on or before 1 September 1465 but who subsequently falls completely out of view, Geirnaert suggests that this Damman and 'Jan Van Mimnelinghe Hammans', as Memling's name appears in the *Poortersboek*, are one and the same person.[32]

At some point, the now financially stable Memling married a woman named Tanne, and three children followed – Hannekin (named after his father), Nielkin and Claykin. Tanne's family name is not recorded, but she may have been the daughter of Lodewijk de Valkenaere, one of the guardians appointed to ensure the well-being of the couple's children on the occasion of her death.[33] At that moment, in 1487, the three children were still legally minors, which in fifteenth-century Bruges meant under 25 years of age (since the oldest was still a minor at Memling's own death, this suggests that the couple could have married soon after 1470, but later dates are also possible). At the time of Tanne's death, in accordance with Flemish custom, the children inherited half the household wealth in trust, and their material interests were subsequently looked after by two guardians, both of whom speak to Memling's social position and contacts within the artisanal class of Bruges society.[34] De Valkenaere is recorded as a *boucraenverwaere* – that is, a dyer of buckram (a fine textile that was used particularly for doublets) – with membership of the guild of the *culcstickers* (quilt-stitchers or flockers). He also appears in the civic records of 1488 as part of the new artisan-led revolutionary government's law enforcement organization. The second guardian appointed to the Memlings' children, Dieric vander Gheere, is recorded as a goldsmith. He appears to have been relatively wealthy (based on loan records of 1487) and had some professional status, serving in the year of Memling's death as an official in his guild.[35]

The patterns and rhythms of patronage over the course of Memling's career in Bruges reflect the complex political circumstances of his time, their effect on the economy and the fortunes of the different subgroups among his clientele. Memling arrived in the city with a good reputation perhaps already established and a handful of influential contacts, and his early career developed in the relative political and economic stability of the reign of Charles the Bold, with ample opportunities for income provided by the community of local and international businesspeople that thrived in this environment.

In the first years of his residency in Bruges we find Memling producing works that were carefully tailored to suit the existing market in the city, but we also find him as an imaginative innovator. One of his earliest works, a Madonna and Child preserved in the Nelson-Atkins Museum of Art in Kansas City, Missouri, demonstrates the highly marketable approach of his early career (illus. 8).[36] The Madonna, clad entirely in red with gold embroidery and grey fur on the hems and cuffs, sits in a loggia, the patterned tiled floor of which is partially covered by a simple, creased green carpet. Decorative finials are the only visible suggestion of her ornamented chair. Supported by her right hand, the child toys with the pages of the book she holds, and she seemingly attempts to keep her place in the text with a carefully placed index finger. Two

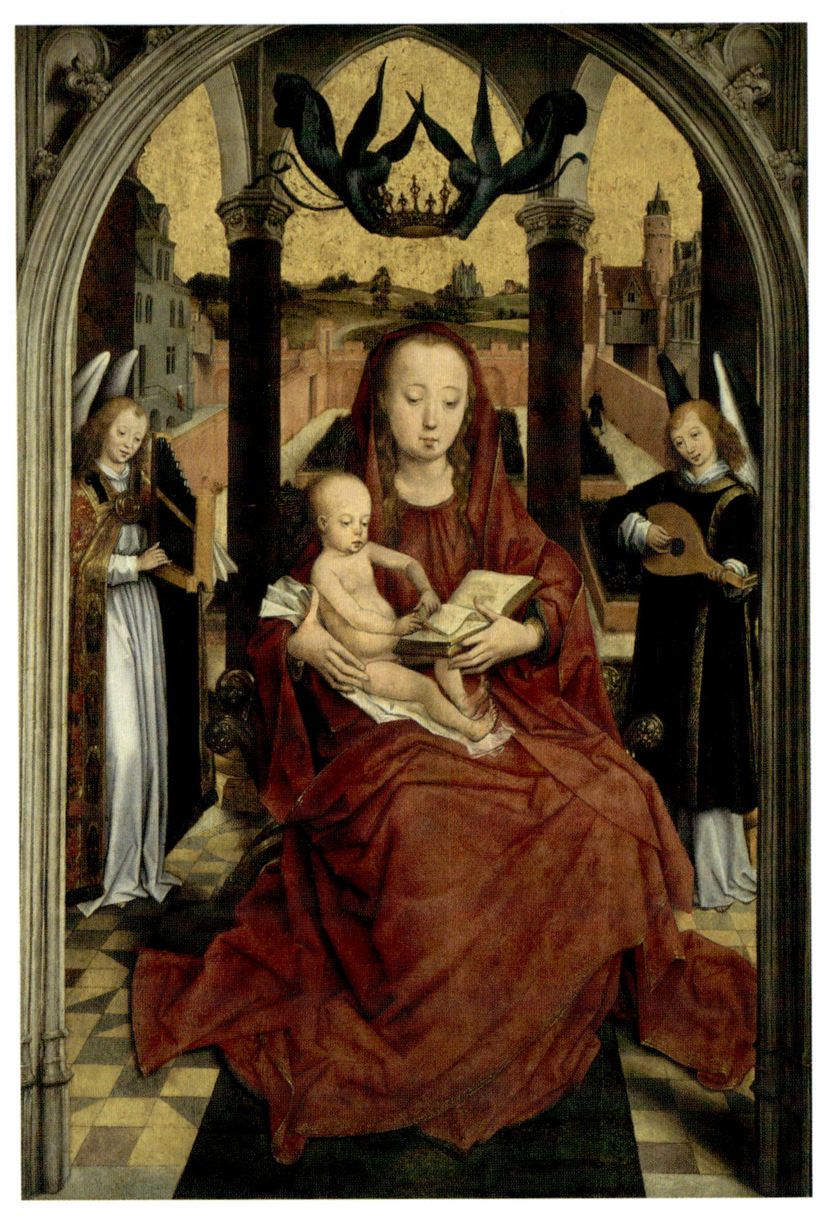

8 Hans Memling, *Madonna and Child Enthroned*, c. 1465–70, oil on wood.

angels stand to the sides, one clad in a purple and gold vestment and playing the lute, the other carrying a portative organ and wearing a white alb and sumptuous embroidered cope fastened by a golden morse. Beyond two maroon marbled columns that support the pointed arch of the loggia's vaulting, an enclosed garden, the surrounding cityscape and a distant landscape climb into the steep background. By this time the gold leaf of the sky would have been somewhat antiquated or nostalgic, and it must have been rendered at the request of the unidentified individual who commissioned the work. As in the *Annunciation* for Ferry de Clugny, the general approach here is reminiscent of Rogier and others of that generation, but the most striking influence of that master's work is the small, bird-like appearance of the two navy-blue angels who hold a jewelled crown aloft above the Madonna's head and the grisaille arched surround that frames the scene – both elements that respond to Rogier's Miraflores altarpiece.[37] At only slightly more than 0.5 metres (1½ ft) wide, this work is like many panels that would follow from Memling's workshop: criticized in the modern era for its standardized and arguably unimaginative approach, but clearly highly in demand in his own time on account of its tranquil beauty and painstaking craftsmanship.

At the same time, we find Memling already at his most inventive in these years, even as he served the same class of clients. The panel depicting scenes from the Passion of Christ, now in the Galleria Sabauda (Savoy Gallery) in Turin (illus. 9), appears to have been commissioned by the Florentine Tommaso Portinari, who had in 1465 become manager of the Bruges branch of the Medici bank after the ousting of Agnolo Tani, the patron of the large *Last Judgement* in Gdansk. Only 1 metre (3¼ ft) wide, Portinari's work presents a panoramic view of roughly two dozen episodes from the Passion and related events in a single complex landscape setting. A host of tiny figures can be traced from the distant countryside at the upper left of the panel, where Christ,

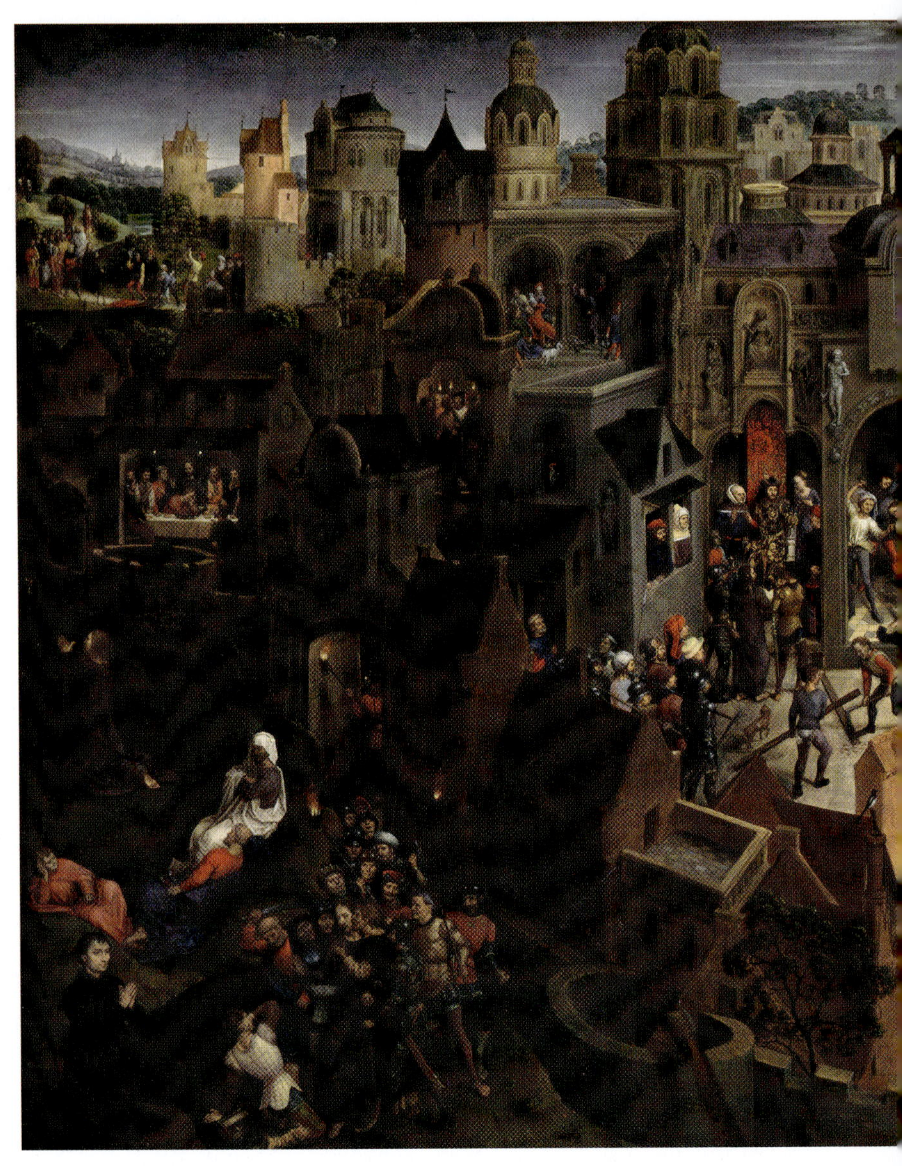

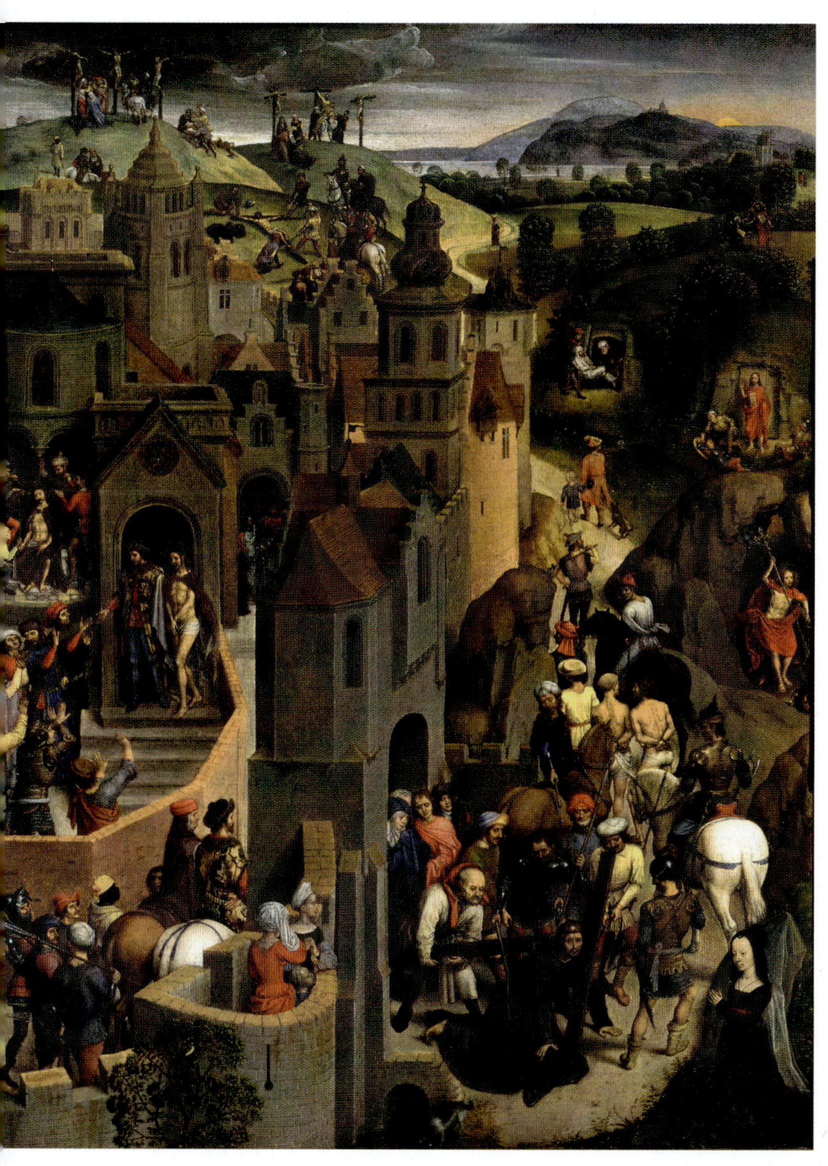

9 Hans Memling, *Passion of Christ, c.* 1470, oil on oak.

met by a throng of residents, makes his Palm Sunday entry through a gate into a detailed Jerusalem cityscape. In another vignette at upper left Christ drives the moneylenders from the temple, while nearby the disciples meet for the Last Supper; here Judas, dressed in green and yellow, rises to leave, and he is recognizable in an adjacent episode collecting his silver and gesturing towards the city gate. At the bottom left-hand corner of the panel, outside the walls of the city, Christ prays in Gethsemane as his followers sleep; a tiny chalice is visible at the edge of the panel. He is subsequently arrested by a mass of soldiers who still emerge from the city, as Peter strikes the ear off a soldier near the figure of Portinari, who kneels in prayer.

In the centre of the composition a series of episodes are distributed like spokes radiating from a courtyard bathed in sunlight: the appearance before Caiaphas and Peter's denial (the rooster perches nearby), the Flagellation and the Crowning with Thorns. This urban experience culminates with the interrogation by Pilate and Christ being condemned by the people. In the centre of the courtyard two carpenters work on beams of wood, their arrangement providing a neat visual foreshadowing of the product: the cross that Christ carries out of the city in the foreground. There he collapses near the figure of Maria Baroncelli, Tommaso's wife, who kneels in the bottom right-hand corner, like her husband apparently witnessing the drama unfold in her imagination.

Continuing procession-like into the landscape background, the action progresses further with Christ nailed to the Cross, the Crucifixion itself and the removal of Christ from the Cross in an efficiently compact use of pictorial space. The artist makes use of the upper right-hand corner of the panel to extend the content yet further with the Entombment, the Resurrection, Christ's encounter with Mary Magdalene and his appearance on the Sea of Tiberius. The spatial coherence and narrative continuity of the composition are remarkable, with individual players recognizable in sequential episodes by their distinctive costumes, and the suggestion of a rational path through space from one episode to the next via courtyards and gateways – their function demonstrated by secondary characters – and the only hinted-at passageways that connect them. Even a clever rendering of the passage of time makes use of the light source of the sun on the horizon in the right background, which – simultaneously rising and setting – shines upon the morning of Palm Sunday, while the night-time scenes at lower right are cast into shadow by the city walls; the scenes at the centre of the city are again bleached by the midday sun, and a bank of storm clouds casts a shadow over the evening of the Crucifixion. One of a handful of Memling's paintings that demonstrate such narrative complexity, this panel offers the potential for a detailed devotional meditation on the life of Christ – in the same era as the early development of such devotions as the Stations of the Cross – or even a 'virtual pilgrimage'.[38] Still in the first decade of Memling's career in Bruges, this unprecedented work seems to have caught the attention of artists and patrons in the city, judging by the composition's influence on subsequent artworks. Clearly Memling was not by nature a conservative artist, despite what the appealing and marketable bulk of his studio's output might initially suggest.

Activity at Memling's workshop proceeded briskly into the middle of the 1480s as his reputation became increasingly established, with plentiful commissions from international and local clients, despite the turmoil of Mary of Burgundy's tenure, the fraught political climate of the disputed regency of Philip the Handsome and intermittent rebellions throughout Archduke Maximilian's reign. In this delicate environment the most affluent Bruges families – such as the Moreels and the Van Nieuwenhoves – sought to bolster their status by sponsoring high-profile works for public venues, their family chapels serving as concrete mani-festations of their power scrimmages and political aspirations as they vied for social recognition.[39]

Any potential client not previously aware of Memling or uncertain of his works' appeal would have been persuaded by the completion in 1479 of the monumental St Johns altarpiece, then, as now, visible at the Sint-Janshospitaal, one of the city's chief charitable institutions. The closed view (illus. 10) depicts those responsible for the commission and their patron saints: Anthony Abbot, James, Agnes and Clare (the tentative identi-fications of the donors as particular brothers and sisters of the hospital is in large part based on the presence of these saints). The saints are depicted in understated hues but not the true grisaille used in Tani's *Last Judgement*, and instead of perching on plinths as sculpture they are brought down to earth, standing on the same ground as those they present.

The interior, more than 3 metres (nearly 10 ft) wide when opened, is rendered in vivid colour, with a narrative recount-ing the end of the life of John the Baptist presented on the left interior wing and an imaginative rendering of John the Evangelist receiving the visions of the Apocalypse on the right wing (illus. 11). Additional vignettes from their lives appear in the slices of cityscape that are visible to the sides of the centre panel; the Baptist preaches and is arrested, and the Evangelist is boiled in a vat of oil (the city's crane is visible nearby; the wine-gauging rights the hospital held were, again, its main source of income). This panel depicts the Virgin and Child seated at the centre of a gathering of saints, the interior setting established by marble columns and a tiled floor that is partially covered by an Eastern carpet. Here the two Johns featured on the wings stand with their traditional attributes, the poisoned chalice and the lamb, and two female saints are seated on the floor: Barbara (identifi-able on account of the diminutive tower that rests beside her)

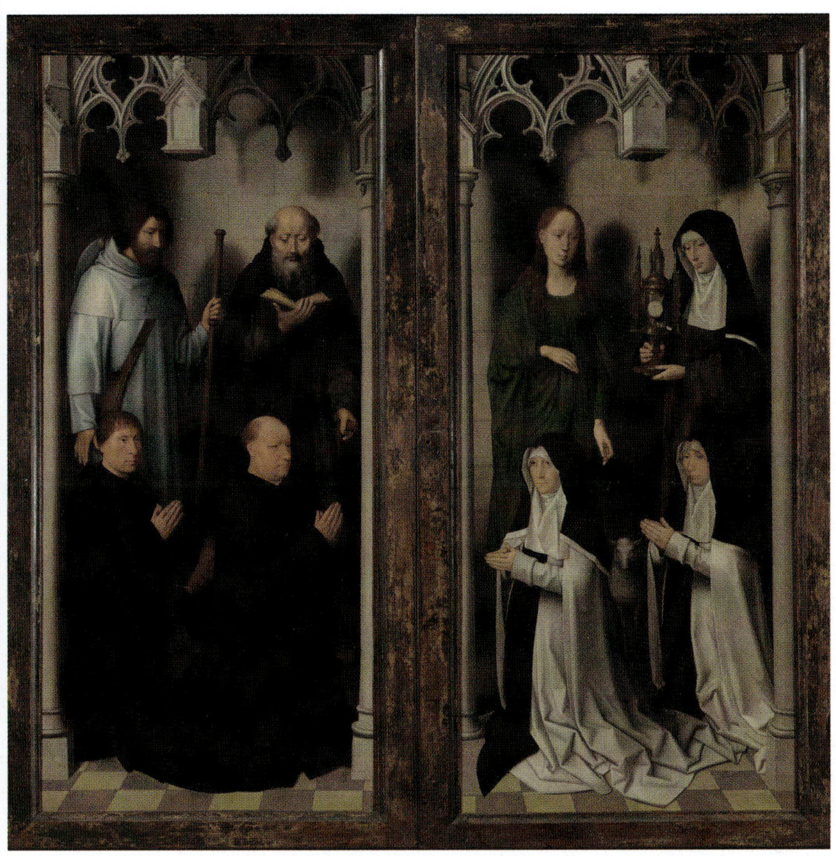

studiously reading a book at the right, clad in eye-catching green and purple; and Catherine of Alexandria, crowned and dressed in white and red with a sumptuous brocade skirt and cape, her traditional attributes of sword and broken wheel laid before her. The infant Christ places a ring indicating a 'mystic marriage' on Catherine's outstretched finger.

The impact of this work on the art-viewing public is clear from a number of Memling's commissions from the 1480s that reuse elements of the composition, probably at the request of his

10 Hans Memling, *Altarpiece of SS John the Baptist and John the Evangelist*, exterior, 1479, oil on oak.

clients. A panel preserved in the Metropolitan Museum of Art in New York, for example, redeploys much of the composition and colour scheme of the centre panel, with the absence of the male saints and the alteration of the appearance of the attending angels; the brocade dalmatic of the angel with the portative organ to the left is replaced by one of luxurious navy-blue with gold trim, and in place of the angel who holds the book through which Mary pages in the older work, a richly attired angel strums a golden harp (illus. 12). The gathering takes place outdoors, on a bed of carefully rendered groundcover plants, rather than in the implied interior and cityscape of the triptych in Bruges (the awkwardly painted bower seems to be a later addition). Behind Catherine a young merchant clad in a black robe kneels and handles a rosary; the purse or badge visible at his hip is the only surviving possible clue to his profession or identity.

Many individual portraits – a speciality of the workshop – survive from the middle of Memling's career. The *Portrait of a Man with a Letter*, dated to the 1480s and preserved in the Uffizi, Florence, provides an example of the high quality and delicacy

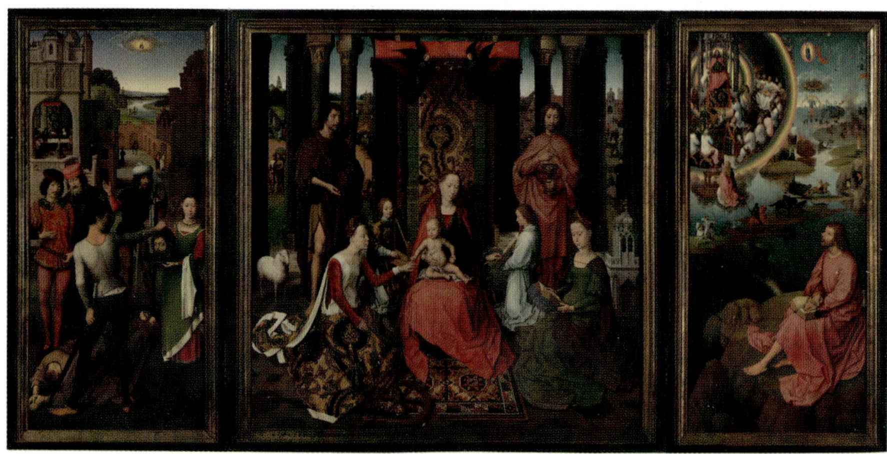

11 Hans Memling, *Altarpiece of ss John the Baptist and John the Evangelist*, interior, 1479, oil on oak.

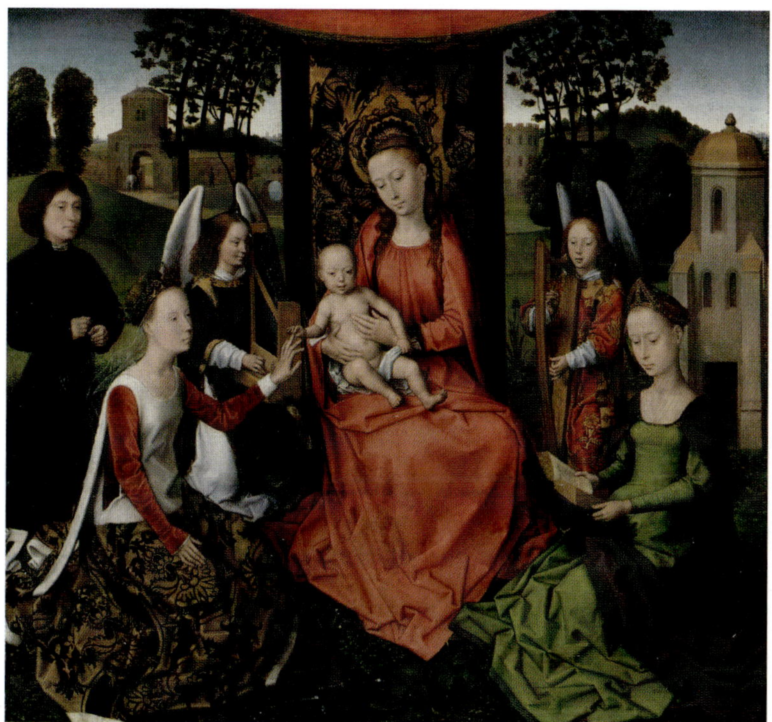

of these works (illus. 13). The male sitter, an unidentified Italian, is depicted at half length with his face presented in three-quarter view. His brown eyes are directed towards the viewer as he rests a hand on a low wall just visible at the bottom of the panel, his fingers grasping a tightly folded paper. An ample white linen collar projects above his entirely black doublet, and despite the chestnut curls that emerge from beneath a matching cylindrical cap, his middle age is indicated sensitively by the careful, delicate lines that have begun to appear at his brow, eyes and neck. Behind him is a landscape of feathery trees and gentle, rolling hills. To the right, two swans float on a calm pond that reflects the line of trees and the sky, and the profile of a church rises on the horizon;

12 Hans Memling, *Virgin and Child Enthroned with ss Catherine of Alexandria and Barbara*, *c.* 1480–85, oil on wood.

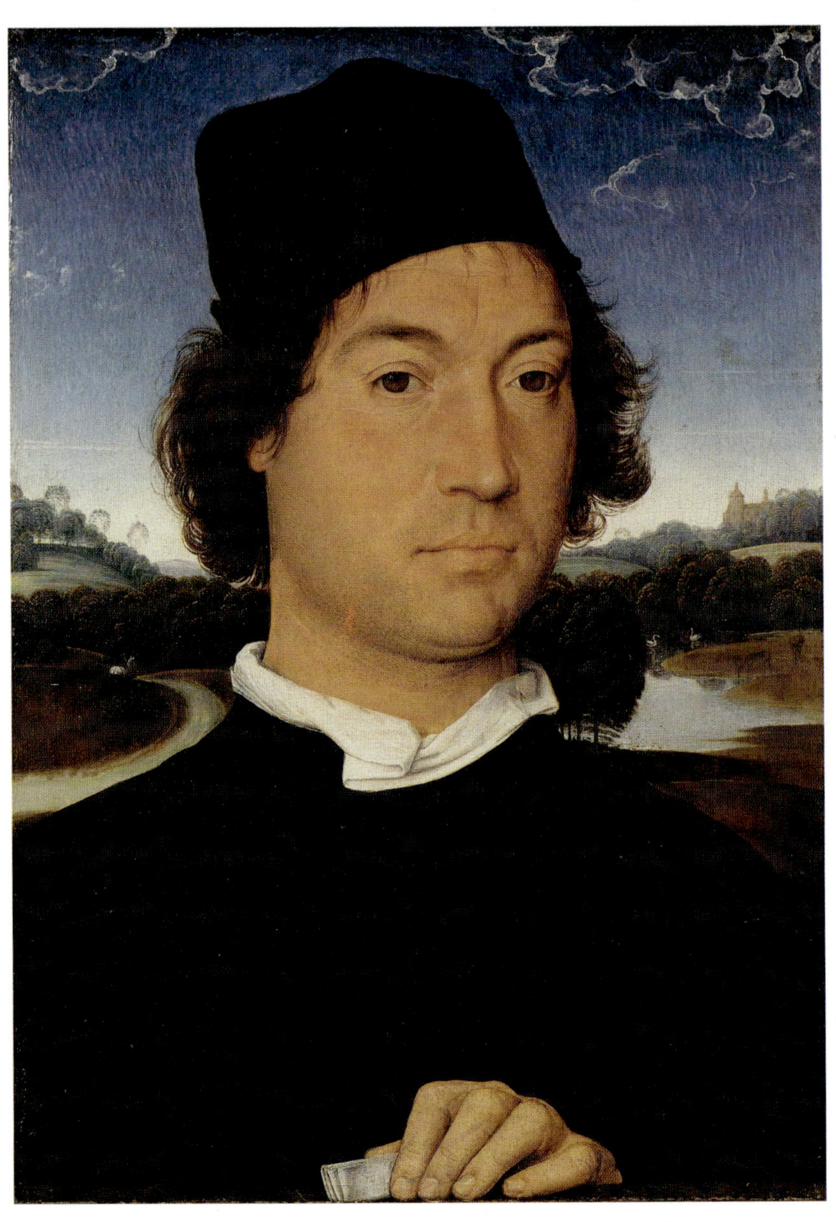

13 Hans Memling, *Portrait of a Man with a Letter*, c. 1485–9, oil on wood.

to the left a solitary horseman rides along a curving road, with overlapping hills appearing cool and hazy as they spill into the far distance. The sky, pale at the horizon and rising gradually to a saturated blue, offers only wispy hints of clouds.

Although now anonymous, the distinctive appearance of this individual is unmistakable and compelling in its veracity, and it is easy to see how such works appealed to Memling's aspiring clients. His concessions to Italian taste are striking; his portraits of sitters placed before tranquil landscapes were particularly admired in Italy, and he seems to have hit a balance between structure and delicacy that appealed greatly to that clientele.[40]

It is possible to detect general patterns in the way the businessman Hans Memling adjusted the style and format of his workshop's productions to appeal to the specific regional tastes of his international clientele. Among the works from the 1480s, for example, that have been characterized as formulaic compositions – perhaps stock types prepared in advance, then customized for the buyers – various panels survive of the enthroned Madonna and Child with a canopy, featuring nude putti and Italianate fruit swags in the antique manner. This indicates a projected Italian clientele or at least the influence of that taste on the market elsewhere.[41]

Tension between Bruges and Maximilian boiled over in the late 1480s and early 1490s, disrupting life and commerce in the city, and the troubled economy was further injured by Maximilian's dispersal of the international merchant community.[42] It is difficult to locate Memling's own political leanings in this environment, since he is known to have completed commissions for two known patrons supportive of the regency council and crafts-led revolutionary government (alongside, perhaps, his own father-in-law), but he also executed works for at least one client of a family firmly associated with the pro-Maximilian faction in the city.[43] Regardless of any political convictions Memling may have harboured, he seems to have prioritized business.

Whatever the case, over these years of turmoil in Flanders Memling's workshop seems to have remained as busy as always. After the delivery of the prestigious *St Ursula Shrine* to the Sint-Janshospitaal in 1489, and other prominent works, the workshop continued its progress on particularly large and time-consuming commissions that had been arranged earlier, including several large international orders. It also augmented its income by pivoting to the production of small standardized works, with a spike in commissions for unidentified donors.[44] In the imposing Greverade triptych (see illus. 16 and 17), dated to 1491 and probably made for a Lübeck merchant family (discussed in greater detail in Chapter Four), Memling continued to adapt to his clients' desires, invoking a number of pictorial and compositional conventions that are more typical of German and Baltic traditions than of the fifteenth-century Low Countries. Likewise, the large, broad panels destined for the monastery in Nájera, Castile, seem to reflect the requirements of the Spanish retablo format rather than any northern European triptych tradition (see illus. 30).

The 1492 Peace of Cadzand, the gradual return of some foreign merchant communities after 1493 and the restabilizing of the economic environment probably led to additional brokered commissions and the completion of stalled paintings that had awaited materials, but few works have been dated securely to the last years of Memling's life. His death in 1494 may have left many commissions in the hands of the journeymen in his workshop, and this may account for the objects on the margins of his oeuvre that are most often considered to be of lower quality or from closely related but distinct stylistic and compositional hands.

Associated by some with Memling's workshop but not the master's own hand, for example, and generally dated to the last decade of the century, a panel now preserved in the Groeninge-museum in Bruges bears in its spandrels the arms of the della Costa family of Genoa (illus. 14). Probably once a diptych or triptych wing, the panel depicts a crowded, intensely cropped Deposition scene in which three male figures gingerly support Christ's lifeless body, which seems carefully presented to viewers. In addition to Joseph of Arimathea and Nicodemus, a third male figure – in a full-sleeved white doublet with blue lining, its but-tons loosened – hangs by an arm slung around a ladder's rung. While the faces of the men seem consistent with Memling's other work, the landscape appears somewhat awkwardly finished. The reverse depicts a bust-length St Andrew standing in a dark, arched niche before his diagonal wooden cross (illus. 15). His simple, dark blue robe is enveloped by a vivid red mantle with green lining, and he manipulates a set of rosary beads with both hands on a banister at the bottom of the image; his figure, too, appears to be the work of a hand very close to the Memling workshop, either wholly the work of a skilled assistant with access to the workshop materials, or unfinished by Memling and completed by an assistant. The panel was most likely commis-sioned by Andrea della Costa, who served in these years as collector-general to Maximilian and orator of the deanery in Bruges. Marrying into the prominent Adornes family (likewise originally from Genoa but residing in Bruges for several gener-ations), della Costa became a citizen in 1483; Agnes Adornes's family coat of arms and patron saint would probably have been on the other wing, perhaps with the grieving *Mater Dolorosa* accompanying the Deposition.[45]

Memling appears to have been favoured above all by the professional middle class and merchants, who called on him to render the large altarpieces and smaller devotional diptychs with

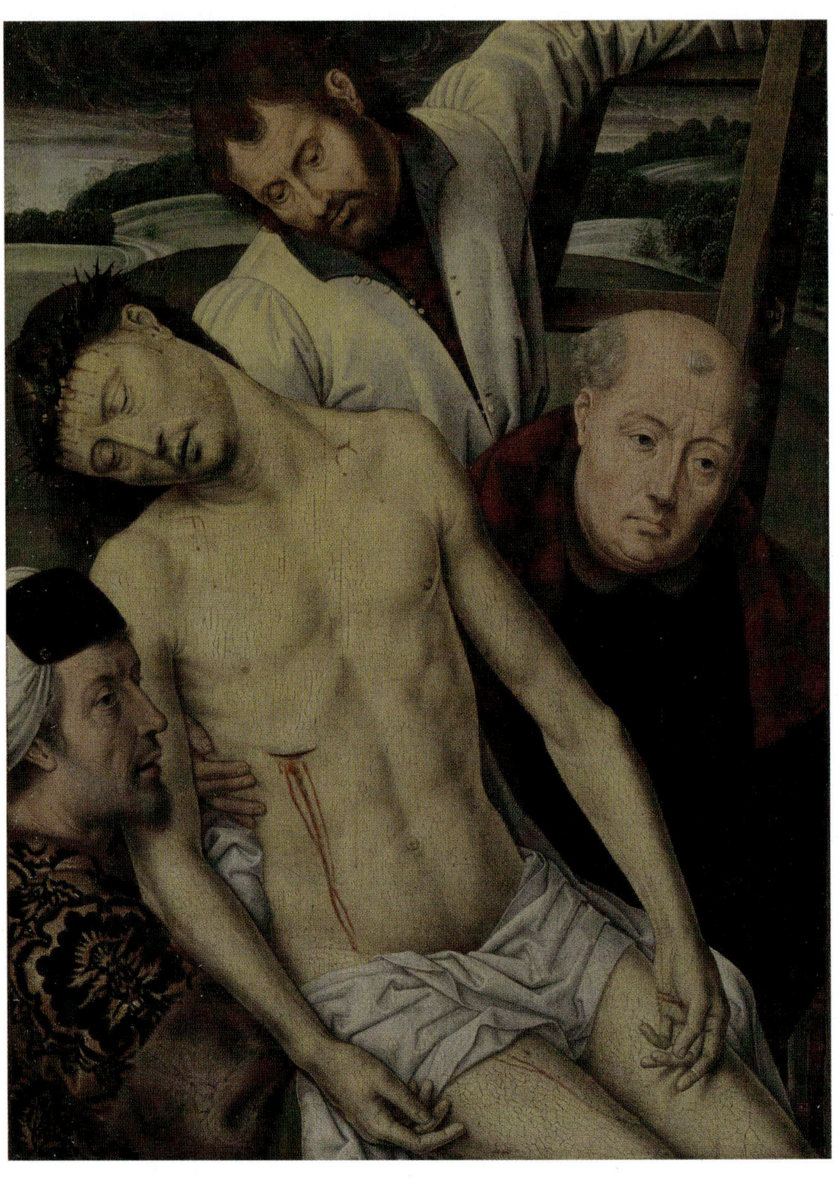

14 Studio of Memling (?), *Descent from the Cross*, c. 1493–1500, oil on oak.

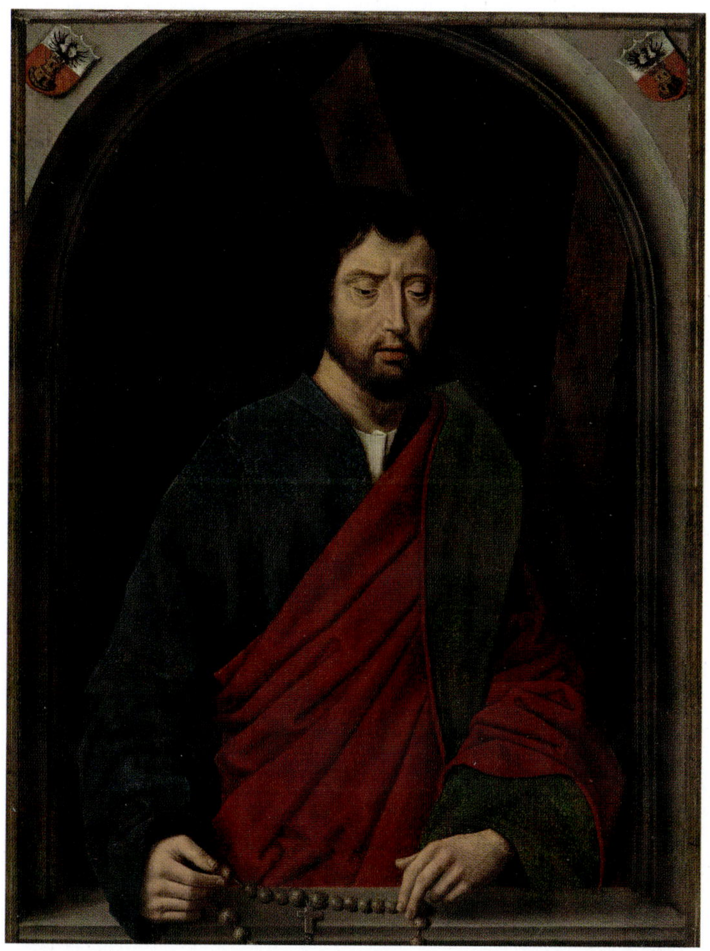

which they adorned the chapels they sponsored in the public
eye, and the devotional works and portraits they commissioned
for their personal use. He also appears to have been highly
regarded by his contemporary artisans. He was certainly respected
by his peers in the Guild of St Luke and Eligius, the corporation
of painters and saddlers. In the obituary list of the guild, the

15 Studio of Memling (?), *St Andrew*, reverse of illus. 14, *c.* 1493–1500,
oil on oak.

notice of his death identifies him as 'Master Jan van Menninghen, Painter'. Out of more than five hundred names listed in this document, only eleven painters are described as 'Master': before Memling only Petrus Christus and Memling's contemporary Pieter Nachtegale (a figure about whom very little is known), then after Memling none until the 1520s with the deaths of Gerard David and Jan Provost, then Albrecht Cornelis (1532) and other mid-sixteenth-century masters, such as Adriaen Isenbrant, Lancelot Blondeel, and Pieter Claeissens and Pieter Pourbus and their sons. Over the same period only two glass-makers and no saddlers are listed as *Meester*.[46] Memling appears to have served no official leadership roles within the guild during his career, nor did he become directly involved in civic politics. He seems to have been respected primarily for his work itself, appreciated as a consummate craftsman wholly dedicated to operating an industrious and professional workshop.

An index of Memling's attempts to position himself socially within his adopted city and develop a professional network of potential clients is his membership from 1473 onwards of the Confraternity of Our Lady of the Snow (Onze-Lieve-Vrouw-ter-Sneeuw).[47] This brotherhood, founded in honour of the August feast day commemorating the miraculous foundation of Santa Maria Maggiore in Rome, fittingly carried out its activities in Bruges at the Onze-Lieve-Vrouwekerk, the Church of Our Lady. Membership originally focused on the artisanal class (it was founded by the tailors' guild), but in the fifteenth century the confraternity had expanded to include merchants, clerics and humanists, such prominent Bruges politicians as Memling's client Willem Moreel, diplomats and members of the nobility, such as Lodewijk van Gruuthuse and even Duke Charles the Bold.[48] Numerous painters featured among its ranks, including Petrus Christus, Jan Fabian, Pieter Casinbroodt, Willem Vrelant and the court painter Pieter Coustain.

Recorded as paying his membership dues of four groats, 'Master Hans, the painter' was one of 81 new members in 1473–4 (and just over 1,000 members in total). The confraternity was not as exclusive as some, such as the Confraternity of Our Lady of the Dry Tree, but it would have offered a wealth of potential clients within its social network and thus may have been better suited to serving Memling's business interests.[49] The citation of a member's occupation in the membership list is unusual, and the use of a title was usually reserved for the nobility – who might be referred to as *messire* or *mynheere/mevrauwe* – and clerics, who would be described as *heer*. Memling thus appears to have been well respected within this broader confraternal community, since of the entire membership in 1473, only seven members were reported as *meester*.[50] He also appears in records of civic and religious institutions as making periodic payments, including property tax payments in his parish of Sint-Niklaas, and contributing to the philanthropic fund for the 'poor-table' at the Church of Our Lady; in the latter accounts he is again referred to as *meester*. His children continued these payments in his name as late as 1514, and the tax records list a 'Johanes Memelinc' making payments well into the sixteenth century, a name that, by then, might refer to his eldest son.[51]

Among the important events that transpired in the year 1494, noted in Jacobus de Meyere's Latin edition of Rombout de Doppere's chronicle, is Hans Memling's death. While brief, the record nevertheless testifies to the high regard in which Memling was held by his contemporaries in Bruges: 'On the eleventh of August died Master Johannes Memmlinc, proclaimed to have been the most skilful and the most excellent painter of the whole Christian world at that time. He came from Mainz, and was buried in Bruges at the church of St Giles.'[52] The year of his death is confirmed by the *obituarium* of the painters' and saddlers' guild.[53] Likewise, as a benefit of his membership of the Confraternity of

Our Lady of the Snow, the accounts of 1493–4 indicate that among the payments for the celebration of masses, one was made sometime between 11 August and 1 September for 'Master Hans, the painter'.[54] Notably, in addition to his burial at Sint-Aegidius cited by de Doppere and these *memoria* in Bruges, it appears that at some point Memling arranged for yearly masses to be celebrated in his home town of Seligenstadt; the records of the family's parish church from the mid-sixteenth century indicate that masses were paid for in 1534 and 1551 in memory of 'Hans Memling, citizen of Bruges in Flanders'.[55]

While recognized across Europe as a leader in art during his own time, Memling, in common with many celebrated artists, fell from view in history. While several early citations of his life and works – by Guicciardini, Vasari and Van Mander, among other authors – set him among the canon of excellent artists of Bruges, little was known of his life, and by the eighteenth century he was largely forgotten.[56] A collection of local traditions, however, emerged around Memling's works and character. Notable among these is the narrative presented in the mid-eighteenth century by the French writer Jean-Baptiste Descamps, who perpetuated a tradition of Memling's birth near Bruges at Damme and his unlikely discovery as an artist while convalescing as a dissipated ex-soldier at the Sint-Janshospitaal; the works that remained at the hospital provided ample material for the Romantic imagination.[57] One early champion of Memling at the turn of the nineteenth century was the critic Friedrich Schlegel, who provided a rare examination of the 'German' school of painting – in which the painters of the Low Countries were included – and who counted Memling as 'having reached the highest perfection in that school':

The already noticed Hemling [*sic*] stands alone in the circle of well-known masters. He has all the pathos and

German feeling of [Albrecht] Dürer, but without his caricature and other peculiarities. In spiritual beauty and devotional feeling, as well as in clearness of meaning, he excels all painters of that school, and can be compared only to Van Eyck; his execution is tender and highly finished, yet his objective profoundness cannot be surpassed even by [Hans] Holbein or any of the Upper German masters, while none of the Lower German school possess equal richness and poetic fancy.[58]

With systematic archival work in the nineteenth and twentieth centuries, what is known of Memling's biography and career began to be documented in greater detail, with such scholars as James Weale uncovering a wealth of information about the painter and his patrons drawn from civic and ecclesiastical archives and other textual sources preserved in Bruges. With the development of art history as a formal discipline, other scholars soon followed, and the outlines of Memling's life have slowly become somewhat clearer, although many mysteries remain.

The scanty archival documentation that has been unearthed concerning Memling's contemporaneous recognition in the city and abroad serves to confirm the evidence of his excellence provided by the surviving works themselves. The image revealed of the painter Hans Memling is one of a meticulous, skilled, adaptable craftsman, highly respected by his contemporaries, operating an effective and industrious workshop in the busy commercial centre of Bruges. In common with many of the artists and other professionals working in Bruges in the fifteenth century, he was an immigrant who sought a career in the trading capital of northern Europe, over time establishing a workshop, building a family, integrating into the community through membership of his professional guild and religious confraternities, and fostering a network of potential clients in the city and abroad. How the members of this relatively new community of patrons made their livelihoods and the environment in which they and Memling encountered one another shaped the character of the works they requested from the artist, and the purposes for which these commissions were intended.

TWO

Memling's Bruges

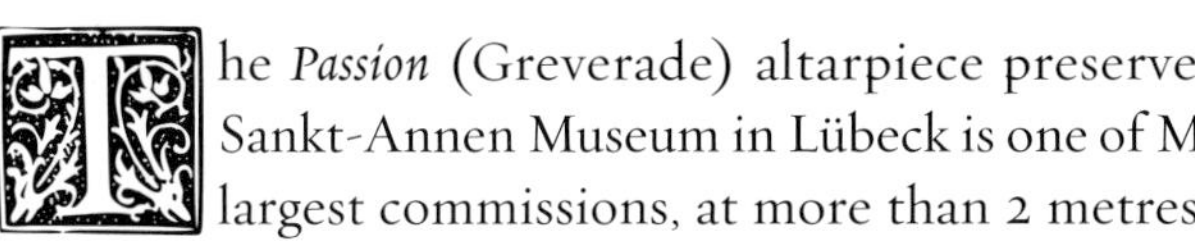

The *Passion* (Greverade) altarpiece preserved in the Sankt-Annen Museum in Lübeck is one of Memling's largest commissions, at more than 2 metres (6½ ft) high and almost 3 metres (9¾ ft) wide (illus. 16 and 17). Probably the last work of significant size of his career, completed in the early 1490s, it is nearly as large as the monumental *Last Judgement* for Agnolo Tani that heralded the start of his career. In its completely closed state the altarpiece has the appearance of a triptych and depicts the Annunciation in a manner that would have been familiar to viewers of the time. The archangel Gabriel on the left wing gestures towards Mary on the opposite wing, who, holding her prayer book, seems to respond demurely to his announcement. Both figures are rendered in grisaille, and this treatment, combined with the arched niches within which they stand on projecting plinths, creates the general impression of marble sculpture in the round, placed in an architectural setting. The more vivid hues of the geometrically patterned tiled floor at the bottom of the panel support this illusion, while the ceramic vase of lilies and irises seems cleverly to bridge the two realms of reality.

Similar in conception to other triptych exteriors in Memling's oeuvre and those of other Flemish artists (similar treatments occur, for example, on the exteriors of Rogier's Beaune altarpiece and Hugo van der Goes's altarpiece in Florence for Tommaso

Portinari), this presentation would not have prepared the viewers who encountered it in his Bruges workshop for its opened state. Here, rather than the broad centre panel and interior left and right wings that they would have expected, four vertical panels of identical dimensions are revealed. Each depicts a standing male saint, nearly life-sized and taking up much of the height of the narrow panel on which he appears: Blaise and John the Baptist to the left, and Jerome and Egidius to the right. Blaise, furthest to the left, stands in his bishop's mitre and a purple chasuble, decorated with an elaborately embroidered orphrey that itself depicts additional standing saints. In one hand he carries his ornamented crozier and in the other a long taper candle; at his feet rests the fuller's comb with which he was martyred. John the Baptist, in the left-centre panel, appears as he does elsewhere in Memling's work; he directs his gaze towards the viewer and gestures to the lamb that accompanies him. At the centre right, Jerome appears in the vivid red habit of a cardinal, with underlayers of grey and black visible, and carries a jewelled processional cross in a gloved hand. His mature years are indicated carefully by the network of lines that detail his face – the same care that Memling takes with his portrait sitters – and he casts his gentle gaze down to where, using tweezers held in his right hand, he removes a thorn from the paw of the appreciative small lion that stands at his side. At the far right Egidius, clad in entirely black habit, stands stoically with an elaborate crozier. He caresses the head of the small deer at his side, seemingly undisturbed by the arrow that still projects from his lower arm. The four narrow panels appear to share a common setting, placed in a shallow vaulted chamber with a pair of tall lancet windows and a round glazed window on each side wall. All four figures appear to stand at the edge of a step built into the colourful tiled floor, and slices of stone columns with decorated capitals appear at the edges of each pair of panels, seemingly supporting a carved wooden lintel.

The altarpiece – not strictly a triptych, but rather a polyptych – opens further yet to reveal another scene, now a vast unified landscape spread across three panels. The left wing presents a condensed and vertically orientated variation on the narratively dense approach to the *Passion* that Memling had used more than a decade earlier for Portinari (see illus. 9). As the rising sun casts a pink light on the horizon, Christ prays at Gethsemane and is arrested nearby. In a tightly packed cityscape copiously ornamented with a diversity of architectural settings, the sequence of Judgements, the Flagellation and the Crowning with Thorns all proceed with spatial efficiency. In an episode depicted in larger scale and taking up the bottom half of the panel, Christ emerges through a city gate carrying the Cross and accompanied by more than a dozen additional figures; the donor kneels at the corner of the panel, dressed in a black garment with fur-lined cuffs.

This procession to Calvary continues on to the centre panel, where additional structures and the outer wall of the same city are visible in the distance, opening up into a deep landscape with wooded hills and rugged mountain peaks. The thunderclouds that gather on the left panel continue here to develop and to darken the sky. The episode depicted is the Crucifixion, but with a wealth of detail and additional narrative content unlike most Flemish renditions of the topic. In the bottom left-hand corner, Mary swoons and is supported by John and a female follower; the stylishly dressed figure of Mary Magdalene kneels nearby, wringing her hands as two women join her in her grief. These figures are echoed compositionally in the opposite corner by a vividly dressed group of soldiers, who demonstrate a different response to the event as they play dice and laugh. Across the middle ground a cast of characters appear at the foot of the three crosses: a mounted centurion in armour to the right of Christ bears witness to his conversion experience by gesturing directly to the viewer, while to the right of the Cross the blind centurion Longinus, assisted

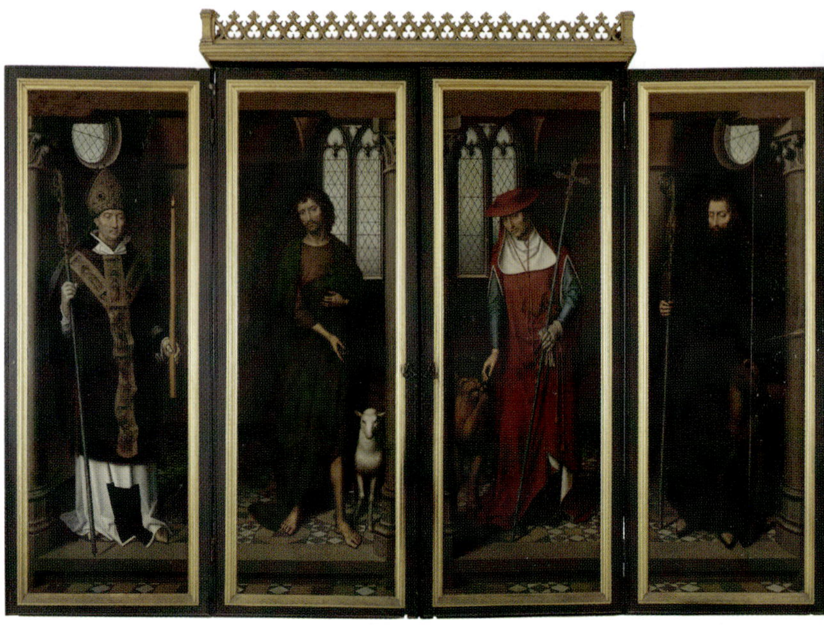

by another soldier, pierces Christ's side with a spear. Among the crowd the figures of Pilate and Caiaphas are recognizable from earlier episodes, as are other supporting characters, such as Nicodemus, who also appears among the smaller group present at the *ecce homo* scene on the left wing, and who stands at the Crucifixion with his back to the viewer, wearing a long black mantle and red chaperon, looking very much like a fifteenth-century merchant witnessing the scene. Other figures less clearly tied to the narrative may be portraits of contemporaries, and more than thirty individual figures appear on the centre panel. The altarpiece culminates with the episodes – again condensed in a manner similar to that of Portinari's *Passion* – on the right-hand wing, which also shares a landscape horizon with the centre panel. Christ is laid in the tomb and appears in Resurrection in close proximity to later events as the sun once more sets in the distance.

16 Hans Memling, *Passion* (Greverade) altarpiece, first closed position, 1491, oil on wood.

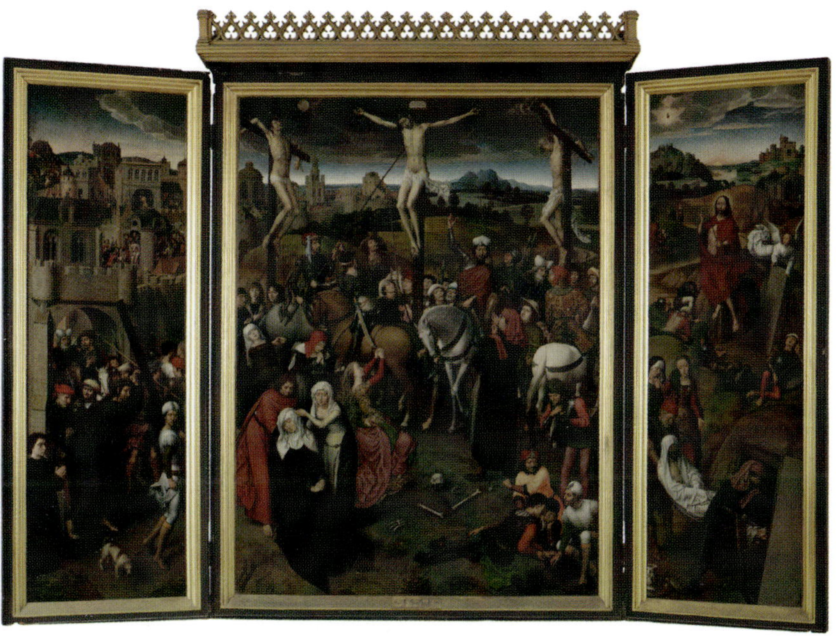

The aspects of this altarpiece's construction and composition that would have been most surprising to a Flemish audience – namely, the polyptych structure with two sets of wings and the heavily populated Crucifixion – would have been very familiar to its probable patron, who was not himself from Bruges but rather from further east. This work seems to have been executed for one or both of a pair of brothers, Heinrich and Adolf, of the patrician Greverade family of Lübeck. The Hanseatic merchants, expelled from Bruges as part of Maximilian's retribution on the rebellious city in 1488, had largely returned in 1491, and, in common with other members of his family, Heinrich was active in Flanders trade, a merchant and director of an exchange bank who spent periodic stints in Bruges and kept a residence there. Adolf later took up a spiritual career, but in 1493 he is listed as a merchant burgher, managing the currency exchange in Lübeck

17 Hans Memling, *Passion* (Greverade) altarpiece, open, 1491, oil on wood.

alongside his brother; it is impossible to tell which brother is depicted kneeling on the left wing of the open altarpiece.

The work itself appears to have been destined for the Greverade family chapel founded, after some delays, in 1493 in Lübeck cathedral, where it was reliably documented in 1504, but it may not have been installed there until after Memling's death. During the perhaps ten years between its completion and its installation in Lübeck, it may have been installed at the Carmelite church in Bruges, where the community of merchants of the Hansa held their services.[1] In the late fifteenth century the Hanseatic League was well established in Bruges, which they used as one of their five chief trading hubs for the distribution of goods, such as Baltic timber and fur, and the purchase of commodities from across northern Europe and the Mediterranean. These northern Germans were a powerful economic and political bloc in the Flemish city, operating out of a spacious and splendidly ornamented headquarters in one of the city's commercial centres; the individual Hansa merchants who made their careers partially or wholly in Bruges themselves purchased property, joined religious organizations, and funded masses and chapels at the city's churches.

The encounter between the Greverade client who ordered this grand work and the painter's workshop on which he called for its creation depended on a distinctive urban environment. When Memling arrived in Bruges and established a workshop in 1465, the city still enjoyed enviable economic prosperity. In 1468 Anselm Adornes, a prominent Bruges burgher but himself of Genoese descent, visited Scotland as an ambassador to James III and there described the city of Bruges as 'que mercature universitas est, ymmo ut ita loquar, in ea arte universitatum mater': like a mother university, but one of commerce.[2] As a side effect of this concentration of wealth, Bruges had become a cultural centre as well. The courts of the counts of Flanders and later dukes of

Burgundy spent seasons in the city intermittently, and a range of collegiate churches and mendicant orders thrived among its vibrant population. Memling, however, was a painter favoured above all by members of the international merchant community and the urban bourgeoisie, whose distinctive activities the city's infrastructure and architecture had developed to facilitate. The environment of Bruges as a commercial and social centre was inextricably linked to its character as a place where these groups interacted.

From its origins in the Frankish period, Bruges developed as a site of trade rather than as a political or military centre. In the twelfth and thirteenth centuries the heart of commercial enterprise in northwestern Europe had been the circuit of the 'Champagne fairs' centred on Troyes and Provins, as a locus for the exchange both of goods and of currency and other credit instruments; the bill of exchange first developed at this meeting point for the vendors of Europe.[3] Even before the emergence of the Champagne fairs, however, the counts of Flanders had encouraged economic growth in the more immediate region through the establishment of a number of fairs that would become integrated with the Champagne circuit, enabled by improvements to major roadways and transport. The first four great fairs in Flanders west of the Schelde were launched by Baldwin V in 1127, and later a fifth fair was added at Bruges even further to the northeast.[4] A major land route linked Bruges and the other Flemish fair cities to those of Champagne and the rest of France, while a second major route – via Ghent, Brussels, Leuven and Maastricht – led eastwards to Cologne and the Rhineland.[5]

The *Encomium of Queen Emma* of 1042 indicates that a great deal of sea trade between England and the *portus* of Bruges was already occurring by that time; the author notes that the town 'enjoys very great fame for the number of its merchants and for its affluence in all things upon which mankind places the greatest value'.[6]

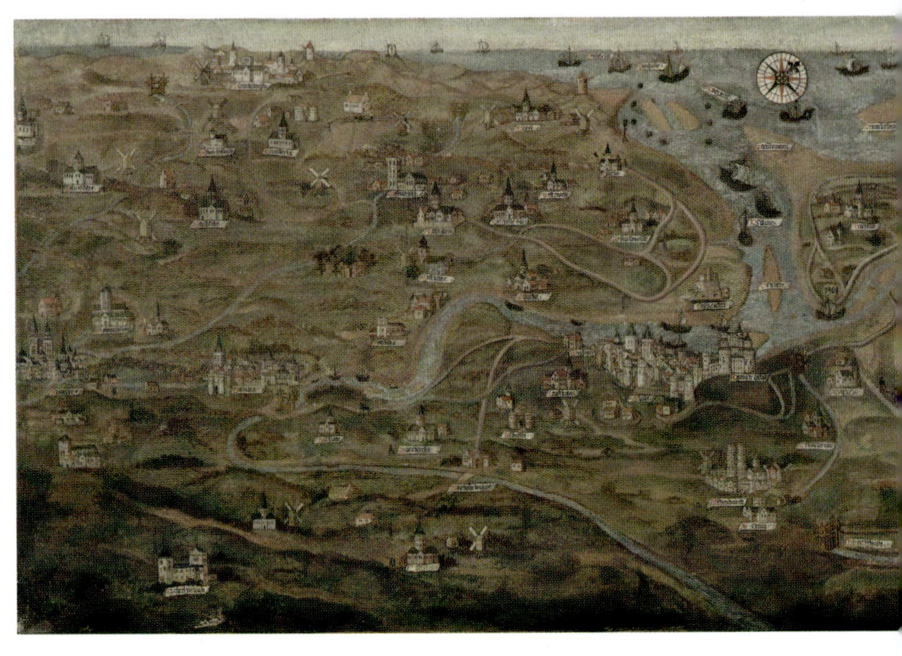

18 Jan de Hervy, *Map of the Zwin Delta*, detail, 1501, oil on canvas.

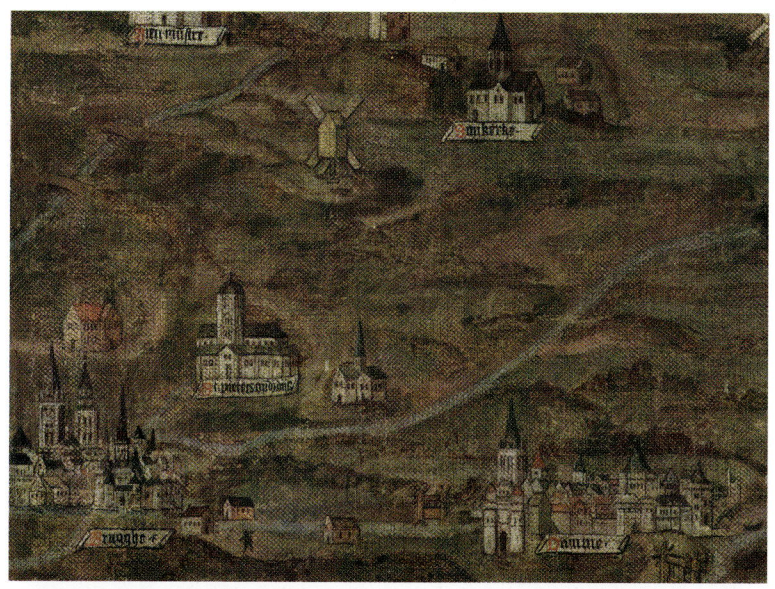

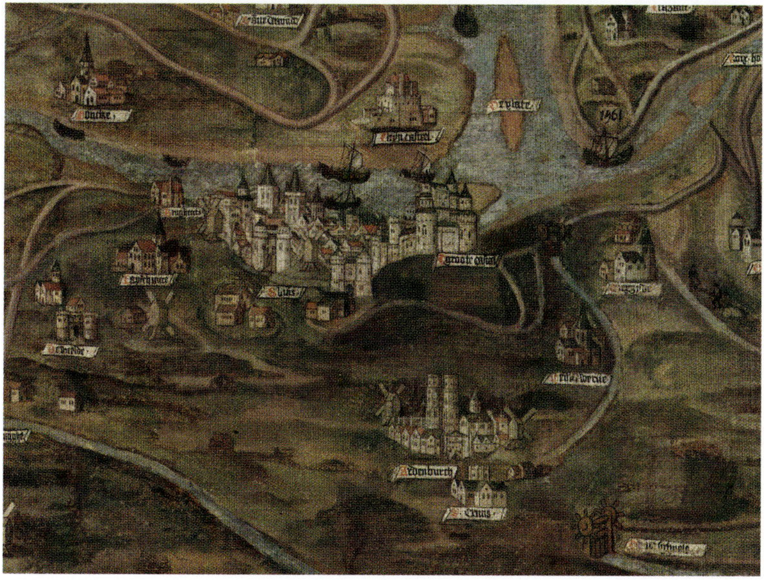

19 Jan de Hervy, *Map of the Zwin Delta*, detail of Bruges and Damme, 1501.
20 Jan de Hervy, *Map of the Zwin Delta*, detail of Hoeke and Sluis, 1501.

Maritime access to Bruges was permitted early on by the Reie, which provided an early but limited port within the city itself. Expanded commerce was supported later by the Zwin and the network of artificial canals, dykes, dams and sluices that augmented it, since the Zwin was prone to a build-up of silt (a natural process probably aggravated by reclamation projects; illus. 18). As part of a coastal development campaign Philip of Alsace had ordered the construction of a substantial dam to stabilize the course of the widest channel of the Zwin where it met the Reie near Bruges, a site subsequently known as Damme (illus. 19). By 1280 access to Damme was unreliable, leading to the establishment in 1290 of Sluis, the most successful of these ports in the following centuries.[7] The use of increasingly large ships – the cogs and even larger *hulken* – exacerbated the situation, and, despite a deepening of the canal between Damme and Sluis in 1421 and the launch of a piloting service in 1472, even Sluis become difficult to access. By the late fifteenth century larger ships had to be unloaded as far away as Middelburg on the coast on to barges or wagons for transport to the city (illus. 20).[8]

Canals were economically crucial infrastructure, and their construction and dredging were administered by Bruges and by autonomous local water boards; the canals linking Bruges to Damme and Sluis were maintained by the city government, which regulated these subordinate ports tightly. Economic competition resulted in the thirteenth-century attempt by the Hansa to develop Hoeke as an alternative to Damme and Bruges, for example, and in more serious conflict, such as the burning of Sluis by Bruges in punishment for violating the larger city's claim as an exclusive distribution point.[9]

Bruges's efforts to develop and maintain land and maritime routes to the rest of Europe were, of course, in the service of commerce. The so-called commercial revolution of thirteenth-century Europe was certainly felt in Flanders, and in 1470 this was one of the most heavily urbanized regions in Europe, with a third of the population living in cities, largely in the dominant 'three members' cities of Bruges, Ghent and Ypres, but also in smaller cities, such as Dendermonde, Lille and Poperinge.[10] In Flanders, as in Tuscany and England, one of the most important trade goods was wool. The artisans involved in textile manufacture were central to civic and economic life, and the merchants who specialized in the distribution and sale of these products prospered. The social origins of this Flemish merchant class that later formed the core of Memling's clientele are unclear, but it may have emerged from local agricultural trade and county administration, or even descendants of serfs and immigrants into the city; early Bruges merchants also invested in waterways and fishing rights, peat exploitation, brickyards, and rents and subleases on property in the city.[11]

While the merchants of Bruges were initially active in trade abroad, by the later medieval period the city was catering increasingly to international merchants as a centre for import and distribution, both seizing the advantages of its geographical location and responding to trade embargoes and increased competition in finished textiles from other centres.[12] In this era, various cities were designated 'staples' by regional rulers. These staples were, as Lodovico Guicciardini described them, public sites with princely privilege at which all international trade in certain goods was required to be conducted.[13] For example, the staple for the distribution of English wool on the Continent was for much of the time assigned to Calais, but goods were transported to Bruges for further exchange and distribution.[14] The most important commodity remained textiles: no longer simply raw wool and finished woollen products, but also luxury textiles, such as the silk, damask, woven gold and brocade production of Lucca and Venice that flowered with the decline of Byzantine industry. A more regional market existed as well, for tapestry from Arras and Tournai, damasks from Kortrijk and fine clothing tailored in Brussels and Lille. Raw

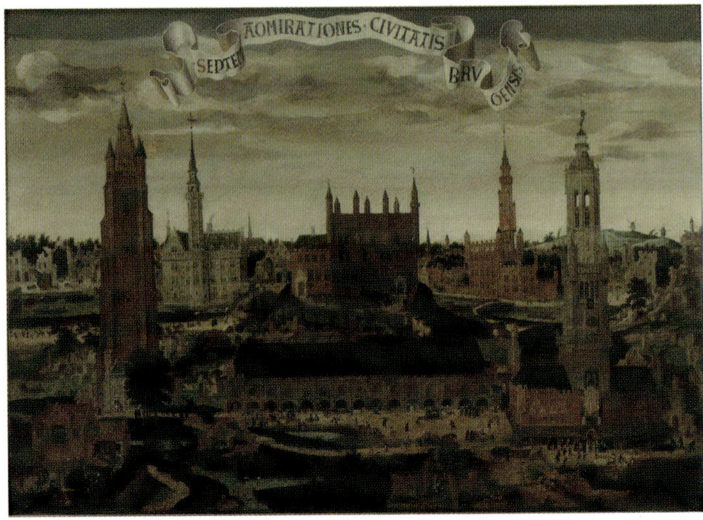

materials were also traded in large quantities in Bruges. Crucial to textile production were the dyes brought from Mediterranean ports and the trade in the alum that was used to fix those dyes, which was imported in massive quantities.[15] Spices and foodstuffs from the Mediterranean and further east – oranges, figs, dates, pepper, sugar – were brought in and distributed by international traders, as were such luxury items as ceramics, carpets, fine leather and jewellery (illus. 21).[16]

This flowering of trade in Europe in the late Middle Ages was facilitated by the development of innovative commercial practices and technology. Literacy and mathematical ability became crucial for anyone occupied in commerce, and the increasingly complex opportunities offered by international exchange are reflected in a proliferation of handbooks for reckoning sums and converting weights, measurements and currency.[17] An example of accounting practice in Bruges is provided by the surviving ledgers of the merchant and money changer Collard de Marke from the second half of the fourteenth century, which use a

21 Pieter Claeissens the Elder, *Cityscape of Bruges* (*The Seven Wonders of Bruges*), 1551–60, oil on canvas.

single-entry bookkeeping technique with transactions in chronological order, Roman numerals and a range of painstakingly
converted currencies.[18] In the fifteenth century nearly all record-
keeping remained in Roman numerals; Arabic numerals were
still limited to highly specialized literature and only slowly adopted
into commercial bookkeeping in the second half of the century.
Complex calculations could be performed using a table abacus,
whereby counting tokens were arranged on a table marked with
inlaid lines or covered in an embroidered cloth. These tokens
had been used in Bruges since at least 1284, and were often minted
with propagandistic imagery, as was done under Philip the Good
(illus. 22).[19] During much of the Middle Ages currency in Flanders
was notoriously confusing. English merchants operating in the
region were warned by a 1460s manual that 'it is right necessary

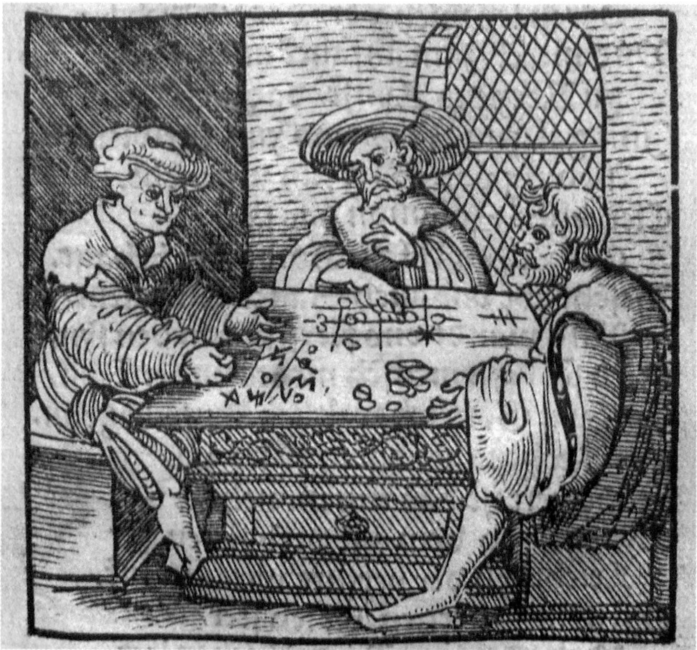

22 Merchants calculating with a counting table and by hand, title-page
illustration from Adam Ries, *Rechnung auff der Linihen und Federn* (1529).

for a merchant to know the value of the gold in that country, for there are many diverse pieces of gold and diverse coins with diverse names, and if a man knows not their value, he may easily be beguiled and lose money.'[20]

The decline of the Champagne fairs in the thirteenth century coincided with the establishment of standing partnerships between merchants (replacing an older model of temporary single-venture agreements) and of regional branches or resident agents of mercantile and banking houses, enabling a more efficient and lucrative trade environment. In the case of the Italians, these branch agents were merchant bankers – combining trade and finance – who represented headquarters in Italy; they would ship and be shipped commodities on consignment, and arrange financing and credit. In 1466, for instance, the Medici functioned in Bruges through a branch manager, an assistant manager, six agents or 'factors' and one apprentice (fifteenth-century banks were lean operations in comparison to the huge Italian banks of the previous two centuries). Some companies' branches abroad – their *filiali* – were interconnected and would be operated by the firm's factors, who would receive a salary and share profits, and who might act as branch managers with legal power of attorney to act on the firm's behalf. Other firms, such as the Medici, were much more loosely organized, with individual partnerships acting as separate legal entities and shareholders investing capital in enterprises, but under the ultimate authority of the family itself. In doing business with one another, Medici agents would charge commission and interest, even while recognizing one another as *i nostri*, essentially 'one of ours'.[21]

The emergence of companies with stable branches in diverse locations likewise permitted early forms of chequing, as cumbersome notarized payment mechanisms were replaced by the more informal bill of exchange. This operated as a letter through which a merchant or financer in one city – who would have received investment funds from a second merchant in that city – instructed an agent in a second city to make a payment on his behalf to the second merchant's agent in that city. By 1300 this practice had developed into a European merchant-banking network, also reducing the hazardous need for merchants to travel with coin.[22] The various banks maintained accounts with one another, and by 1300 there were about eighty banks operating in Florence; it has been estimated that in 1400 one-tenth of adult men in Bruges had bank accounts.[23]

While many merchant bankers of the fifteenth century specialized in this lucrative line of business, generally they diversified and continued their commodities trading in textiles, spices, alum and other goods, since their awareness of exchange rates and ability to exploit available capital made it possible to nimbly take advantage of commercial opportunities. A number of courier services in the fifteenth century also developed to serve merchant communities in the timely delivery of letters of exchange, news (such as updated prices and exchange rates), and personal and commercial correspondence. In 1464, for example, the Medici's representatives in Bruges reported a profit-cutting alum surplus and recommended withholding further shipments. The *scarselle dei mercanti fiorentini* (named after the leather mail pouch used by the couriers) served routes from Bruges to Florence and Pisa, via Cologne and Milan or Paris; in the 1420s one could expect a courier to reach Bruges from Florence within 25 days.[24]

While shipping in the fifteenth century was still sometimes exorbitant, it was deemed worth the expense, and various insurance mechanisms developed. In the early fifteenth century the freight cost of cloth, wine and spices was roughly 10 per cent of the value of the cargo, but transport of Baltic timber from Gdansk cost 79 per cent and Portuguese salt 85 per cent of the value.[25] Goods transported to Florence and Rome were generally routed through Pisa and other coastal ports, where

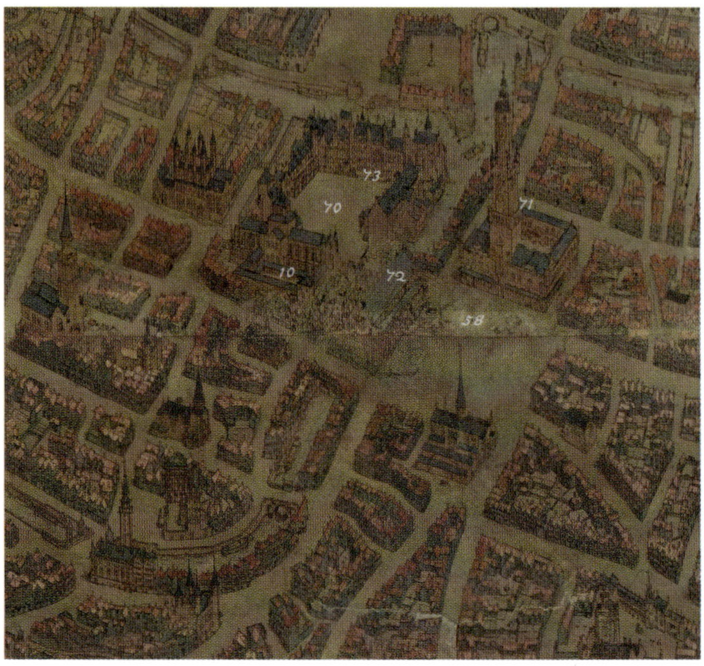

they would be transferred from ships to land transport. Many shipments of artwork were arranged in bulk for resale (such as '60 canvas paintings'), but other artworks were shipped as special personalized items.[26] The development of maritime insurance allowed merchants to reduce costs by shipping goods via a single carrier, rather than distributing shipments among several carriers or vessels to cut potential losses to piracy or misadventure; Genoa's financiers had developed the model by which one would pay a premium and be compensated in the event of damage or loss.[27] Some risk remained and necessitated the resolution of disputes, however. The case of the two galleys built in Pisa for Philip the Good (intended for an abandoned crusade) and subsequently acquired and operated by the Medici has been well studied. Their first journey transported alum to Sluis and Southampton

23 Marcus Gheeraerts, *Map of Bruges*, 1562–3, detail. Locations of the Burg (70), Sint-Donaaskerk (10), the Grote Markt (58), Hallen/Belfort (71), Waterhalle (72) and Stadshuis (73).

and returned to Porto Pisano with English wool; the second
carried more alum and wine – under arrangements made with
34 Florentine individuals and families – but on the return trip
one of the galleys, carrying alum, cloth and the *Last Judgement* altarpiece by Memling intended for Florence, was taken by Hansa
privateers.[28]

With this rise in commerce the initially small settlement of
Bruges had developed a stable population and a more robust
environment to house expanding business and trade. In 1477 the
city housed perhaps 42,000 residents (a quarter of whom belonged
to the trades or the patriciate), seasonal migrants and travelling
merchants.[29] By the mid-fourteenth century the city's infrastructure had taken shape: its essential waterways, paved streets and
a heterogenous set of fortifications comprising gates, a double
moat, earthen ramparts, timber palisades and walls of brick and
stone.[30] The construction of a brickyard in the same era permitted

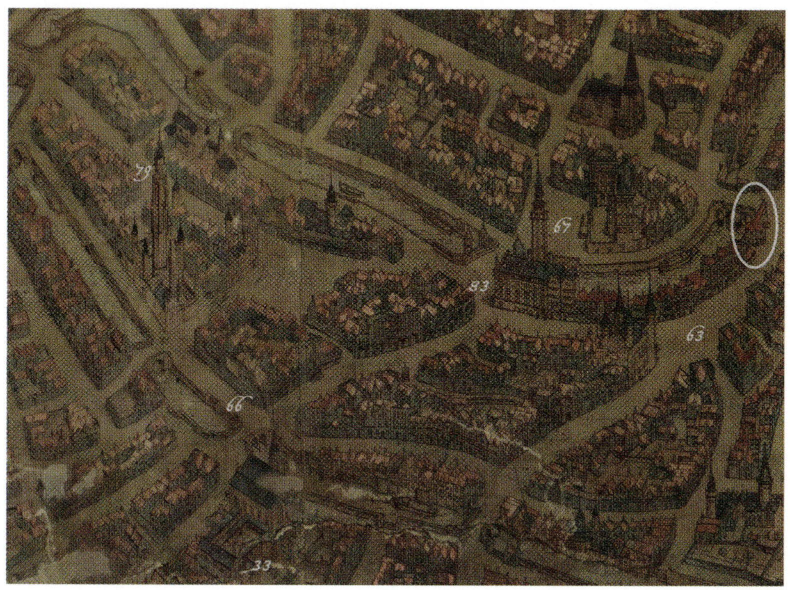

24 Marcus Gheeraerts, *Map of Bruges*, 1562–3, detail. Locations of the Beursplein
(63), Poortersloge (83), Kraanplein (crane visible by the bridge near 63),
Biscayerplein (67), Castilian nation house (66), Augustinian monastery (33)
and Oosterlingenhuis (79).

the increasingly common use of more fire-resistant building materials throughout the city.[31]

While in some ways rather generalized, the ground plan of the city commissioned from Marcus Gheeraerts in 1561 provides an overview of primary infrastructure (illus. 23; see also illus. 3). The Burg square, the original heart of the city, still served in the fifteenth century as a centre of civic administration and religious life for Bruges. It featured the collegiate church dedicated to St Donatian of Reims and the Virgin Mary (the Sint-Donaaskerk), and since the thirteenth century the Chapel of the Holy Blood at the church of St Basil (the Heiligbloedkapel at the Sint-Basiliuskerk) across the square had housed the city's most sacred relic: traces of the blood of Jesus in a rock-crystal vial, venerated as the focus of the city's largest annual procession in May.[32] The old residence of the counts of Flanders nearby had been abandoned in the late thirteenth century and acquired by the civic government, and in 1376 a new city hall was constructed on the same square, the first of the grand late Gothic city halls of Flanders.[33] The Burg also served as the seat of the officials of the Brugse Vrije or Franc (sometimes translated as 'the Liberty of Bruges'), the rural district that surrounded the city. In earlier centuries a range of stalls clustered near the Sint-Donaaskerk sold various goods, but by the fifteenth century commerce on the Burg was limited to books, art and the productions of professional scribes.[34]

Nearby to the west, connected to the Burg by a bridge over the Kraanrei canal, was the true commercial centre of the city at the Grote Markt, the city's grandest marketplace.[35] Most prominent among the buildings here was the complex of the 'Halls' (Hallen) and their bell tower. The Hallen served until 1280 as a civic administrative centre, but in the fifteenth and sixteenth centuries it was a place of commerce, the vast chambers of its four wings dedicated to trade in spices and dyes, gloves and other goods, and above all textiles.[36] The symbolic power of its imposing bell tower – the

Belfort or Halletoren – was recognized with numerous campaigns to increase its height, and the top third was constructed only in 1482–6.[37] Its bells marked the hours of the day and announced the opening of yearly markets, festivals and other important events.[38] Between the Burg and the Grote Markt was the New Hall, or Waterhalle, 95 metres (312 ft) long. It was built in the 1280s and 1290s over the course of the Reie canal so that barges could pass under the adjacent bridge for the loading and unloading of shipments within the great vaulted lower floor of the building itself, connecting the centre of the city directly to the waterways leading to the North Sea. Fourteenth-century expansion had added a two-storey arcade of shop stalls, and the upper floors served as warehouse space for goods. By the fifteenth century the stalls of the *wissel* – the currency-exchange centre – had been relocated from the Halls to the north side of the Waterhalle, and the bridge leading towards the Burg thus became known as the Exchange Bridge.[39]

Outside the Grote Markt, further commercial activity was concentrated to the northeast (illus. 24). Along the old course of the Kraanrei canal was the Kraanplein, the site of the largest city crane. This elaborate wooden structure, operated with a circular treadmill by the 'children of the crane', weighed shipments that were too heavy for the Waterhalle infrastructure, such as barrels of wine and beer (illus. 25).[40] Further along the canal at the Sint-Jansbrug stood the Poortersloge with its impressive tower, serving as a nexus between civic government, burghers and merchants, as well as the headquarters of the Brotherhood of the White Bear, known for holding annual jousting tournaments and festivities.[41] At this intersection stood also the toll house and the hall (1470) of the Rijkepijnders – the porters – who oversaw the lading and weighing of goods.[42]

The primary accommodation for the various foreign merchant communities was conveniently situated in the immediate vicinity

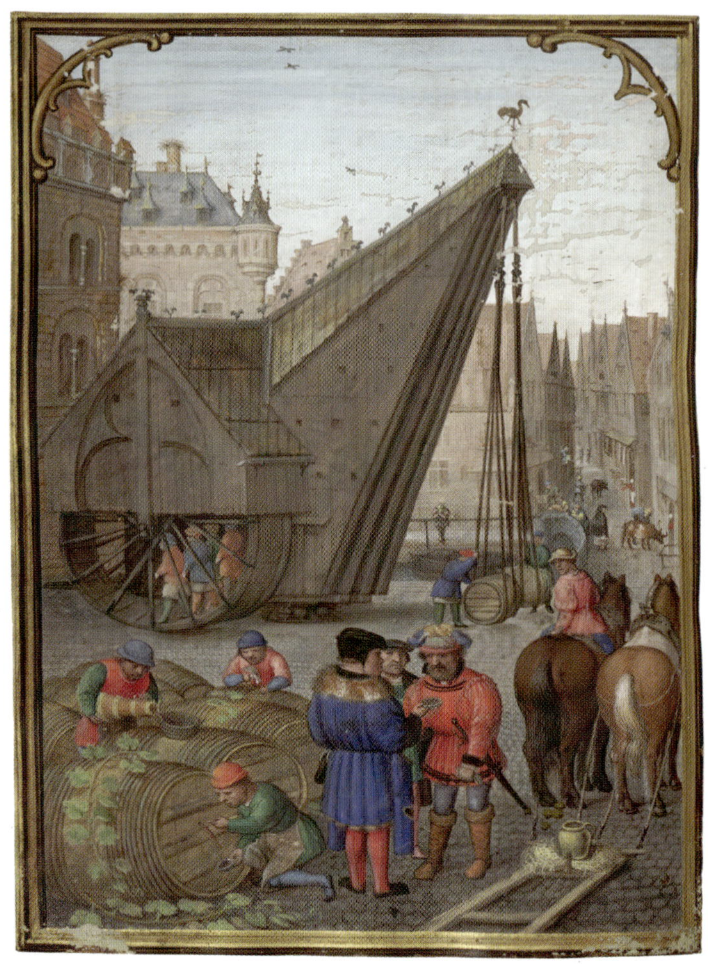

of the Kraanplein and Sint-Jansbrug, particularly at the Beursplein, where Florentines, Venetians and Genoese lodged at hostels and later kept their nation houses (illus. 26). Originating with the hostel run by the Van der Beurze family, this square served as a gathering place for the exchange of securities and a space for trade separate from the main marketplaces, and was

25 Simon Bening, *October*, calendar miniature from a Book of Hours, 1520–25.

referred to in texts as the *Forum Mercatorum* or *Der Cooplieden Beurse*:
the merchants' forum or merchant *Beurse*. The regulations gov-
erning trade at the Beursplein are poorly documented and appear
to have been conventional or customary; it operated separately
from the market hours of the city (indicated by the ringing of
a bell) and was overseen by a special bailiff.[43] In the 1470s and
1480s merchants from Lucca, Florence, Venice, Genoa and Pisa
are documented as active there, as well as some from Aragon and
Castile.[44] A letter of 1458 between representatives of the Florentine
Salviati merchant-banking firm in Bruges reported a return
address 'at the Beurse where the merchants congregate'.[45]

On the periphery of this same international quarter were
assorted buildings and squares controlled by various merchant
nations, other prominent hostels, such as that of the Metteneye
family, the mansion of Pieter Bladelin (purchased by the Medici
firm in 1472) and the Carmelite church, where several international communities held services. Very close by, across the bridge,
perhaps 300 metres (985 ft) away, Hans Memling established
his workshop in close proximity to his primary clientele; one

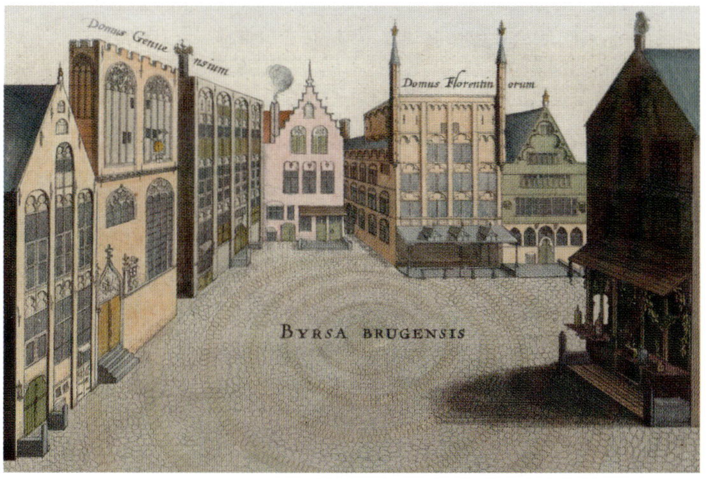

26 Beursplein with the nation house of the Genoese, the Huis ter Beurze,
the house ter Ouder Beurze (used by the Venetians) and the nation house
of the Florentines. From Antonius Sanderus, *Flandria illustrata* (1641).

neighbour was the illuminator Willem Vrelant, and other artists would follow in setting up shop in the neighbourhood.

In addition to its commercial and civic institutions, Bruges contained a range of abbeys and mendicant churches, lured by the economically diverse population and trade in which they, too, participated.[46] The first to arrive were the Regular Canons of St Augustine, at Eeckhout Abbey in the centre of the city from the 1130s, and in 1188 the Rule of St John, one of the earliest hospital rules, was established at the Sint-Janshospitaal, outside the original city fortifications.[47] The international communities would be most active at the four mendicant monasteries, where they founded altars and chapels and safeguarded their records and weights.[48] The Franciscans and Dominicans arrived in the 1230s, and later that century the Carmelites settled near the business district, as did the Austin Friars (the Black Friars of St Augustine).[49] In 1466 a group of reform Franciscans – the Friars Observants – were donated land outside the Ezelpoort by Tommaso Portinari, the agent of the Medici family and Memling's repeat customer.[50]

The foreign merchants of Bruges, who comprised a large proportion of Memling's clientele, focused on the export and import of goods but also took part in other lucrative operations, such as international finance. While usually excluded from participation in civic governance, many of them served the ducal court in various capacities, especially fiscal appointments.[51] Over time, organized consulates represented twelve foreign communities in Bruges: the cities of the Hanseatic federation; the Italian peninsular cities of Florence, Venice, Lucca and Genoa; the Iberian regions of Castile, Biscay, Aragon and Portugal; and England and Scotland (merchants from other cities, such as Milan, were present but not formally represented or recognized by local officials as 'a nation').[52]

Unlike many centres of international commerce in the era, in Bruges the foreign merchants were not separated from one

another or from the local population in walled enclaves or exclusive districts, but instead mingled freely in the inns, pubs and
brothels, bought property, occasionally married and purchased
permanent citizenship, endowed masses and founded altars, and
commissioned artworks for their chapels and altars.[53] Key to the
success of these communities of foreigners was their securing
from the city and other authorities various economic privileges
and legal rights, which required periodic renegotiation and
renewed enforcement. For example, as early as 1319 the Venetians
were granted a number of rights by the Count of Flanders: to
operate a consulate holding jurisdiction over their own affairs,
to sell wholesale and retail goods, and a reduction of charges levied
on them by Bruges brokers, among others. In return, the foreign
nations pledged, for example, to keep their staples in Bruges rather
than some other port, or to offer their goods in Bruges before
continuing to England or elsewhere.[54]

It is difficult to quantify precisely the number of foreign merchants present in the city, since their presence depended on both
seasonal and political climate. One frequently cited index has
been the description by the chronicler Nicolaas Despars of the
merchant groups participating in the 'Joyous Entry' of Philip the
Good in December 1440, which notes the presence of 150 Italians
(40 from Venice, 40 from Milan, 36 from Genoa, 22 from Florence
and 12 from Lucca), 136 Hansards and 48 Castilians.[55] This is
probably a conservative count owing to the 'off-season' timing
of the event, which might account for the absence of several entire
nationalities; Despars mentions no French or English merchants,
nor the Basques, Aragonese and Portuguese, and it is even more
difficult to determine how many foreigners from such regions
as Brabant, Hainault, Picardy and Artois would have been present.[56] Likewise, three hundred merchants were described as
participating in the procession held on the occasion of the
wedding of Charles the Bold and Margaret of York in 1468, but

the total number of foreign merchants active in the city may have been as high as 2,000; it has been estimated that 15–20 per cent of the city's 45,000 residents in the fifteenth century spoke a foreign language as a native tongue.[57] Among Memling's clients who have been identified with some certainty we find Florentines, Bolognese, Venetians, Castilians, Germans, English and, of course, the native Flemings.

Best represented in Bruges were the merchants of the Germanic Hanseatic League, known in Bruges as the *Oosterlingen*, 'Easterlings', including the brothers Greverade, the commissioners of the large polyptych now in Lübeck. This trade confederation of numerous cities stretching from the Netherlands to Estonia was represented by its dominant cities of origin Lübeck and Cologne (especially in later years), as well as Dortmund, Hamburg, Gdansk, Reval (Tallinn) and others.[58] Receiving privileges from the count of Flanders in 1252, they were the earliest foreign merchants to organize formally in Bruges (illus. 27). On numerous occasions the staple was moved temporarily to other cities, most frequently as a way to leverage more favourable privileges.[59] Unlike at the other three early Hansa regional offices, or *Kontoren* (at London, Bergen and Novogorod), the Germans in Bruges were not permitted to construct a separate enclave and instead mingled among the locals and merchants from other nations, lodging at inns and in rented houses.[60]

During the first centuries of the Hansa merchants' presence in Bruges, the posting of official announcements, meetings and decisions affecting the collective was done at the refectory of the Austin Friars, and they kept a set of their standard weights in a shrine at the Franciscans from 1347; by 1442 the Hansa *Kontor* was using an office near the Beursplein.[61] In 1457, when they returned their staple to Bruges – an event marked by a ceremonial entrance in which more than two hundred merchants participated – the city offered the use of a square close to the

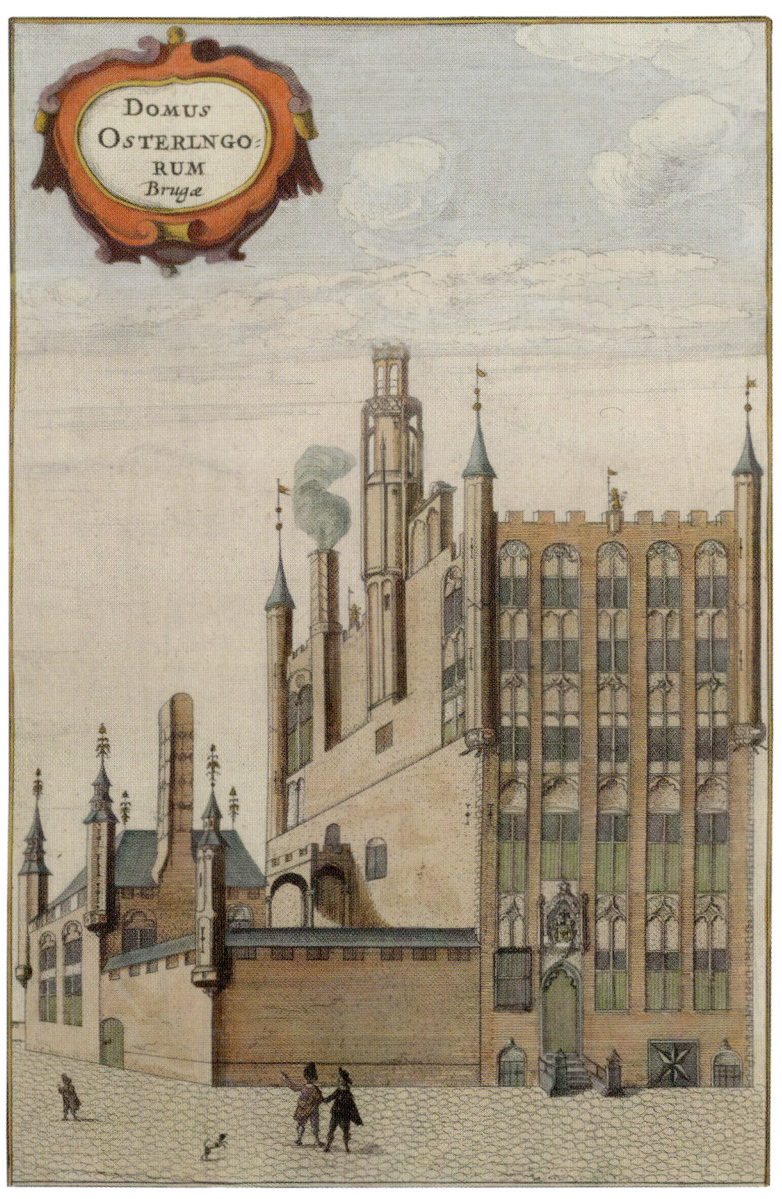

27 Nation house of the Hanseatic League (Oosterlingenhuis), from Antonius Sanderus, *Flandria illustrata* (1641).

toll house, subsequently known as the Oosterlingenplaats.[62] In 1478 construction began on the Oosterlingenhuis, an impressive brick structure featuring several turrets, a tower upon which an image of Emperor Frederick III was placed, and flags with imperial eagles further marking the Germanic presence. They also possessed on the square seven small buildings and a public clock, its maintenance paid for by the Hansa *Kontor*.[63]

The Hansa merchants left many indexes of their incorporation into the urban social fabric, such as marriages, property purchases and membership of local religious confraternities, such as Our Lady of the Snow.[64] In 1260 the Hansa merchants helped to found the Carmelite monastery, where they would bury deceased members at a common sepulchre in the chapel dedicated to Thomas Becket, administered after 1457 by the English colony.[65] The Hansa preferred operating in Bruges to elsewhere in Brabant or Holland; the city of Lübeck, particularly, increasingly tied its fortunes to Bruges in the later years of the fifteenth century even as the merchants of other German cities began to drift towards Antwerp and Utrecht.[66] As a southern German living in Bruges in the fifteenth century, Memling was not alone, for in addition to this northern coastal Hanseatic presence, contingents of merchants from southern German cities operated in Bruges as part of their circuit to the markets at Bergen-op-Zoom and Antwerp. Although less numerous than their northern German counterparts, merchants from Constance, Nuremberg, Augsburg and a branch of the Grosse Ravensburger Handelsgesellschaft were present in Bruges.[67] Occasionally profiting from troubles between the city and the Hansa – rewarded by the counts and dukes, for example, for breaking Hansa embargoes against Flanders – the southern German merchants had become more prominent in Flanders by the late fifteenth century.[68] Like their Hanseatic colleagues, these southern Germans organized at favoured brokerages and inns and participated in local religious foundations and brotherhoods; the merchants of Nuremberg, too, held a daily mass at the Austin Friars.[69]

Merchants from the various states of the Italian peninsula comprised the largest group of foreigners in fifteenth-century Bruges, collectively outnumbering even the Germans, and constituted a significant proportion of Memling's clientele. The permanent presence of dozens of Italian merchant-banking houses in Bruges was distinctive in northwestern Europe, a product of their impressive assets and their advanced commercial technology.[70] The most active Italian communities in Bruges were those of Venice, Genoa, Lucca and Florence; merchants from Siena, Pisa, Bologna, Piacenza, Milan, Arezzo and Como were also present, their interests often bundled together with the negotiations of the larger Italian representations.[71] As did the merchants of the Hansa, these groups organized to protect their members' economic and political interests, received trading privileges from the city and regional princes, and integrated both corporately and individually into the fabric of civic life in Bruges. As one index of this integration, between 1309 and 1507 some 55 Italians became citizens, fully joining Bruges society, including the Genoese businessmen Giovanni Arnolfini (Van Eyck's client) and Andrea della Costa.[72] Marrying into the prominent Adornes family, itself originally from Genoa but residing in Bruges for several generations, della Costa became a citizen in 1483, as did the Florentine Tommaso Portinari, who was still conducting business in the city.[73] Portinari, as we have seen, was a repeat customer of Memling, and in the 1490s della Costa ordered a diptych that has been linked to Memling's atelier (see illus. 14 and 15).

One of the earliest Italian merchant communities to conduct significant business in Bruges was that of Genoa. This maritime republic was not a major producer of goods of its own, but was ideally located to take advantage of shipping other Mediterranean and Levantine products, especially luxury goods, spices, citrus fruit and woad; it also held a near monopoly on alum from Asia Minor before its territories were absorbed into the Ottoman Empire in the mid-fifteenth century.[74] By 1277 the Spinola family – early leaders in trade and finance – was operating in the city, and by 1298 regular trade between the two cities had been established; in 1397 the Genoese formed in Bruges an association of all the heads of merchant houses who had been present for a year.[75]

The Venetians were the first Italian merchants to organize formally as a 'nation' in Bruges, arriving in 1314 and establishing a consulate in 1332.[76] Their galleys arrived at Sluis with commodities from the Mediterranean including spices, almonds, rice, oil, fruit, cotton and other textiles, woad, soap, sugar and wood for longbows, and in 1358 they were granted privileges for trade without constraints over the month and a half after their arrival each season.[77]

Both the Genoese and the Venetians in Bruges operated from the Beursplein, where in about 1397 the Venetians rented a former property of the Van der Beurze family; in 1441 the Genoese consulate was in a nearby structure that resembled the later Hansa headquarters in its monumentality and ornamentation. Likewise, both groups focused their religious activities at the Austin Friars, where they held daily masses; the Genoese paid for a set of pews for the choir, and the Venetians established an altar dedicated to San Marco.[78]

Lucca, which had established privileges in Bruges in 1369, remained in the fifteenth century a major textile centre, producing a range of high-quality silks for brocades and liturgical garments. In the early fifteenth century the residences of the Lucchese merchants were clustered just west of the Beursplein, in the same neighbourhood that the Florentine Medici would occupy some years later.[79] That century brought new competition from Bologna, Venice and Florence, however, and by 1478 only twelve Lucchese merchants were still active in Bruges. The Lucchese were also occupied as merchant bankers, money exchangers and insurers, and a number of them had served the counts and dukes as head of the mint.[80] Their corporate body in Bruges was notably devotional in character; their statutes, while outlining commercial rules, are presented, 'first for the praise and reverence of the Holy Face [*Volto Santo*] and the maintenance of our chapel, then for the honour of our city and for peace, concord and union of all the inhabitants of Lucca who are and will be found in the future in these countries'.[81] A member of the brotherhood in Bruges appears to have sponsored a painted version of this *Volto Santo* – a crucifix in the cathedral of Lucca modelled after a miraculous image of Christ – for the minstrels' guildhall in Bruges, and the Lucchese practised the same devotion at their chapel dedicated to the Holy Cross at the Austin Friars, where individual members (among them Arnolfini and his brother) established foundations.[82]

While active in Bruges as early as the late thirteenth century, the Florentine presence had dwindled after the collapse of the Bardi and Peruzzi family firms in the middle of the fourteenth century. Their fortunes, however, increased again in the fifteenth century, and they became one of the dominant foreign presences in the city, establishing a consulate there in 1427; they would become one of the largest blocs of Memling's clientele. The Florentines initially operated from a loggia on the Beursplein, and in the 1430s the Medici set up a branch operation in Bruges, alongside other Florentine merchant-banking juggernauts, such as the Pazzi and Strozzi.[83] From the 1460s Piero de' Medici leased Pieter Bladelin's old mansion near the Beursplein, from which the Medici's Florentine factors operated, focusing on wool, linen and fine silks, but also financing, working with letters of exchange and cash deposits.[84] After the discovery of alum deposits in the Papal States, the Medici began to trade huge amounts of it in Bruges, holding a practical monopoly and ending Genoese dominance of that market.[85] From 1414 the Florentines maintained a chapel dedicated to Francis of Assisi at the Franciscan church, and in 1466 Cosimo the Elder and Portinari supported the construction of an Observant Franciscans' cloister on land donated by Portinari.[86] The Florentines supported chapels at Sint-Jakobskerk, which served as the parish church for many – including Portinari, whose chapel there was probably the destination for one or more of Memling's works. Members of the Florentine *nazione* in Bruges held a two-day celebration of their patron saint, John the Baptist, and joined such confraternities as Our Lady of the Dry Tree (drawn by its dedication to the Franciscan-supported theme of the Immaculate Conception), Our Lady of Roosbeke and the Crossbowmen of St George.[87]

The historical relationship between England and Flanders was politically and commercially complex. In the Middle Ages Flemish merchants pursued an active trade in finished wool cloth in Gloucestershire, the Cotswolds and northern England, and British merchants operated in Flanders and Bruges. By the thirteenth century, however, 35 per cent of wool imported into Flanders was English, and they would leverage this dominant position politically and economically, moving the wool staple from Bruges to Calais in the fourteenth century.[88] As merchants began to import finished cloth woven outside Flanders, its competition with locally manufactured cloth resulted in a ban on the sale of English cloth in Flanders and caused the English to seek alternative outlets for this trade; Antwerp, which had little textile industry of its own to protect, soon benefited.[89] While the Hundred Years War and related embargoes, piracy, smuggling and monopolies further disrupted trade with England, the English did continue to have some presence in Bruges during the fifteenth century, and operated a scale and weigh-house until 1586.[90]

The Scots remained active in the import of wool and finished textiles at Bruges throughout the period, since their coarse, low-quality cloth was not seen as a threat to local manufacture. Only in 1470 did Charles the Bold attempt to control Scottish imports to protect Flemish industry; they were able to keep their staple in Bruges until 1498 and continued to trade there into the sixteenth century.[91] The English and Scots, too, were active in religious and civic life, the English in the neighbourhood around the Sint-Walburgakerk and the Scots centred on the nearby Sint-Maartensplein (later called the Schottenplaats). A confraternity dedicated to Thomas Becket was founded with two chapels at the Carmelite church, and a Scottish chapel was dedicated to Our Lady and St Ninian; in 1422 an English Augustinian friar was brought to Bruges to preach in English, and enough Scots dyers were operating in Bruges to warrant establishing their own altar dedicated to St Andrew at the Sint-Gilliskerk.[92] A governor of the Merchant Adventurers of London, William Caxton, is best known to English-speakers for having collaborated in 1473 with Colard Mansion in Bruges to print the first book in English, and for introducing the press to England.

Bruges hosted a number of Iberian merchant communities: those of Castile, Biscay, Catalonia, Navarre and Portugal. The Catalonians were the earliest Spaniards to organize in Bruges, founding a consulate in 1330, and encompassing merchants from Barcelona and also such Aragonese cities as Valencia and the island of Majorca; they imported, among other goods, pottery from Valencia by the mid-fourteenth century.[93] From the 1350s they rented space on the Beursplein alongside the Italian communities, and in 1483 they transferred their consulate to a site neighbouring the German Hansa headquarters.[94] In common with other nations, the Catalonians and Aragonese maintained communal grave sites at the monastic churches and made use of the high altar at the Carmelites from 1389.[95]

A population of Castilian and Basque merchants had arrived in Flanders in the late thirteenth century and flourished in the fifteenth century.[96] In grouping themselves as a common 'nation', the subjects of the king of Castile (initially encompassing both Castilian and Basque merchants) received greater privileges from the Flemish authorities than they did at their other principal trading colonies, including the right to select their own magistrates and govern their own affairs.[97] Burgos served in the fifteenth century as the centre of Spanish wool production and export, its merchants bringing merino wool to Flanders and returning to Castile with Flemish wool; the Basque merchants imported Cantabrian iron and French wine to Flanders for distribution in the north.[98] By the 1440s the Castilians in Bruges were operating from six commercial buildings, each run by a small staff of factors.[99]

In 1455, however, this northern Iberian merchant presence in Bruges fragmented as the Basque merchants separated from

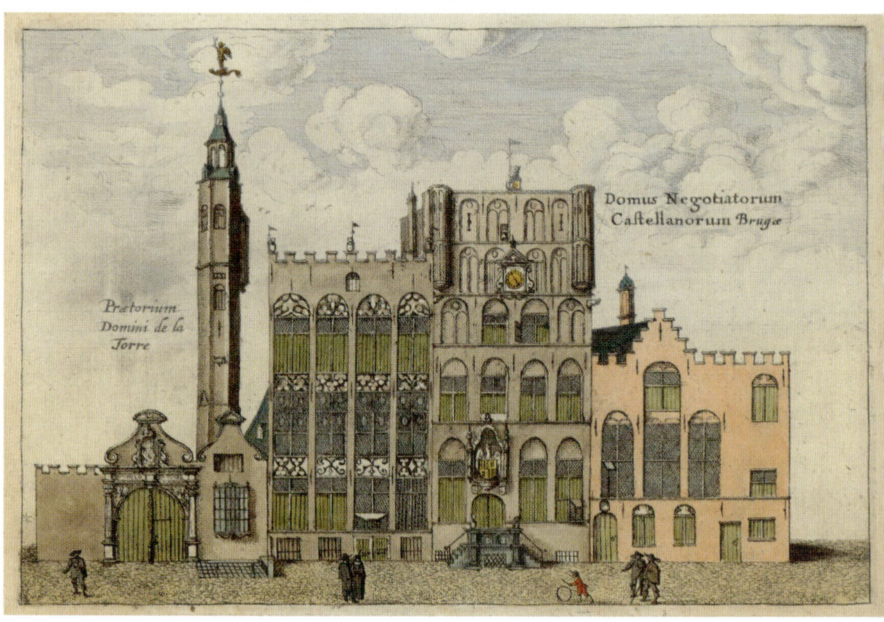

28 Nation house of Castile, Huis de la Torre, from Antonius Sanderus, *Flandria illustrata* (1641).

the interior cities, resenting perceived assertions of dominance by the Castilians.[100] In 1413 or 1414 the northern Spanish established a chapel in the Franciscan church dedicated to St James, their national saint, and the Castilian group established altars at the Austin Friars and the Observant churches in the late 1460s and 1470s.[101] Having boarded earlier at the Huis ter Beurze, in 1483 the Castilians established their consulate in a house previously owned by one of their merchants, and the merchants of Biscay operated from separate quarters nearby from 1494 onwards (illus. 28).[102] Amid the political turmoil of Maximilian's era, the Spanish were quick to return to Bruges in 1484 and 1494 as their wool staple was reconfirmed by the emperor, and in the sixteenth century they would be joined by the merchants from Navarre, present earlier but only now formalizing a consulate.[103] A side effect of the robust trade in wool between Bruges and Castile was several major commissions for Memling late in his career, exported to Spanish destinations but arranged by Castilian merchants in Bruges as intermediaries.

The marriage of Philip the Good to the Portuguese *infanta* Isabella of Bourbon in 1430 contributed to the sudden rise of the Portuguese trading presence in Bruges. Some Portuguese merchants were already importing wine, olive oil and warm-climate fruit, such as figs and raisins, into the city at the beginning of the thirteenth century, but their global exploration and exploitation in the fifteenth century expanded their range of wares to include spices (such as west African pepper), exotic wood, African ivory, dyestuffs (including orchil) and – particularly later in the century – sugar from Madeira.[104] In 1410 the Portuguese founded their own chapel dedicated to the Holy Cross at the Dominican church, with rights to celebrate masses and bury their dead, and decorated it with their arms.[105] Soon afterwards they received further privileges from the city and organized as a corporate body, and in 1417 the king of Portugal installed a factor in the city.

In 1438, after the marriage of Philip and Isabella, the Portuguese were given the right to elect their own councillors and settle internal disputes.[106] While the number of Portuguese merchants in Bruges increased rapidly through the 1470s, their activity would run a short course. Only in 1494, as part of the attempt to return commerce to the city, did the city magistrates offer the Portuguese merchants a building, although it is unclear whether they ever actually used it; the colony departed permanently for Antwerp in 1499.[107]

This vibrant presence of international merchants was what made fifteenth-century Bruges distinctive, but the natives of the city maintained some exclusive privileges as well, and both groups would be central to Memling's clientele. Many families of Bruges themselves participated in import and export activities, and banking and finance; retail trade remained the domain of the local merchants and artisanal guilds, who dominated the market in such luxury goods as finished textiles, fine clothing, spices and fur. The local spice merchants appear to have been particularly prosperous, and several were among Memling's clients (illus. 29). A number of specialized occupations – essentially a robust service industry – existed symbiotically with the merchants and were restricted to or predominately offered by citizens of Bruges: brokers, pawnshops, longshoremen and the vast hospitality industry of innkeepers and hostellers, alehouses and brothels.

One of the key industries supporting international trade in Bruges was that of the brokers and the hoteliers (*waarden* or *hosteliers*), two occupations that very often overlapped (the hoteliers would either offer brokerage services themselves or contract a broker to facilitate transactions on site) and that were administrated through their own guild.[108] From the end of the thirteenth century onwards, any wholesale trade or transaction amounting to more than five Flemish pounds between foreign merchants was required to pass through the hands of an intermediary domestic broker. Only native Flemings with Bruges citizenship could pursue these occupations, so many of these families, among them the Van den Beurze, became very rich and politically powerful.[109] The inns not only provided food, board and brokerage services for the visiting merchants, but were also a site for the exchange of information: updated market trends, deals and regional events that might affect trade. Hoteliers connected merchants with transport and lading businesses, insured cargos, served as guarantors and legal witnesses, and connected merchants to the local banking networks with which these hoteliers naturally held accounts.[110] Hoteliers could also provide for the storage of goods, renting out their cellars or neighbouring buildings; such access was laid out explicitly in a nation's privileges, and some hoteliers specialized in the storage of specific wares, so that certain nationalities tended to work with particular hoteliers.[111]

Money-changing was another vital service for anyone doing business in Bruges. It was a carefully controlled occupation that initially carried the legal requirement of *poorter* status, although by the fifteenth century it seems to have become less socially respected, and more foreigners purchased citizenship in order to enter the trade. Most large transactions were done through bills of exchange, but any remaining imbalance had to be reckoned with bullion, and while the notoriously complex coinage situation in Flanders had been ameliorated by the fifteenth century, the availability of coinage and its risky and heavily regulated export remained problematic, as did the wide range of dominations in circulation.[112] Similarly, pawnbrokers and other licensed usurers could extend credit, as would more illicit lenders willing to account in their budgets for whatever penalties might be imposed. Like the money changers, the pawnbrokers served an important role in the economy of the city owing to the relative shortage of circulating coinage across all social groups, exacerbated by

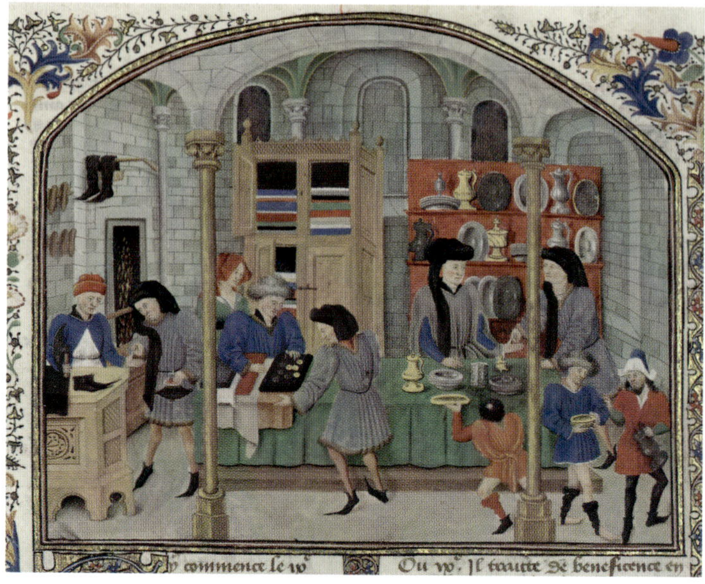

merchants' reluctance to tie up their capital. Temporary trade in precious items served to even up accounts or provide emergency credit.[113]

The commercial activity of late medieval Bruges took place under the watchful eye of regional, civic and corporate authority. Class relationships in the city were complex and the control of power fluid, with quickly shifting power blocs among the guilds, the patricians and economic elite, and the traditional nobility, as well as the motivation of the dukes and their occasional physical presence in the city.[114] By the mid-thirteenth century civic authority lay in the hands of count-appointed officers: the bailiff (*baljuw*) and the urban sheriff (*schout*).[115] The guiding documents for administration were the statutes or privileges, which were frequently renegotiated; the number and composition of the board of aldermen, for example, was in continual dispute.[116] The civic government also had a direct hand in the governance of the trade

29 Retail trade in the Middle Ages: *The Mint*, miniature from a French translation of Aristotle's *Ethics, Politics and Economics* by Nicholas Oresme (1453–4).

guilds, which covered occupations from textile manufacture to grocers, glovemakers, porters and of course the painters and saddlers' guild. Membership of the city's elite *poorterie* conferred a special legal status and, while reserved for those who possessed citizenship of the city, was in practice narrower, differentiated from the working and artisanal classes on account of its economic prosperity and other selective criteria. Access was effectively limited to the very wealthy and some ecclesiastics; perhaps a tenth of the population in Bruges belonged to this group.[117]

Class was to some extent conventional, and those who belonged to the urban patriciate, such as the hoteliers, were recognized as such in the moment, regardless of their low status elsewhere.[118] The holders of leadership positions in the guilds – especially in the construction trades – were increasingly social climbers who sought social and economic profit, often at the expense of the collective, further complicating our view of relationships between the artisanal class and the elites.[119] The line separating the nobility (the other traditional estate) from the economic oligarchy of the urban bourgeoisie was also permeable, since they sustained themselves less through agrarian land ownership and increasingly through not only military and ambassadorial service but the leasing and taxation of property, land reclamation and peat exploitation, and commercial activity.[120] The noble lifestyle, however – *vivre noblement* – was partly performative. The perception of fluidity between these classes would have appealed to many of the merchant class, and the material trappings associated with the noble life were available to those who could afford them.[121]

While the economic and social milieu of the city in which Memling lived and worked was complex and power was fluid, the processional and performative life of the city provided one arena in which the stakeholders in the community reasserted their rights and clarified their position within civic life. At such events as the yearly Procession of the Holy Blood, the trade and artisanal guilds, merchant nations, monastic and ecclesiastical groups, wards of the state, civic officials ranging from aldermen to clerks, philanthropic organizations and representatives of the city districts and of the royal court all assembled to represent their place under their banners and in a predetermined order.[122] Despite that year's struggle between the city and the monarchy, for the visit of the emperor and archduke in 1485 the civic government, merchant nations, guilds and religious communities all decorated their corporate houses and arranged stages for performances of *tableaux vivants* and similar dramatic events; the Waterhalle and Hallen were decorated with banners in the city's colours of red, white and blue, coats of arms and other paintings, and one hundred flaming torches.[123]

Despite such performances of unity, the Flemish Middle Ages were punctuated by periods of increased friction between the monarchs and the cities, the territorial ambitions of the former often threatening the economic interests of the latter. The cities of Flanders did not dependably present a unified front but frequently acted in individual political or economic self-interest and were often fractured within their own walls with factional and class conflict.[124] Continual economic tension, such as that between Bruges and Sluis, was manipulated by the dukes as a lever against the larger city, resulting in numerous uprisings throughout the thirteenth and fourteenth centuries. The city's simmering resentment and an English blockade of wool exports from Flanders erupted into the rebellion of 1436–8, resulting in a year-long siege of Bruges and blockade of the Zwin by the Duke of Burgundy; starved and humiliated, the city ultimately surrendered. Costly reparations imposed by the duke in retaliation and the ban on the sale of English cloth stressed the cities of Flanders further.[125]

In Memling's time political, economic and social tension remained high, and following the comparatively peaceful and prosperous reign of Philip the Good, his death in 1467 initiated a period of crisis that badly disrupted life and commerce in Bruges.[126] Philip's son Charles the Bold had a rockier relationship with the Flemish cities, eroding their traditional semi-autonomy and requiring staggering amounts of credit and significant taxation for his military campaigns, levied above all on prosperous Bruges. His abrupt death at the Battle of Nancy in the early days of 1477 left Burgundy in the hands of his nineteen-year-old daughter, Mary, who had a few months earlier become betrothed to Archduke Maximilian of Austria. The Flemish cities seized this opportunity to reclaim some of the rights of self-governance and free trade they had lost during Charles's reign, resulting in the 'Grand Privilege' negotiated in February 1477, which, however, was deemed insufficient by the new Bruges government – now dominated by the trade guilds – which destroyed its copy in a publicly theatrical manner.[127] Armed demonstration of Bruges's guilds in the market square and a snap election of city aldermen followed, and additional charters that year expanded the city's trading rights.[128] Following Mary's death by accident in March 1482, many in Brabant and Flanders refused to recognize Maximilian's claim as her son Philip's guardian, and factional conflict intensified as the pro-Maximilian party took control of the civic government and again reduced the power of the trade guilds.[129] Following further resistance from the city, in 1484–5 Maximilian insisted on a temporary relocation of foreign merchants to Antwerp, in retribution; for much of 1485 Bruges was blockaded from Sluis, further disrupting trade, and in 1486–7 no Italian or German ships unloaded at Bruges.[130]

In late January 1488 Maximilian was prevented from leaving the city, and in the days that followed was seized and imprisoned in Bruges. Guild militias took to the streets, installed a revolutionary government and carried out a series of executions over the following months, including the decapitation of leaders of the pro-Maximilian faction.[131] For some months Bruges and other cities of Flanders remained tense and fractured, anticipating the eventual intervention of the emperor. The Procession of the Holy Blood on 3 May was still carried out, but with little festivity; there were no trumpets, nor were civic representatives provided with new livery. The trade guilds were absent from the procession. On the previous day they had met as a group to discuss an end to hostilities, but a confrontation outside the city that same day resulted in the death of the dean of the painters' guild and the holding for ransom of several others.[132]

The threat of the approaching imperial army resulted in a treaty that promised to restore the Grand Privilege, Flemish autonomy and a regency council to govern during Philip's minority, and Maximilian was released on 16 May.[133] He immediately reneged on the agreement, however, gathering troops in Brabant and suppressing the city; the following month the foreign merchants were again commanded to leave Bruges and their consulates officially transferred to Antwerp.[134] With the withdrawal of support from France and Cleves, at the end of 1490 Bruges capitulated; Ghent and Sluis, however, held out until 1492, preventing the return of some of the international merchant community to Flanders until 1493, while other groups did not return at all.[135] These events, of course, had a catastrophic effect on trade and commerce in Bruges, leaving the city in shambles, and perhaps 5,000 houses remained in ruins or abandoned.[136] By the time of the inauguration of Philip the Handsome in late 1494, just months after Memling's death, Bruges had largely been supplanted by Antwerp as the centre of commercial activity in the Low Countries. While artistic life in Bruges would enjoy a burst of creativity and productivity in the sixteenth century, Memling would not witness it.

In 1465, however, Memling would have arrived as one of many international immigrants to a prosperous city that still busied itself with mercantile activity and the import and export of commodities from every reach of Europe and beyond. The stakeholders in this collective economic project were varied: not only local and foreign merchants and merchant bankers, but the local hospitality industry, brokers and financiers, porters, the construction sector, and money changers and pawnbrokers. The industries and trades were integral to this system, producing goods that would be exported by these merchants and directly consumed by them as users and clients. Power, money and luxury objects were available not only to the nobility and the traditional patriciate, but increasingly to a newly prosperous and aspirational economic elite, who saw a possibility of social mobility and emulated those they envied. The perception of economic and class fluidity nurtured an interest in the formation of identity and the projection of status (real or hoped-for) that could be realized through, among other activities, the commissioning of art. Perhaps this complicated, shifting environment is part of what made possible the distinctive character of Memling's career, bracketing this last generation of the Burgundian era.

THREE

Memling's Career in Bruges: The Painter's Workshop

A set of nine panels would have been one of the largest works produced by Memling's studio and would have consumed much of its efforts in the years just before 1490 (illus. 30).[1] The three surviving panels, recently restored and now preserved in Antwerp, depict God the Father and singing and music-making angels. Probably only an upper register of the original ensemble, these panels would not have been the largest of the assemblage, but still they render their half-length subjects in enormous scale: approximately twice life-sized, and together almost 7 metres (23 ft) wide.

God the Father appears in the centre panel wearing a crown bedecked with pearls and gemstones, as is the woven-gold orphrey that borders his richly lined velvet chasuble. His garments are fastened by a large circular brooch ornamented with pearls and three remarkably large gemstones that mirror the reds, greens and blues of his vestments. The white leather stole draped over his shoulder is likewise festooned with gems and pearls, and is tipped with decorative bells. Eyes cast down towards what would have been the primary scene of the complete retablo – perhaps an Assumption of the Virgin reflected in later copies – he holds his right hand up in blessing, and with the other he steadies a rock-crystal orb topped by a cross, again ornamented with jewels. On each side stand three youthful angels with golden hair and vividly feathered wings, singing from the large hymnals that they together hold; the coloured sewing at the spine, decorative metal bosses and closure straps of the bindings are rendered carefully. The fingers of the angel immediately to God's right are visible gently lifting God's garment to free his gesturing arm. The angels, too, wear liturgical garments decorated with floral brocade and geometric patterns, and the three-towered castle motif and lion rampant found on their stoles indicate the kingdom of Castile and León, the work's destination. On each of the side panels, which are slightly wider than the central panel, five angels, similarly attired in richly ornamented liturgical garments, play a range of musical instruments: to the left a psaltery, a stringed *tromba marina*, a lute, a trumpet and a shawm, and on the right a fiddle, a harp, a portative organ and two additional trumpets.

All seventeen figures appear against a golden background surrounded by a tidy bank of clouds; these clouds are now tarnished and dull, even after restoration, but in the years just after the work's completion they would have been brightly silver. The work was unlike any other created in a Bruges workshop: a monumental polyptych following Spanish retablo traditions, and a clear response to the demands of a client, which would have been agreed on in advance according to specific traditions.[2] Destined for a Cluniac Benedictine monastery in Nájera, Castile, the commission was probably arranged for the institution through one of several merchants from the region known to have been active in the wool trade in Bruges.[3]

After the death of the prior who ordered the work, documents suggest that his successor verified that the retablo should be completed 'at any cost'; it was delivered and installed in 1494, eleven years after the original commission, at a relatively high total cost of 239,383 *maravedies*, which probably included its transport from Bruges.[4] Other factors that contributed to the price would have been the raw materials required for its creation: the huge oak panels (imported from the Baltic by Hanseatic merchants) on which it was rendered and the pigments with which it was painted. These included both relatively inexpensive colours produced locally or even in the yard behind the artist's studio, and those that had to be imported from a great distance and at great cost, obtained in small amounts from the city's spice merchants and apothecaries, and originating as far away as present-day Afghanistan, an index of the reach of late medieval trade. The work makes use of a number of different grades of gold leaf, which was also expensive, but the variation in the quality seems to suggest a shift in the studio's working method, perhaps a need to economize or the stress of a compressed timeline for completion of the work. The sheer size of the work, larger than anything the studio had produced before, would have required the participation of several journeyman assistants in addition to any apprentice then being instructed in the workshop, and the existence of small colour notations in the preparatory underdrawing confirms the fact that a number of hands took part. The division of labour and working conditions of the staff would have been tightly regulated by statutes issued by the city, and under the close watch of the painters' and saddlers' guild.

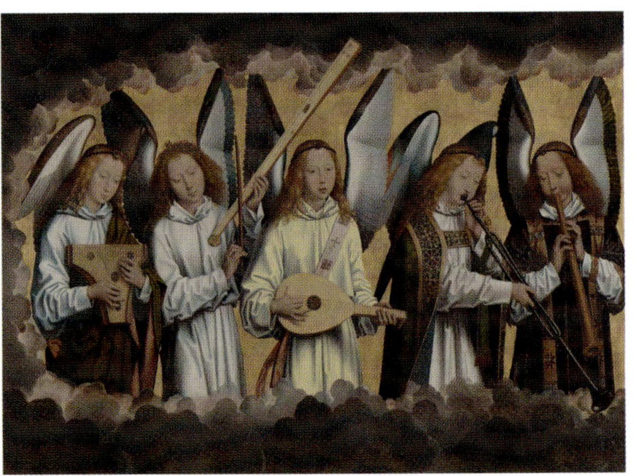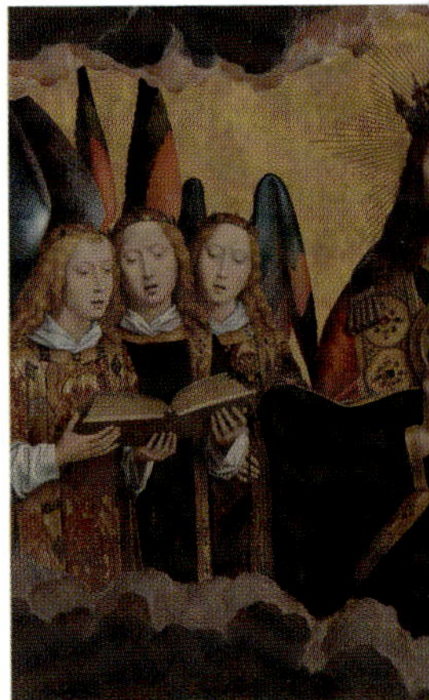

In 1465 Memling arrived in Bruges to find a thriving international commercial centre populated by a prosperous potential clientele, and he operated in a similar way to other painters of his era. During his early career he integrated himself into the local community, established a local reputation, cultivated a network of potential clients, secured property for workshop space and responded to the expectations and artistic traditions that had been established by his predecessors in the city. In his later career, busy with numerous commissions, he adapted to the growing demands of the market by taking on assistants, increased his workshop's efficiency and productivity by various means and responded to the stresses on supply chains generated by political and economic conflict. Investigation of the intersections between commerce and the concrete operations of the painter's workshop, such as relationships between clients and artists, workshop practices, the economics and sourcing of materials, and the guild guidelines that regulated artists and their workshops, demonstrates the ways in which Memling's activity was fashioned by the wider socio-economic environment of Bruges in which he participated.

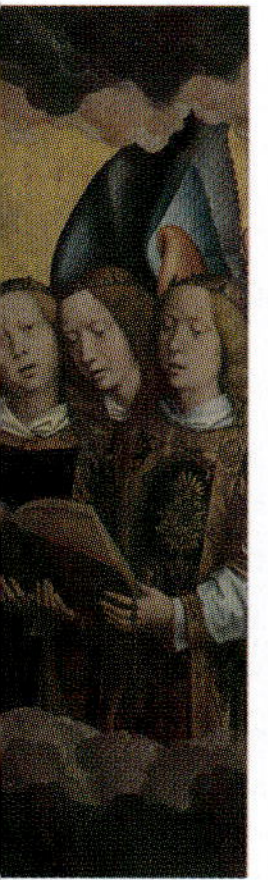
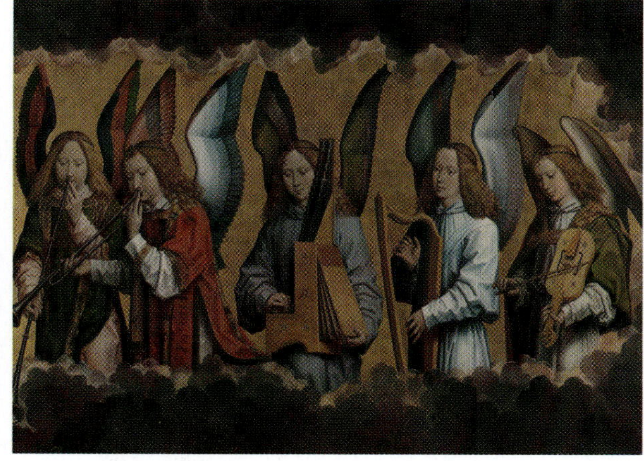

30 Hans Memling, *God the Father with Singing and Music-Making Angels*, 1483–94, oil on wood.

Memling would have assimilated into an already thriving artistic environment in the city, adapting his style to popular local conventions and making space for himself in a crowded market. Of his contemporaries in panel painting about whom we have a dependably reconstructed oeuvre, most prominent in the generation in which Memling arrived was Petrus Christus, who had become a citizen of Bruges in 1444 and who would be active there until his death in 1475 or early 1476, ten years after Memling's arrival. Christus was, like Jan van Eyck and Memling, an immigrant to the city, arriving from Baerle-le-Duc, near Turnhout in Brabant near the current border.[5] He was thoroughly integrated into the community, like Memling a member of religious confraternities – Our Lady of the Dry Tree and Our Lady of the Snow, in Christus's case – and he served the first of these confraternities as well as the Guild of St Luke a number of times as a representative in legal matters. In addition to working for private citizens, he received commissions from the civic government, including, with other artists, the decorations for the ceremonial *Joyous Entry* of Philip the Good in 1463. His son Bastyaen Christus joined the guild in 1476, probably in order to take over his deceased father's workshop, and he in turn passed the business on to his own son Petrus Christus II in 1500.[6]

In Memling's time Pieter Coustain served as painter to the Burgundian court of Philip the Good, a position he had held since 1450, but the only surviving works that can be firmly tied to his name are a series of coats of arms for members of the Order of the Golden Fleece, from which his figural style is difficult to extrapolate. Gerard David – from Oudewater in south Holland and perhaps educated in Haarlem – appeared in Bruges and joined the painters' guild as a master in 1484. He married the daughter of the dean of the goldsmiths' guild and held representative and leadership positions in the painters' guild, serving as *vinder* in 1495, the year after Memling's death, and becoming its dean in 1501. He might have been a rival for Memling's clientele, but in fact the two artists appear to have been sought out for different perceived specialities. David, for example, executed very few portraits, while such works remained central to Memling's enterprise. He also executed a high-profile commission for the civic government of Bruges, the *Judgement of Cambysses* for the city hall, for which no analogous work is known from Memling's career.[7] Attempts to connect the names of other apparently respected panel painters of these years known from textual sources are tantalizing but may remain inconclusive unless archives or technical investigations disclose new information.

Bruges was also recognized as a centre of manuscript production. Among the most prominent manuscript illuminators in the city was Memling's client Willem Vrelant, who in 1454 was registered as a founding member of the new illuminators' and librarians' guild, which comprised manuscript painters but also scribes, binders, papermakers and other artisans associated with book production.[8] By 1473 book-printing had emerged in Bruges, practised by scribes from the librarians' guild who seized the lucrative opportunity.[9] The printer Johannes Brito specialized in inexpensive works, such as schoolbooks, and Colard Mansion, who had previously specialized in luxury manuscripts, began producing high-end printed matter, including collaborations with William Caxton. In common with so many other entrepreneurs, however, Mansion left Bruges in 1484, and by the end of the century the printing industry had virtually disappeared from the city.[10] Tapestry, as part of the luxury textile industry, remained an important product in Bruges into the sixteenth century, with a strong export market of both speculative production and personalized commissions, such as coats of arms, which were popular especially among the Italians and Spanish. The various artistic media in Bruges influenced one another, and products of the tapestry industry often reflect directly or indirectly the designs of such painters as David, Ambrosius Benson and Lancelot Blondeel.[11]

While it is clear that Memling was held in high regard among his contemporaries in the city, his oft-cited financial success – he is sometimes described as one of the wealthiest citizens of the city – is less robustly confirmed by the surviving documentation. The few pieces of evidence that directly indicate financial transactions do seem to suggest, however, a reasonably successful artisan. We have no surviving written contracts for Memling's works, and only one set of records of payment for a work by him. This commission, carried out in 1478–9, was arranged by Vrelant on behalf of his trade guild. Installed in the guild's chapel at Eeckhout Abbey, this seems to have been a carved wooden altarpiece with painted wings, for which Vrelant and the other members of the guild collectively paid a total of four pounds and three shillings.[12] Such a project would constitute roughly four months' work, and this amount was on a par with payments made to Memling's contemporaries for similar commissions.[13]

Memling seems to have enjoyed sufficient financial success to purchase previously rented property in 1480, some fifteen years after his arrival in Bruges, in a comfortable but not extravagant neighbourhood favoured by artists and artisans.[14] In 1480–81 he was one of the citizens from whom the city extracted a compulsory loan; the evidence indicates that he fell within a privileged but not exclusive economic class. His client the spice merchant Willem Moreel, for example, was levied six times as much as Memling.[15] By the loan expropriations of 1487–90, Memling no longer appears on the lists of the most wealthy citizens, a fact that perhaps reflects a deterioration of the family's finances as a result of Tanne's death or a combination of the hardships that befell the city over the course of the 1480s. At his wife's death the household was valued at 24 Flemish pounds, of which half was placed in trust for the children. At the end of Memling's life in 1494 the estate held only eight pounds: sufficient to secure his burial in the churchyard of his parish church of the Sint-Aegidiuskerk, but not to cover the cost of a space inside the building, which would have been exceptional for any painter's income.[16]

Overall, Memling appears to have been comfortably prosperous, but his fortunes waxed and waned alongside those of the city as a whole in the turbulent final decades of the century. While those holding guild administrative offices, especially those in the construction trades, seem to have been prone to ambitious social climbing and to have become relatively wealthy, the rank and file of the artisanal guilds, including painters, were on average working class; at the end of the fourteenth century sample tax lists indicate that the painters' and saddlers' guild included a distribution of income similar to that in the city as a whole, with no painters or saddlers in the highest bracket at that time.[17] Such figures as Petrus Christus, Memling and David may have earned more than the average painter, but they were not among the economic elite.

The actual operation and 'home economics' of Memling's workshop were subject to tradition and regulation. On his arrival in Bruges Memling registered his membership of the Guild of St Luke and Eligius, as was required of all master painters of images (*beeldemakers*) in the city.[18] Not all the masters in the guild were painters on panel, however; these comprised about 40 per cent of the membership. Another quarter were canvas painters and 12 per cent glassworkers, and smaller numbers worked as mirror-makers, printers (before their absorption into the librarians' guild), vellum- and parchment-preparers, saddlers, pommel-makers and those who worked on other specialized saddle components.[19] The panel painters were recorded in numerous disputes with the new librarians' guild as they attempted unsuccessfully to compel the painters of manuscript miniatures to join the older guild and to prevent the import of foreign miniatures.[20] The canvas painters were differentiated in the statutes from the image painters:

permitted to paint objects, including wooden and stone sculptures, as long as they did not show those objects in their shops, they were nevertheless forbidden to use oil paint or render portraits.[21] Other arts that we might today see as kindred to painting – silver-smithing and the sculpture of images, for example – belonged to different guilds; the silversmiths fell within the greater smiths' guild, and the sculptors were split between those who worked in wood and were tied to the joiners' guild, and those who worked in stone and were grouped with masons.[22] These associations of different trades were conventional and specific to Bruges. The corporation to which panel painters in Ghent belonged, for example, encompassed painters, sculptors, glassworkers, illumi-nators and scribes, while in Antwerp the painters, wood-sculptors, goldsmiths and glassworkers were grouped together.[23]

The statutes (*keuren*) of a guild laid out rules that governed the lives and livelihoods of its members, clarifying how workshops were to be run and business conducted, and regulating the par-ticipation of the artisans in the city's ritual life. The city of Bruges maintained oversight of the administration of all the trade guilds, granting each organization control over pricing, compensation, technical regulations, the training of assistants and requirements for advancement through the ranks.[24] In 1252 the city government put in place statutes regulating oversight of the drapery sector's guilds in order to maintain quality of product, and other trades followed suit.[25]

In 1441–2 all the guilds' charters, including that of the paint-ers and saddlers, were revised in a uniform manner. The revision provided that each guild would be led by a handful of administra-tive positions, each elected for a one-year term: the *deken* or dean, seven *vinders* (roughly 'investigators') and two financial and bureau-cratic executors. These offices would be elected internally each year, and practitioners of a trade had to grant them access for workplace visits.[26] The registers of the painters' guild record the identities of these individuals each year, in addition to the names of new masters and apprentices.

Membership of the painters' guild required a payment of two Flemish pounds for previous residents of the city and three for those arriving from elsewhere; costs were also lower for anyone whose father belonged to the trade.[27] The Bruges guild appears not to have required the demonstration of a 'masterpiece' for new membership, as was the case with guilds in some cities.[28] Some exceptions to the rules were made for painters with an appointment to the ducal court. A legal dispute in 1472, for example, between the guild and Pieter Coustain (painter and *valet de chambre* to the duke) determined that he should be permitted to execute works for the duke and officers of the court without paying duties to the guild, although he was required to be a member.[29] Almost a third of new masters registered in the painters' guild were immigrants, like Memling. In the late fifteenth century a quarter of members were the sons of previous masters in the guild, and 40 per cent of new masters were described as 'half-free' (in other words, they had been apprenticed in Bruges rather than arriving from elsewhere).[30]

While the statutes suggest an ordered competitive environment, the many legal actions brought before the guild authorities and civic government indicate an enduring need for formal guidance, interpretation and enforcement.[31] Strict divisions between different specialities were either laid out in the statutes themselves or clarified via lawsuits brought before the city and recorded by the guilds, such as those between image painters, canvas painters, manuscript painters and printers. Activity that would give artisans a perceived unfair advantage was curtailed; members, for example, could not buy stockpiles of material without extending an opportunity for purchase to other members.[32] The Bruges statutes in general applied a lighter touch regarding workshop practices for painters than those of some other cities, where the thickness of wooden panels might have been regulated or specifications laid out concerning the use of gold leaf or pigment substitutions.[33] Other statutes stipulated that members could not operate on Sundays and obligatory holidays, with the lucrative exceptions of important weddings and funerals, jousting tournaments and other festivities (for which they were granted permission from the guild authorities).[34] During the month-long spring fair, trade was permitted in imported raw materials for painters without the intervention of brokers. While altarpieces and wooden sculptures were displayed during the fair – including even those from outside Bruges – it seems that paintings were not shown there, since they allowed the exhibition of painters' works only in shops and at counters; this was the case for manuscript painting, as well. Likewise, while in 1482 the Bruges sculptors' guild built an open market space for the sale of wooden sculpture, paintings were not yet sold in this fashion; perhaps these sculptures were produced in a more standardized manner or served a larger speculative market abroad, or maybe the materials were deemed more tolerant of the environmental conditions at fairs.[35]

The guild also concerned itself with the spiritual well-being of its members, providing a site for collective religious practice and arranging funerary masses. In 1427 the dean of the guild purchased a building for corporate use, and in about 1450 an independent chapel structure dedicated to SS Luke and Eligius was built on an adjoining piece of land.[36] In 1455 Philip the Good ordered that members of the guild attend daily mass in this chapel.[37] By the 1470s the guild as a corporate body had received from an adviser to the ducal court some valuable donations of property, as well as funds for the service of two chaplains for the chapel and its furnishing with additional masses and supplies.[38] On the feast of St Luke and the anniversary of the chapel's foundation the guild would exhibit a painting by Jan van Eyck (and, after the mid-sixteenth century, a second by Lancelot Blondeel).[39]

Members represented the guild in the city's most prominent annual celebration, the Procession of the Holy Blood held on 3 May, and attended the related feast (those who refused to participate or wear the requisite livery were fined). Similarly, the guild regulated the moral fibre of its membership, levying fines for extramarital affairs and for hiring prostitutes.[40]

While the marketing of art would change substantially in the following century, in the years in which Memling worked nearly all major artworks – especially panel paintings – were created on commission for specific patrons, rather than speculatively for the open market. By the beginning of the following century, some painters were offering their works in such places as shop windows, market stalls and special depots called *panden*, a practice earlier developed for the sale of sculpture.[41] Among the artists who adapted to this sales model was Memling's co-tenant and possible assistant in his early career, Lodewijk Boels; Boels was among those painters renting stalls during the yearly fair by 1513, and after his death his widow continued to sell presumably leftover stock at the *pand*.[42] Florentine merchants, additionally, documented the purchase of some items – including canvas paintings – on spec at the biannual Antwerp fairs; in the 1460s, for example, Tommaso Portinari corresponded with Piero de' Medici about the availability of *pannetti depinti* (painted cloths) to purchase in bulk.[43] In Memling's lifetime, however, personalized commissions remained the norm for panel painting, and this was certainly the case for his atelier.

While driven by individual bespoke commissions, by the last years of the century many workshops – including Memling's – sought ways to streamline production. A number of his commissions seem to be copies of earlier motifs or patterns requested by patrons. Many of his clients, for example, would have seen the St Johns altarpiece at the Sint-Janshospitaal and may have requested their own variations on the composition; the few surviving contracts suggest that this sort of stipulation was relatively common.[44] The John Donne altarpiece (see illus. 56), for example, is so closely modelled on the earlier prominent St Johns altarpiece (see illus. 10 and 11) that the commissioner may have specified in the contract its use as a model. A composition in the Metropolitan Museum of Art offers an even closer variation on the centre panel, copying much of the placement of figures and the colour scheme, but placing the scene in a garden setting, removing the male saints and inserting the unidentified donor in place of John the Baptist (see illus. 12).[45]

Other panels – especially such popular generic topics as the Madonna and Child – may have been produced confidently in advance. Two small roundels depicting the Virgin nursing the Christ Child – one in the Met and the other in a private collection – are of similar dimensions and format (the composition is probably based on the work of Robert Campin). The former

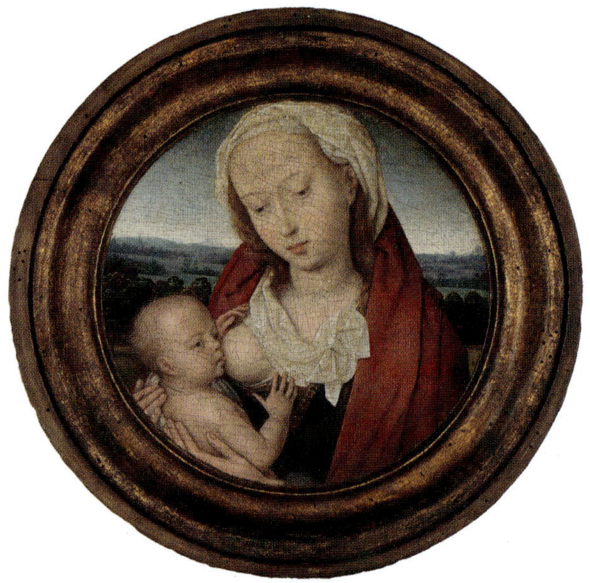

31 Hans Memling, *Tondo with the Virgin and Child, c.* 1480–85, oil on oak.

depicts Mary in a voluminous red mantle and blue gown, the hem of which is richly bejewelled with rubies and pearls; a golden kirtle, its laces loosened, is visible underneath, and a white cloth partially covers her breast (illus. 31). Despite the small scale of the work, the landscape is meticulously rendered, and beyond a line of trees the spires of buildings are visible before the mountains of the distant horizon. In the latter image the landscape has been replaced with gilding – producing a differently sumptuous effect – and the costume is simplified to a more modest blue gown; just visible under the edge of Mary's head-covering, however, is a gem in a gold setting, a less conspicuous indication of regal status (illus. 32).

Likewise, the appealing *Madonna and Child with Angels* in the National Gallery of Art in Washington, DC (illus. 33), bears no mark of specific ownership, and has a great deal in common compositionally with the centre panel of the Pagagnotti triptych

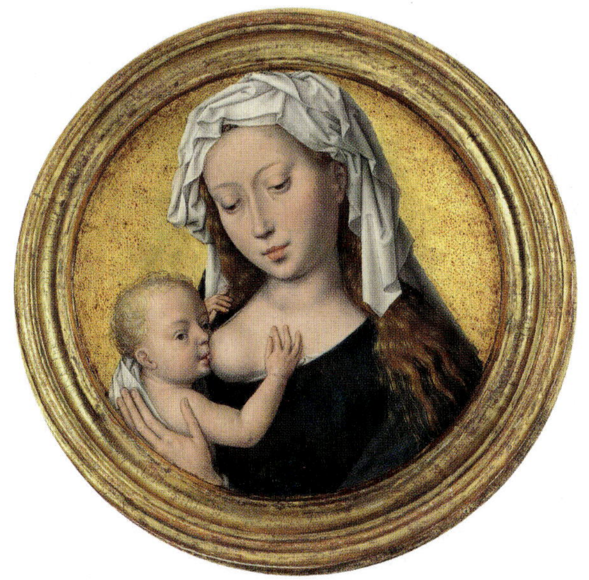

32 Hans Memling or workshop, *Tondo with the Virgin and Child, c.* 1485–90, oil on oak.

(see illus. 48 and 49). Each of these panels places the figures on Eastern carpets before brocades and red canopies; the ornamented painted archways are derived from the work of Rogier van der Weyden and others, but the garlands of laurel leaves and fruit held by putti that mark the Pagagnotti triptych as being destined for the Italian market are replaced in the other work by sculpted figures rendered in grisaille paint: putti integrated with the architectural surrounding and small figures of King David and the prophet Isaiah in decorative niches. Some works produced by the studio may have been largely completed in advance and had personalizing details added at the request of a client (such as family arms or saints selected for the wings of a triptych): a combination of on-spec work and bespoke commission.[46]

As a result of traditional bureaucratic and legal procedure, exceedingly few documents serving as contracts survive for painting commissions in early modern northern Europe. In Bruges, private contracts could be witnessed by the clerks of the civic court, but that body did not preserve these documents before 1484 and only a handful of clients' copies exist (it is likely that some arrangements even remained oral agreements between the patron and artist).[47] The handful of surviving documents and corroborating sources reveal that these contracts would note the basic wishes of the client, agreed price, terms of payment, delivery deadline and penalties for failing to complete the assignment. Additional details could include a work's destination, desired content, whether it was intended to copy an existing model, its size and the quality of the materials to be used, such as gold leaf (and whether it would be burnished) and fine pigments.[48]

A contract dated 1464 and relating to Dieric Bouts in Leuven stipulates the required subject matter – upon which two university theologians would be consulted – and payment schedule, and a requirement that Bouts would work on the piece exclusively

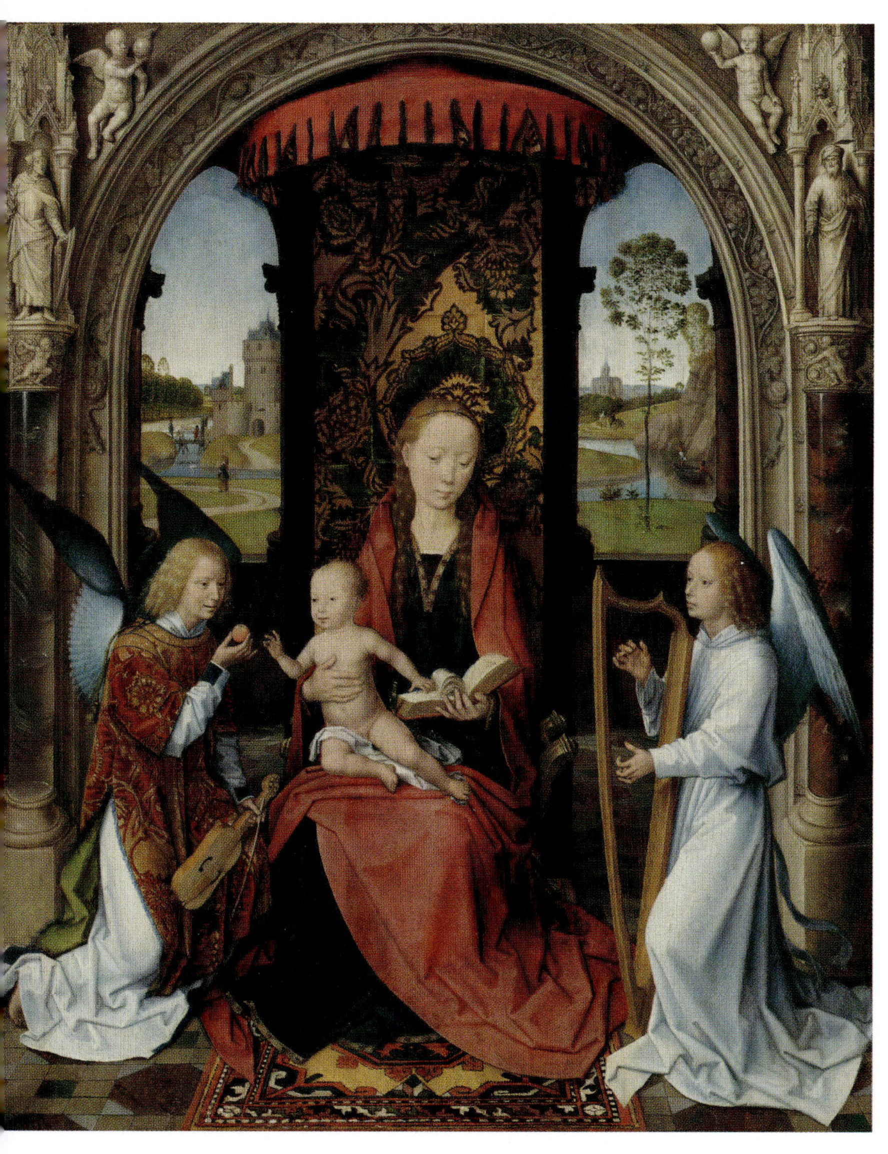

33 Hans Memling, *Madonna and Child with Angels, c.* 1490, oil on panel.

until its completion.[49] Accounts documenting a polyptych from the 1490s by Aert van den Bossche of Brussels indicate that he was paid an advance and for an initial design; after its approval by the commissioners a contract was prepared and an additional payment made for a copy of the design, probably kept by them as a sort of receipt of agreement.[50] The most information to survive in regard to Memling's workshop concerns the altarpiece for the librarians' guild chapel at Eeckhout Abbey, described earlier. Here we find that the guild purchased from a carpenter four wooden panels, two of which were then supplied to Memling for painting. A separate document also describes the requirements for any altarpiece that might be needed to replace this work at the abbey if the guild were to abandon the site, taking Memling's work with them. Probably comparable to the original specifications demanded of Memling's work, any new work must be as large as the chapel, be painted in oils and represent four or five figures.[51]

Memling's operation required studio space within which he and any assistants could work. For some time after his arrival in Bruges and his purchase of citizenship, it appears that he rented two adjoining structures – one of which is described as a 'large stone house' – in St Nicolas parish, between Wuulhuusstraat and the Vlamingbrug (illus. 34).[52] In 1470 the taxes on one of these were paid by Boels, another painter, who may likewise have been a tenant in the building (and who made further payments after Memling's death).[53] This is probably the same property that Memling paid off in full and took ownership of in 1480, after solidifying his economic and social position in Bruges with the completion of the highly visible commissions at the Sint-Janshospitaal. The property, which appears to have had a courtyard and a small gated structure behind it facing Jan Miraelstraat, was still owned by the family at the time of Memling's death; his children seem to have kept possession of it until 1509.[54]

The most prominent features of this neighbourhood were the Austin Friars' cloister (a location favoured by foreign merchant nations) and the halls of the crossbow guild of St George, and it was convenient for the northern part of the economic core of the city, at the Beursplein and adjacent infrastructure.[55] This proximity to potential clientele seems to have appealed to artists in the fifteenth and sixteenth centuries. In Memling's time, the manuscript illuminator Willem Vrelant lived five houses further

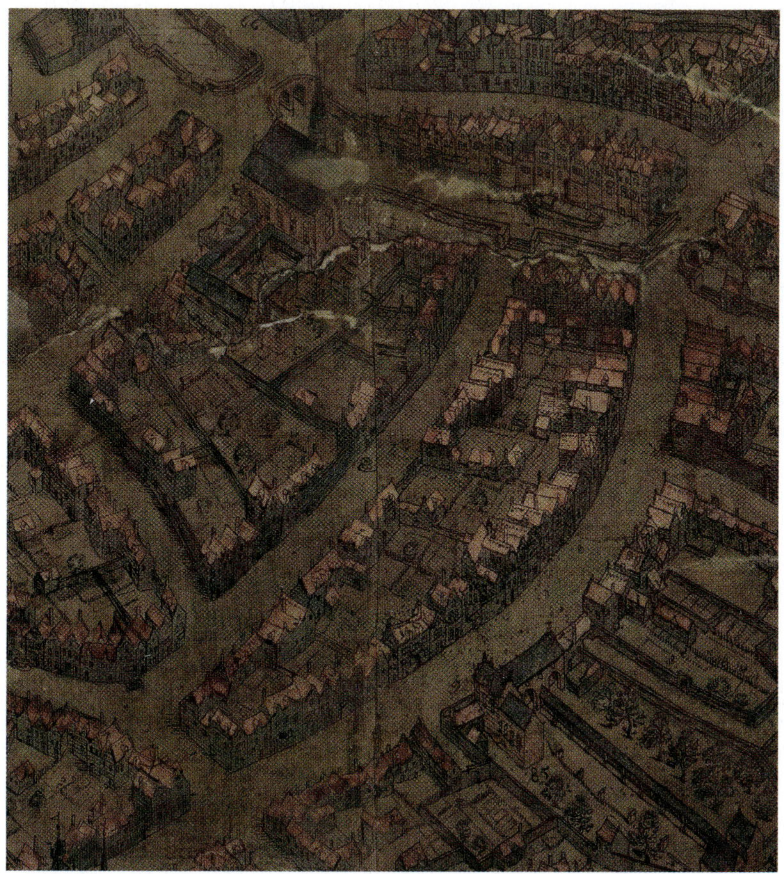

34 Marcus Gheeraerts, *Map of Bruges*, 1562–3, detail of the approximate location of Hans Memling's property.

down, and, perhaps capitalizing on Memling's and Vrelant's earlier presence, Gerard David and many of the more prominent sixteenth-century artists – including Jan Provost, Lancelot Blondeel, Antoon Claessens and Pieter Pourbus – would all take up residence in the neighbourhood.[56]

The property in which Memling's family lived served as the location of the painter's studio, where he and his assistants operated with the materials, techniques and division of labour typical of painting workshops of the second half of the fifteenth century. Collaboration within a workshop could take different forms by which a master might make the executive decisions regarding composition, colouring and so on, and delegate the completion of various aspects to one or more assistants, depending on the demands of each commission. In the later medieval and early modern eras an artist would begin a career as an apprentice in the workshop of an established master, performing small tasks and menial labour in the workshop, such as grinding pigment and sweeping the floors, and drawing copies of studio compositions. In this period fewer than half of the painting workshops in Bruges took on apprentices. Those that did probably had a robust clientele and demand, and Memling's operation would have counted among this narrow slice of particularly attractive ateliers with established reputations.[57] Depending on the success of the business and the demands of commissions, a workshop might also employ one or more journeymen – or *compagnons* – who would already have completed their apprenticeships and developed reasonably competent skills, and who would assist the master with the completion of large or less important commissions. These journeymen were not required to join the guild (and those who did were not recorded in guild records) but would be obliged to do so if they themselves became masters and took on apprentices of their own. In the second half of the fifteenth century most painters who completed their apprenticeships remained journeymen for the rest of their careers, working as assistants in the workshops of other master painters. Workshops in the fifteenth century, however, remained relatively small in comparison to some in later centuries; workshops of the era might employ up to three painters in addition to the master, while some remained one-man businesses.[58]

In this era, a master who took on apprentices would usually have one or two at a time; they would pay what amounted to a tuition fee and might live among the master's household. According to the statutes of the painters' guild of Bruges, an apprenticeship lasted for four years and a master could oversee only one apprentice at a time.[59] Memling appears in the surviving guild records as accepting an apprentice twice during the course of his career in Bruges. The first, Hannekin Verhanneman, is listed in in the guild records of 1480 but does not appear again in Bruges records; if he continued his career as a painter, it is possible that he pursued his remaining training and career in another city, or remained a journeyman and kept a low profile in the city.[60] The second apprentice recorded was Passchier van der Meersch, registered in 1483, and about whom there is slightly more information.[61] It is unclear whether he became a master and, if so, in what year, since the guild recorded no new masters between 1493 and 1498 — probably simply a lapse in documentation or a gap in surviving records. He, too, may have remained a journeyman for the duration of his career, but he must have joined the guild in some capacity because he appears in the obituary lists of the guild, dying sometime between 1501 and 1503.[62]

Memling quite possibly also trained one or more of his own children in his craft, and they could have assisted as apprentices or journeymen and even continued the workshop's operations after his death. If they never registered as masters in the guild their activities would have gone unrecorded, since free masters' sons trained by their fathers were not reported in the guild rosters.[63]

It is very likely that Memling employed one or more journeymen in his workshop, especially later in his career as he received commissions for large works. Again, because these assistants were not recorded in guild documents and there was no statute that limited the number who could be employed, their number and identity are impossible to determine with any certainty. Within the context of the creation of commissioned artwork in the fifteenth century, however, it is clear that there was no room for individual creativity on the part of these assistants. A unified hand was expected in the finished product, and any idiosyncrasies of style among the various painters in the workshop must be suppressed in favour of the workshop style, making it difficult to determine the precise division of labour or even the number of hands involved. Despite these challenges, some individual personalities have been suggested based on archival clues or perceived stylistic influence. Passchier van der Meersch may have remained in Memling's studio for many years as a principal assistant following his apprenticeship, even possibly continuing the production of paintings in the workshop style for some years after himself becoming a master following Memling's death, benefiting both from the workshop's reputation and from access to its pattern drawings and compositions.[64]

Another assistant may have been Boels, the painter noted earlier as paying tax on the property at which Memling was also living in 1470.[65] Boels, probably a native of Bruges, is documented in 1476–80 as serving an apprenticeship with Nikolaas van Keersbach, a painter from Cologne who arrived in the Flemish city a few years after Memling.[66] Boels himself became a master with the Bruges guild in 1484, serving on occasion among its officers, and took on a series of apprentices before his death in 1522. It is possible that in the early 1480s he worked as an assistant to Memling, and the idea that the painters would have shared some immersion in the Cologne tradition is an intriguing proposition.[67] They do seem to have had a personal connection; after Memling's death in 1494 Memling's children continued to live at the family property, for which Boels paid some expenses in the first decade of the sixteenth century on Memling's behalf.[68]

Among the individuals with known oeuvres who have been proposed as possible journeymen or assistants in Memling's studio, the suggestion of Michael Sittow – from the Livonian Hansa city of Reval (now Tallinn) – is tantalizing and to a degree less speculative than some.[69] While the stylistic similarities between the two masters are clear (modulated by the additional influence of Hugo van der Goes and Gerard David), archival evidence supporting this suggestion remains circumstantial.[70] Sittow was born in 1469 and apprenticed with his father in Tallinn as a painter and woodcarver, and he seems to have travelled in early 1484 'to Bruges in Flanders to learn my art and office', according to later court statements. He appears in Spain working for Isabella of Castile by 1492 at the latest, and there he remained for some time before reappearing in Tallinn in 1506.[71] An *Assumption of the Virgin* by Sittow (National Gallery of Art, Washington, DC) may reflect a lost panel of the Memling workshop's retablo that included the large *God the Father with Singing and Music-Making Angels* from Nájera from late in Memling's career (see illus. 30), but whether Sittow's knowledge of it was derived from workshop drawings or participation, or simply from later viewing, is unclear.[72] Juan de Flandes, who likewise pursued a career in Castile working for Isabella from 1496 onwards, has also been proposed as a potential assistant to Memling, but is even less well documented.[73] In any case, neither artist appears clearly in the Bruges *Poortersboek* or painters' guild documents. If either Sittow or Juan were present in Memling's workshop in the 1480s, it could not have been as an apprentice, which would have been recorded, and he could not have overlapped with the documented presence of Hannekin Verhanneman or Passchier van der Meersch, but must have been a journeyman and thus might not feature in guild documents.

A workshop, whether a group of artists working under the coordination of a master or a solitary artist, would make use of a collection of drawings and patterns in order to increase its productivity and the speed with which it could complete commissions. These standardized figures, motifs and details, such as drapery effects or facial expressions, could be studied and implemented within fuller compositions, and account for the sometimes pastiche-like resemblance between portions of different works from the same master or workshop. Such drawings might even be transferred to a new composition. These were valuable resources, and a well-documented lawsuit from 1519 between David and his journeyman, Ambrosius Benson, offers testimonies from a dispute over two trunks filled with sketchbooks, workshop pattern books and other materials that Benson claimed to have collected from other artists and left at David's workshop after his departure.[74]

Some art historians have suggested possible divisions of labour based on technical analysis, in particular infrared reflectography, which reveals the underdrawing layer of a painting. We know from infrared reflectography studies that many Netherlandish masters frequently composed directly on the prepared panel, so separate preparatory drawings survive in fewer numbers in the north than in Italy.[75] These studies suggest that Memling completed this early stage of composition himself, without assistance and with a very idiosyncratic approach and technique, but many of his paintings reveal greater detail in the underdrawing, suggesting an intention to guide other artists' hands in completion.[76] Colour notations even appear in the underdrawings of the large Nájera panels (but not elsewhere, to date), but workshop participation has been suggested in the case of some relatively small works, as well.[77] Variations in the finished paint surface

that might suggest the participation of Memling's assistants —
judged by the degree of finish or perceived ability in the brushwork
— might also be based in economy, schedule or the individual
aesthetic taste of his clients.

The resources Memling's workshop needed to produce finished
paintings reflect the complexity of the market, and many basic
supplies were imported, some at great expense: wooden supports,
media for drawings and the preparatory layer, paint media and
pigments, metal foil and other necessary resources. A considera-
tion of the techniques and materials involved provides additional
insight into the intersections between Memling's artistic production and larger patterns of commerce and international trade in
the late fifteenth century: the availability, prices and sourcing of
these materials, how he at times adapted his practice to appeal
to patrons or to increase productivity, and in some cases further
indications of the possible division of labour within his workshop.[78]
Memling's paintings and those of his early Netherlandish
contemporaries were most frequently executed on supports
constructed from wooden panels. Canvas was at times used in
Flanders, such as for ephemeral decorations, but it was not yet
the dominant support it became throughout Europe. Memling's
workshop used oak — which was preferred for its slow growth
pattern and its density, which made it resistant to warping — both
for its largest known paintings (such as the enormous Nájera
panels) and for small devotional roundels. Through dendrochronological analysis and the study of shipping records, the origins of the oak used by Flemish workshops can be traced specifically
to the Baltic region (northern Poland, among other locations),
transported to Bruges by merchants of the Hanseatic League.[79]
One known exception in Memling's oeuvre is the *Cellier Diptych*
in the Louvre, for which he appears to have used walnut — a material more commonly used for sculpture and unusual for panel
painting in the southern Netherlands, but not unheard of along

the Rhine, including the Cologne school; perhaps the patron Jan du Cellier, a spice merchant in Bruges, provided the material (see illus. 58).[80]

A number of Memling's paintings still feature their original frames, also oak, and in some cases the painting and frame have been constructed from the same small piece of wood (such as the small roundel in the Metropolitan Museum of Art in New York; see illus. 31).[81] The surviving documentation regarding Memling's work for the librarians' guild indicates that this sort of auxiliary carpentry work would be completed by artisans outside the painter's workshop and guild. The wooden support would then be coated with a preparatory ground layer to smooth out any irregularities in the surface and to provide an evenly coloured starting point for the painting process. The ground layers of Memling's paintings most commonly comprise chalk bound in glue, typical of painting practice in northern Europe. In the Nájera panels in Antwerp, again an especially large and time-consuming commission, Memling appears to have used a mixture of materials, somewhat unevenly applied. These include chalk mixed with gesso, which is very unusual for an early Flemish painting and a decision made for unknown reasons.[82] In addition, Memling frequently applied a very thin imprimatur layer to reduce the absorbency of the ground layer; in various cases he used a bone white or lead white pigment, and at times he added a touch of earth pigment to lightly tint this imprimatur.[83]

With the support prepared, Memling would then have executed the underdrawing, determining the composition and position of most of the principal figures and the basic details. These underdrawings would not be visible in the finished product, being covered by the numerous layers of paint, so they often reveal peculiarities of style and method that have provided historians – since the development of infrared reflectography – with additional stylistic information that can assist with efforts

towards attributing a work and determining a workshop's division
of labour. Over the course of Memling's career he used a range
of media for underdrawings. In addition to the use of a brush
with ink or paint, he may at times have used some pigment (black
chalk) mixed with a binder and cut into sticks like modern drawing chalk.[84] Some of Memling's smaller works and certain portraits
show minimal or no underdrawing at all through infrared reflectography, and it has been suggested that in these cases he used a
medium such as iron gall ink (which would be invisible to infrared imaging) or silverpoint (which would result in a very fine line
that would likewise not appear to infrared).[85] On the other hand,
it is possible that this lack of obvious underdrawing in the portraits in particular is caused by Memling's specific method in
those cases, in which he would begin with a basic template and
add personalized features directly from the model, based on a
drawing or from a sitter present in the studio.[86]

At times favoured patterns would be traced from workshop
drawings, resulting in the same motif occurring in several compositions. For example, the same brocade pattern for a cloth of
honour or an ecclesiastical garment – to within a millimetre – re-
appears in four known works, suggesting the use of a mechanical
transfer method, such as pouncing or squaring.[87] The colour notations that appear in the underdrawings of some Netherlandish
workshops appear very rarely in Memling's works; the single
known instance appears to be in one panel of the large *God the
Father with Singing and Music-Making Angels* from Nájera (possibly
evidence of the hand of assistants guided by these instructions).[88]
In addition to the underdrawing, other preparatory composition
and adjustments were worked out throughout the painting process as indicated by faint incisions and indentations detectible
in the ground or initial paint layers, made with a stylus or the end
of a brush. At times these incisions appear to have been intended
to preserve the visibility of guiding lines after gilding or the first

layer of paint was applied, and in some instances they clearly relate to larger compositional and perspectival schemes.[89]

Although it was not as frequently called upon in the Low Countries in the late fifteenth century as it had been in earlier decades, Memling at times applied gold leaf or other metal leaf to his paintings using a range of methods, resulting in a luxurious, reflective effect that naturally still appealed to some patrons. Gold leaf was a relatively precious material and appears generally to have been provided to artists by spice traders, apothecaries and other merchants who dealt in small quantities of expensive products; the amount of gold used would typically be one of the conditions agreed in advance between artist and patron.[90] The leaf would be applied to limited portions of the prepared support panels, often before other paint pigments. In one technique, mordant gilding, the gold leaf would be laid upon a thin layer of resin and a siccative (drying) oil, often incorporating lead for that purpose and to provide a warm-coloured tint. In water gilding, the leaf would be applied to a 'bole', a tinted clay whose fine grains were suspended in water-based glue; gold applied to this soft base could be burnished to a shine.

Gold and other metal leaf is used in only a handful of Memling's works, and only a few panels have received detailed enough technical analysis to determine which of these methods was used. A great deal of gold was applied, for example, to the large Nájera panels, possibly as a concession to the local taste of the retablo's original destination in Castile (see illus. 30). This appears to be mordant gilding, with the gold leaf applied to an ochre-tinted base but not subsequently burnished: a sensible and economical technique for ornamenting such a vast surface area.[91] Additionally, on one panel of this large commission Memling's workshop seems to have used so-called *Zwischgold* or *or parti* (part gold), a lower quality of gold leaf produced by hammering together sandwiched layers of silver and gold foil; at typically half the expense of fine gold leaf, this was probably a cost-saving measure.[92] The gold in the large *Last Judgement* triptych, originally destined for Florence but now in Gdansk, is applied via mordant gilding (see illus. 2), while more limited applications of metal leaf appear, for example, on the reverses of the portraits of Willem Moreel and Barbara van Hertsvelde (also called van Vlaenderberch), where in addition to gold a silver or tin leaf has been applied.[93]

The paint used by Memling and other painters of his time and place was generally composed of powdered pigments suspended in a medium of linseed oil or occasionally walnut oil, depending on the desired colour (walnut oil was used for some lighter tints of cool hues); this oil paint would be applied in numerous translucent glazes that together produced a rich and complex colour. At times artists, including Memling, would use linseed oil that had been prepared by heating for some hours in order to reduce the paint's drying time (so-called heat-bodied oil).[94]

Some of the pigments used by Memling and other artists of his time were manufactured locally — in the case of simpler and inexpensive materials — but many were imported from some distance, very much a reflection of the patterns of international trade in the fifteenth century.[95] A number of the common pigments used by painters were predominately used to colour textiles, the most crucial manufacturing activity of the Low Countries during the Middle Ages. Many of the 'lake' pigments used in the textile industry were derived from plants, both local and imported: blue pigments from woad or turnsole, a yellow from 'dyer's weed' and a red from rose madder.[96] More luxurious pigments used for the dyeing of cloth included 'scarlet' red, produced from the 'grain' extracted from scale insects from the Mediterranean or the Baltic (the red lake pigments commonly used by artists were often acquired from waste shearings of previously dyed textiles).[97] Other textile-dyeing materials imported into Europe from distant ports included saffron crocus, sappan wood, lac and 'dragon's blood' resin (the last three were all used to produce red dyes). Additional pigments used by dyers and painters were derived from minerals and chemical compounds, some manufactured locally and some imported. Many of these materials were not used exclusively in the arts but also frequently featured among the materials sold by apothecaries and used across a range of professions; sappan wood, realgar, saffron, orpiment and lac, for example, were all used medicinally.[98]

Technical analyses conducted since the turn of the millennium have revealed many of the specific pigments that Memling used in his works. He seems to have been completely typical of his time and place, using a limited palette to achieve a wide range of hues and values. The palette used in his works is for the most part identical to that used in, for example, the works of Rogier van der Weyden.[99] Some of these pigments would have been relatively inexpensive and easily obtained locally, such as lead white, which appears throughout Memling's works. This pigment, which was also useful as a siccative, was prepared from strips of lead stored in clay pots and exposed to acidic vinegar fumes; these would be stacked in sheds with horse manure or waste left over from the leather-tanning industry, and after a few months the material could be scraped off and further prepared.[100] The most common source of black pigment, bone or carbon black, was ubiquitous, simply obtained by charring wood, grapevines or bone, or by scraping soot from lamps.[101] A range of earth pigments, such as iron-based browns and ochres, were also very inexpensive and easily obtained.[102] The green pigments that Memling's workshop used were verdigris and similar copper-containing intense greens, which appear more saturated than the malachite or *terreverde* used in other painting traditions.[103] They were also relatively inexpensive and consistently available, a crust-like product of the combination of fermenting fruit pulp (such as pomace or marc) stacked with copper plates; a steady supply of imported verdigris was also available from wine-growing regions, such as Montpellier.[104] At roughly twice the price of verdigris, a common source of yellow in the early modern era found frequently in Memling's work was then known as *masticot* in the north, apparently the same pigment called *giallolino* used in Italy in the same period. This lead-tin yellow was produced by heating a combination of lead, tin and additional red lead (*minium*) in a glassmakers' furnace.[105]

A variety of red pigments was used in these years, derived from plant, mineral and even animal sources and varying widely in cost.[106] One moderately priced red pigment that Memling certainly used was vermilion.[107] It is difficult, however, to determine whether the vermilion used by Memling was produced from the natural mineral cinnabar – which was imported from Asia into Italy, and from there to Bruges (closer sources in Andalusia and Germany also existed) – or manufactured vermilion, which appears to have been relatively common by the fourteenth century.[108] He also appears to have used at times the red lead pigment called *minium*.[109] It was called *menning* by Agricola in the sixteenth century, and the Germans produced it for the textile-dyeing industry by simply melting and oxidizing lead. Used by painters as a base layer for more expensive pigments or gold leaf, it was also useful as a siccative.[110] Also common but of greater expense were the red lake pigments, available from a variety of natural sources imported for the textile industry and recycled for use in painting. One such pigment that Memling would have used was produced from the rose madder plant, which was grown in various parts of Europe, including France and the Low Countries, and imported into Flanders for the textile industry – although the creation of the original lake textile dye required specialized skill, contributing to its moderate cost.[111] Kermes lake, on the other hand, was relatively expensive, second only perhaps to ultramarine, and was obtained by the precipitation of extract of the female kermes insect with alum. This *graan* or 'grain' was the same dye that was used to colour the expensive and luxurious 'scarlet' cloth, and was known variously as *granum, lacca, vermiculum*, crimson and carmoisine red.[112]

The most common source of blue pigment used by Northern artists was azurite, occurring in many parts of the world as a feature of copper ore deposits and supplied to artists in early modern Europe from mines in southern Germany, Austria, Hungary and Slovakia. The pigment was available in qualities ranging from a coarsely ground form of dark blue to a finely ground powder that provided a lighter colour.[113] Different grades of *azur* are recorded in purchases made by the court painter Pieter Coustain in 1468: a high-grade *delié azur* and the less expensive *azur d'Allemaigne*. Prices for pigments were volatile throughout the period, so only general patterns are clear, but at that moment in Bruges the less expensive grade of azurite cost seven and a half times as much as vermilion, and the dearer grade of azurite eleven and a half times as much as vermilion.[114] Memling and other artists would have combined the varying grades of pigment economically. In the Nájera retablo panels and the large *Last Judgement*, for example, Memling used azurite for almost all of the blue, but mixed and applied it in layers to achieve variations in tone; in early paint layers the workshop would use a lower grade of azurite pigment with larger grains and more greenish particles, then a higher grade of azurite would be applied with smaller, more saturated blue particles.[115]

The second blue that has been detected in Memling's paintings is ultramarine, an extravagantly expensive pigment. When this pigment appears in shipping manifests and valuations it is, like saffron, listed by the ounce, rather than by the pound as was the less expensive azurite. Inventories of shipments from Genoa and Venice list values for both the unprocessed lapis lazuli stone and the prepared ultramarine pigment.[116] A Florentine merchant

working for the Bardi company in the 1340s informed his readers
of a valuable technique by which to differentiate ultramarine
powder (*oltramarino*) from the *azurro della Magna* – German blue,
that is, azurite.[117] The quarries at Badakshan in the Kokcha River
valley of Afghanistan seem to have supplied the bulk of the medieval European market's supply of lapis, and early records refer to
the pigment as *azur de Acre* – Acre blue – pointing to its source in
the Middle and Near East.[118] Supplies available in the north seem
to have been imported primarily via Venice.[119] Late fourteenth-
century documents indicate that the pigment was provided to
painters at the Burgundian court by spice merchants – *espiciers*
– in Troyes, Dijon, Paris and Bruges, and at least one order for
the court painter Jean Malouel was provided by Jacques Rapondi,
a Lucchese merchant active in Paris and Bruges; in these larger
markets Italians seem to have been a frequent source. Having
no medicinal value, ultramarine was not standard apothecaries'
stock, so opportunistic buyers seized on any fortuitous availability; on one occasion the early fifteenth-century painter Melchior
Broederlam's expenses were paid to travel to the southern
Netherlands for a shipment of the pigment, and he seems to have
spent more than a month there awaiting its arrival.[120]

Memling used ultramarine sparingly, of course: it would, like
gold leaf, be an expense that would be agreed in advance with
the commissioner of a work, and a certain cost earmarked for it.
He frequently applied the less expensive azurite in the initial
layers of paint, with a final layer of ultramarine above.[121] In the
immense Nájera retablo panels, for instance, the application of
ultramarine is very limited; it is used only for a number of gems
on God's garments, and even then applied just as a top layer over
azurite underlayers (see illus. 30).[122] In other paintings, however,
such as the John Donne triptych, Memling applied the ultramarine more widely and purely (see illus. 56). The use of this opulent
pigment clearly depended on the specific commission, and art

viewers of the period would have recognized it immediately and been aware of its expense. Memling's clients could have been confident of its intended effect.[123]

Artists working with these pigments suspended in oils applied the paint in several layers of thin glazes, so that the final visible variations of hue and value would be produced through the combination of a number of pigments within one layer or over several layers. Analysis has shown, for example, that Memling used layers of red lake laid over a vermilion base layer; his oranges were produced through a combination of lead-tin yellow with vermilion, and his greens were typically built with three layers: mixed opaque lead white and lead-tin yellow, an opaque copper-containing green that has been identified as probably verdigris, and a top glaze containing that same copper-based green. His reds were likewise complex. In Memling's workshop azurite would be mixed with red lake dye to achieve a violet colour. He seems at times to have applied a thin layer of oil and resin varnish between paint layers to saturate the colours further. From about 1478 onwards the workshop appears to have sought ways to apply pigments using clever painting techniques to achieve luxurious effects with maximum efficiency and economy, such as the use of hatching strokes of different values in lieu of additional glaze layers, or the skilful use of yellow and white pigments to simulate the effect of gold leaf.[124]

In addition to the materials that directly comprised a finished painting delivered to its buyer, a workshop like Memling's needed to budget for numerous other materials and tools. As well as pigments and metallic leaf, lists of materials ordered earlier in the century indicate iron compasses, vinegar, oils, wax, varnish (which could be relatively expensive), various linens, fish glue, chisels, swan-feather quills, pots in which to store materials and the pig bristles, cord and wax used to make thicker brushes.[125] While the Bruges statutes are silent about the expected quality of materials, the Tournai guild statutes of 1480 are specific and can perhaps be understood as a guide to 'best practice' for the period. They have much to say, for example, about the use of specific pigments, gold leaf, the quality of paper used for preliminary designs and the types of brushes and their composition.[126]

As we have seen, Memling's workshop and operations depended on access to materials and supplies, some manufactured locally – perhaps even in-house, in some cases – but some imported from distant sources and made available in Bruges through the trading activities of international merchants. This access would have been as vulnerable to political and economic upheaval as the rest of the city's commercial environment; although no records of his workshop's purchases survive, surely the trade embargoes, naval blockades and dispersal of the international communities of the 1480s would have affected the availability to Memling's workshop of the large, good-quality oak panels shipped to Bruges from the Baltic by Hansa merchants, or the ultramarine pigment that in such preciously limited quantities made it from Afghanistan on to the ships of Venetian or Genoese traders and haphazardly into the spice merchants' inventories in Bruges. Such uncertainty would have taken its toll on Memling's ability to accept new commissions, and perhaps affected the completion of work that had already been initiated.

In common with other cities of the era, Bruges maintained a careful watch over competition and the reputation of its artisanal and trade communities through the guild system. Through its *keuren*, the painters' Guild of St Luke and Eligius regulated an artist's access to the city's marketplace, oversaw the training of apprentices and the participation of other workshop personnel, set limits on a workshop's operations and appropriate use of resources, and provided a group identity in shaping a collective civic and devotional life for its members. In the fifteenth century this trade guild system was, of course, a powerful political arm in

its own right. The collective actions of the Bruges guilds throughout the period served to give their members a voice through which
they asserted their interests against other cities, the dukes and
both the traditional oligarchy of the nobility and the new oligarchy of the wealthy merchant class. It is this last group of affluent
Bruges citizens and their international counterparts who made
their careers in the city that served as the dominant part of Hans
Memling's clientele.

FOUR

Memling and His Clientele

The Moreel altarpiece, now in the Groeningemuseum in Bruges, would have seized the attention of those who encountered it at the parish church of Sint Jakob both on account of its considerable size – roughly 3.5 metres (11½ ft) wide when opened – and for the somewhat unusual focus of its subject matter (illus. 35). At the centre of the opened interior, where a late fifteenth-century viewer would typically expect to find an enthroned Madonna and Child or a Crucifixion scene, the imposing figure of St Christopher carries the infant Jesus on his shoulders. Christopher, brightly clad in a red mantle that billows around his cerulean tunic and its eye-catching lemon-yellow lining, strides through the shallow end of a body of water that stretches into the distance. He gazes up at the flowering end of the staff he carries as the Christ Child raises a hand in blessing, enveloped in a slate-blue cloth and framed by glowing light. Among the dandelions, violets, nettles and other carefully depicted riverbank plants stand two additional men. Maurus, to the left, appears in black-and-white Benedictine habit carrying an ornamented crozier and holding open a book, its detailed clasps spread unfastened to the side. To the right, Egidius (in English known as Giles) holds a closed volume against his body and lays his hand gently on the head of the small doe that stands beside him; he appears undisturbed by the shaft of the arrow that remains embedded in his forearm. The rocky bluffs that line the river descend into forest-edged meadows; a hermit carrying a lamp emerges from a cave nearby, a reference to a different episode from the Christopher legend.

The Bruges merchant Willem Moreel and his wife, Barbara van Hertsvelde, appear to the left and right on the interior wings, accompanied by the sons and daughters of their rather sizeable family. Moreel kneels before a prie-dieu that bears an open prayer book, presented by his armoured patron, William of Maleval, and escorted by five of his sons, who appear behind him. His wife is presented by her name saint, Barbara, who raises her attribute tower in a draped hand, and eleven daughters crowd into the frame, some of them barely visible. The painted

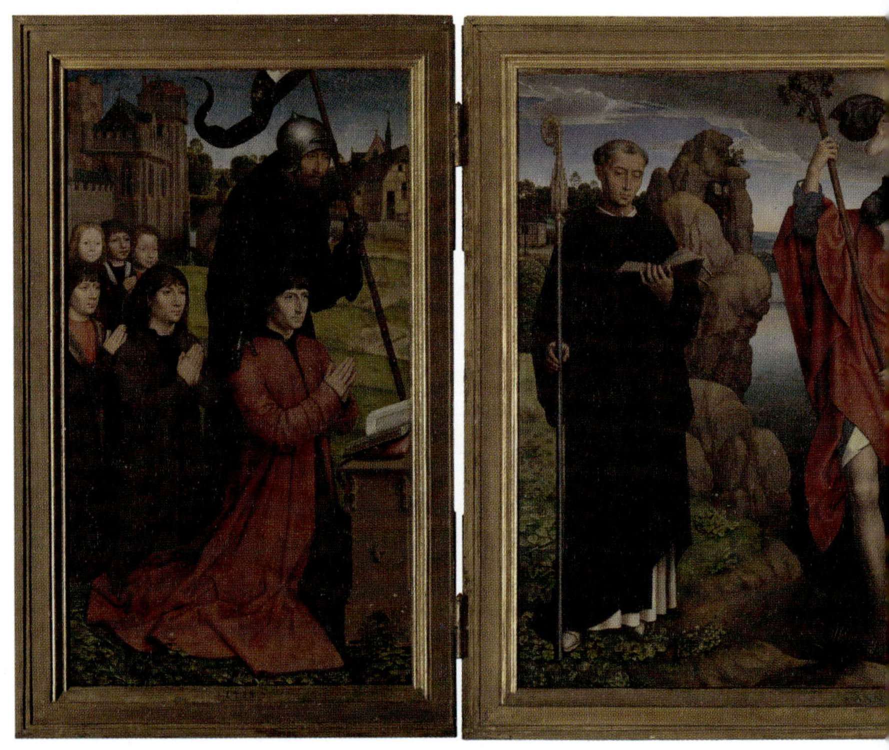

treatment of the children is inconsistent and technical examination confirms that they were not rendered at the same moment;
subsequent to the installation of the triptych – perhaps after
additional births – the heads of six daughters in the right wing
were painted in above the already completed landscape, and the
heads of two sons on the left were adjusted to make room for
an additional son.[1] In any case, the inclusion of eighteen individuals on these wings, in addition to the two saints, would certainly
have posed a logistical puzzle for Memling at a time when the
group portrait as a genre was in its infancy.

The selection of saints is personal and familial. The inclusion of
William and Barbara as onomastic saints – that is, name saints –

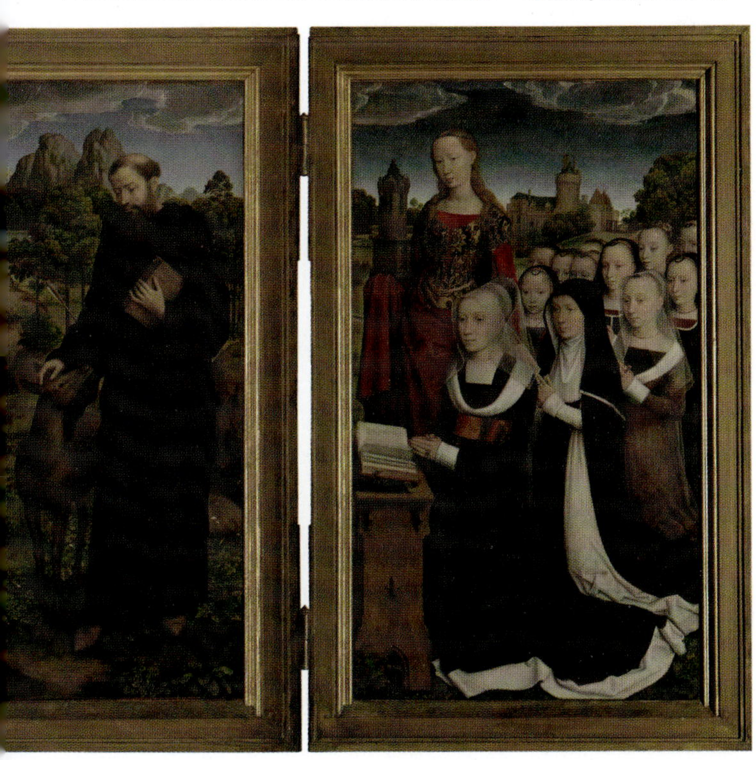

35 Hans Memling, Moreel triptych, 1484, oil on wood.

is easily understood, but Giles and Maurus were also probably chosen in relation to the clients' family names: Giles on account of the deer suggested by Barbara van Hertsvelde ('deer field') and Maurus through an extension of the Moreel name. Christopher was perhaps selected because he shared a feast day with James, the patron of the family's parish church – the Jakobskerk – for which the work was intended, and his presence would also have been appreciated for his intercessory protection against sudden death and death in childbirth, certainly a concern for this sizeable family.[2]

Moreel was among the most prominent of Memling's local clients in Bruges, a merchant and politician, and one of the urban economic elite who had climbed into the lesser nobility. Carrying the title of Burgrave of Roeselare, he had also inherited the title of Lord of Oostcleyhem from his father, who had been granted it in 1435 and purchased a farm estate.[3] In business Moreel was occupied as a spice merchant renting a space at the grocers' hall; he was also a member of the coopers' guild, dealt in property, held several annuities and arranged financing for Italian merchants.[4] Barbara van Hertsvelde likewise belonged to a prominent Bruges business family, and her father operated a company that traded with merchants from Venice and the Papal States.[5] Moreel, like Memling, was a member of the Confraternity of Our Lady of the Snow, which met at the Church of Onze-Lieve-Vrouw; the two men may have become acquainted there, and Memling had worked for the Moreels on a smaller triptych several years previously.[6]

Moreel is best known, however, for his dramatic career in state and civic politics, and was one of the major personalities in the turmoil of the 1470s and '80s. Serving as alderman in the early 1470s, he was outspoken in 1477 on behalf of the interests of the Bruges merchants, was one of the city's representatives appointed to negotiate new privileges from Mary of Burgundy and was elected *burgemeester van de schepenen*, mayor of the aldermen, in 1478 (the more important of two different mayorial positions in the period); he was clearly seen as an advocate for the city.[7] In 1479 he was made a superintendent of finances for Maximilian, who probably hoped to capitalize on Moreel's good standing in the community. Maximilian soon assumed a more negative stance regarding Moreel's popularity, however, and at the end of 1481 he had Moreel arrested on charges of conspiracy to overtake the city 'to the detriment of their Lord and for self-interest'. After five months of imprisonment, Moreel again served as financier to the archduke, but when the anti-Maximilian faction once more took power, after Mary's death, Moreel would again become *burgemeester* in 1483 and serve as a member of the regency council.[8] As power in the city continued to oscillate, in 1485 there was a plot on Moreel's life and he fled the city, returning only in 1488, after the guild revolt, to serve as bailiff and treasurer.[9]

It was in this turbulent period of his public life that Moreel commissioned from Memling's workshop the large altarpiece that bears the date of 1484 in an original inscription on the frame.[10] In that year the Moreel family received permission to dedicate an altar to the saints Maurus and Egidius – both of whom appear on the triptych destined for it – at their family chapel at Sint-Jakobskerk in Bruges.[11] This parish church was renovated in the late fifteenth century in part through the donations of the prosperous families it served, among them the Moreels and the Portinaris. There Willem and Barbara hoped to be buried alongside several family members (but, for some reason, were not, initially, instead resting in the churchyard until their son Jan insisted on their transfer to the chapel tomb).[12] The triptych thus served a number of functions, both pious and political. As an altarpiece it naturally served as a backdrop for the sacrament of the Eucharist and as a fitting and meritorious tribute to their familial saints, and to Mary and Jesus. It also preserved the likenesses and memory of family members and offered a visual memorial as a focus for future prayers for their salvation at their intended grave site. In addition, it represented Memling's client – embattled but at the height of his economic and political career – in a positive light and in a public space visible to his allies and rivals. By calling upon one of the city's leading artists, Moreel ensured that it did so in a conspicuously beautiful and sumptuous manner.

Willem Moreel was representative of the class of ambitious burghers and international businessmen who comprised the bulk of Memling's clientele. Memling's workshop production and the overall trajectory of his career were, as we have seen, dependent on the larger economic and social patterns of late fifteenth-century Bruges, which determined the rules and conventions under which he operated, the availability and value of the materials he used and the size and productivity of his workshop and personnel. The character of the relationship between his workshop and the individuals and institutions he ultimately served was likewise driven by the particular environment in which they interacted, and the political and economic events in Bruges and throughout Burgundy affected larger patterns of patronage across his career. Considering the general demographic trends of Memling's clientele brings focus to the members of the relatively new Flemish and international middle class who provided the better part of his commissions: their national identities, the occupations they represented and their motivation for commissioning artworks – what they hoped to achieve spiritually and socially. Finally, the exploration of a number of better-documented commissions as case studies offers more concrete insight into these individuals and institutions: how their identities, their career paths and the sources of their fortunes fit into these patterns of commercial and social activity within later fifteenth-century Bruges; the life events they hoped to commemorate and how they wished to present themselves to the public; and the destinations for which the artworks they commissioned were originally intended.

About a quarter of the patrons of the 75–100 works that are generally accepted as being from Memling's workshop can be identified with some confidence, while a further quarter of the works provide some hints as to the possible geographical origins or social status of a client – the style of clothing, early provenance of a work or iconographical details, for example.[13] While the phenomenon of speculative production was in these years in its early development, it is clear for about 70 per cent of the works that survive from Memling's workshop that they were commissioned in advance by clients known to him, rather than made for the open market (and it is likely that many of the less documentable cases, too, were commissioned).[14] Most of Memling's large, most prominent and presumably most expensive commissions represent known individuals or the occasional institution – such as the Sint-Janshospitaal – while the many smaller devotional works, especially, were executed for clients that are yet to be identified.[15] This leads, perhaps, to an initial misreading of his average clientele, since the few clerics and high-status diplomats among his clients – and the exceedingly few members of the nobility who may have used his services – are more easily documented, while the many works with now-anonymous patrons are somewhat overlooked in the literature.[16] The economic upper-middle class that constituted the bulk of Memling's patrons – the merchants, merchant bankers and striving representatives of the trade guilds – tended to commission smaller, more generic and less arresting works, and as a result are more frequently unidentified and under-represented in discussions of specific patrons.

Among the more successful of the middle-class patrons of art in Flanders – such merchants as Moreel, especially, who through the social mobility that was possible in Bruges could penetrate the economic oligarchy or patriciate – the commissioning of monumental artworks could serve as a public or semi-public marker of power and prestige.[17] Likewise, in the case of some high-profile commissions, contact with the Burgundian court seems to have inspired these striving bourgeois merchant bankers – among them Agnolo Tani and Tommaso Portinari – to demonstrate their newly achieved success and aspirational lifestyle through activities that were previously associated with the hereditary nobility, such as the founding of chapels and the drive to memorialize and elevate their lineage via portraiture.[18]

This upwardly mobile class of patrons is, to some degree, the same kind of clientele that we find served by Memling's predecessors and contemporaries, including Jan van Eyck, Petrus Christus and Hugo van der Goes, but many more unidentifiable sitters are found than before among Memling's patrons: individuals who are neither noble nor even patrician.[19] Memling, however, was able to capitalize on the fluidity of class in Bruges and the degree to which different populations – artisans and bourgeois clients, the urban patriciate, and even courtiers and the nobility – mingled in their neighbourhoods, parish churches and religious confraternities.[20] Memling very much drew from the international community of which he was a part; about a fifth of the commissions with relatively firm identities are from local or Flemish clients – among them clerics, politicians, merchants and representatives of trade guilds – but almost as many clients have been identified as from the Italian nations, particularly Florence. Others who have been identified with reasonable confidence include several patrons from Castile, one family from the Hansa city of Lübeck and a Welshman in the service of England; also represented, but less firmly identified, are possible patrons from Portugal and from Franche-Comté in eastern France.[21]

These commissioned works appear to have been destined for both private and public situations, and to have served a combination of uses: memorial, liturgical and devotional, and to build status or mark milestones. The large altarpieces clearly worked liturgically as a visual focus for the celebration of the Eucharist, and devotionally in veneration of Jesus, Mary and the saints. That these are so often associated with family or trade-guild sponsorship, and the inclusion of donor portraits in the majority of such works (and even simply the knowledge that a given individual was responsible for donating a work), however, makes it clear that such publicly displayed commissions were also under-stood to have a social function in asserting or reinforcing socio-economic status.[22] Some smaller works, such as small altarpieces, although destined for public and semi-public ritual veneration and liturgical use, could at the same time accommodate intimate and personal devotional use. Devotional activity in particular was fluid, and could occur in collective and even public ways, at times simultaneously with liturgical celebrations.[23] The well-known bust-length portraits of the Moreels from an earlier period of their lives, for example, appear to have originally been wings of a small, transportable triptych. The back of each panel displays the other individual's family coat of arms, putting the arms on the outside of the closed triptych, fitting for a place where it could be viewed by a wider public — such as the family's endowed altar at Sint-Jakob's — but could also have served in a more private devotional setting (see illus. 57).[24] The triptych could thus have served as an altarpiece for liturgical use, a focus for devotional contemplation and also a memorial to prompt prayer that would, among other things, benefit the souls of the Moreels.[25]

A work could be sacred in subject matter, on the one hand, but also commemorate more personal life events for individuals and families on the other. Small roundels, such as the *Virgin and Child* in the Metropolitan Museum of Art (see illus. 31) produced by the workshop, could — similarly to the *desco da parto* or 'birth salver' tradition in Italy — mark marriages and childbirths while also encouraging a family's continuing piety and petitioning the saints for the family's well-being: simultaneously sacred and secular.[26] It is likely that the small triptych that once included the portrait panels of Tommaso Portinari and Maria Baroncelli (which probably originally flanked a central panel depicting the Madonna and Child) was commissioned to mark the occasion of the couple's marriage in 1470; while serving a personalized devotional function, it also indicates an intention to communicate the couple's economic prosperity (although she is dressed in understated black, Maria's necklace and fur collar are comparatively opulent; see illus. 44).[27]

Numerous examples survive of similar works that Memling produced for clients who remain anonymous to us. Both wings are preserved in Munich of a diptych – by Memling or a skilled workshop assistant – depicting the Madonna and Child surrounded by angels on the left-hand panel and a donor presented by St George on the right (illus. 36).[28] The angels, two seated and two standing, are dressed in simple robes of pale blue, pink, violet and yellow, and play a variety of musical instruments, including a portative organ, a lute and a harp; one lays down his stringed instrument to offer a small fruit as the Christ Child reaches across his mother's lap for it. The Virgin is wrapped in a voluminous plain red mantle, but underneath she wears a blue garment with grey fur cuffs and a gold collar richly ornamented with gems and pearls above a silver and gold brocade kirtle. These figures are separated from the background by a hedge of pink and red roses, while the carefully rendered landscape features the edge of a city. A group of buildings, walls and a gate with a bridge over a moat or small pond continue on to the right-hand panel, where the landscape recedes into distant mountain crags, while a number of minuscule figures of people and horses populate the plains. On the right-hand panel the unidentified donor wears an understated but rich fur-lined mantle and kneels facing the opposite panel, a set of red and silver rosary beads hanging

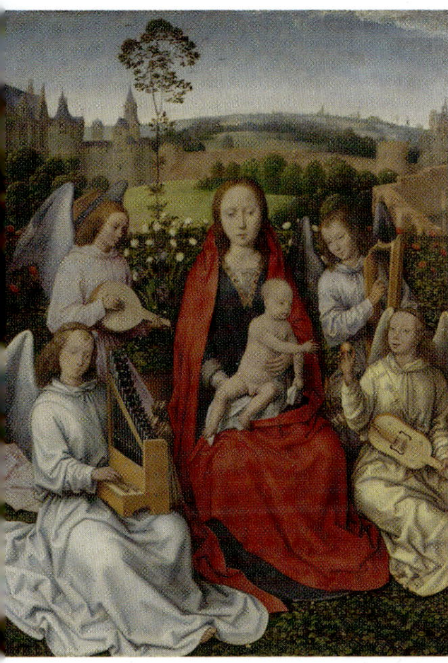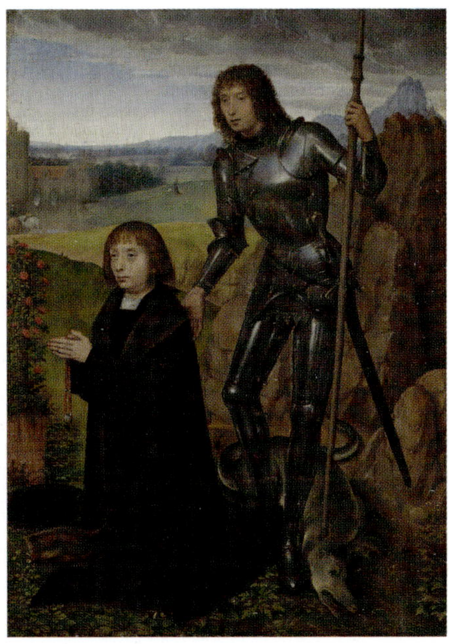

from his clasped hands. St George, who leans over to encourage
the donor with an outstretched hand, steadies an upright lance
that projects from the body of the dragon lying motionless behind
him. An observant reflection of the entire scene of the left-hand
panel, including both the figures and elements of the setting, is
rendered meticulously on the surface of George's cuirass. While
the individual who commissioned the work is today unidentified
(but most likely a George, Joris or Giorgio), such a painstakingly
crafted work would have come at some expense to its affluent
owner.

The many of Memling's smaller panels that can be classified
as portraits are poorly documented in terms of their original
patronage and destinations. A number of panels that appear to
represent individual sitters alone or with a patron saint were
probably initially part of now dismembered religious diptychs

36 Hans Memling or workshop, *Diptych with the Virgin and Child with Angels and
St George with Donor*, c. 1490, oil on oak.

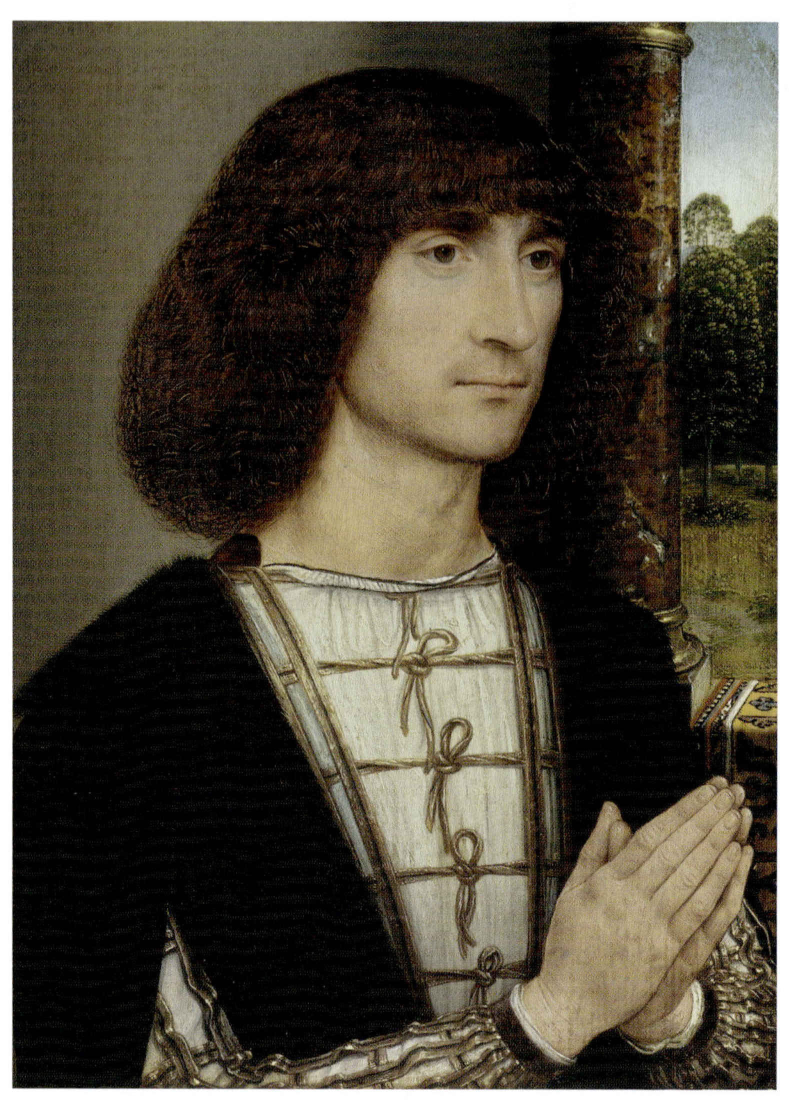

37 Hans Memling, *Portrait of a Young Man, c.* 1485–90, oil on oak.

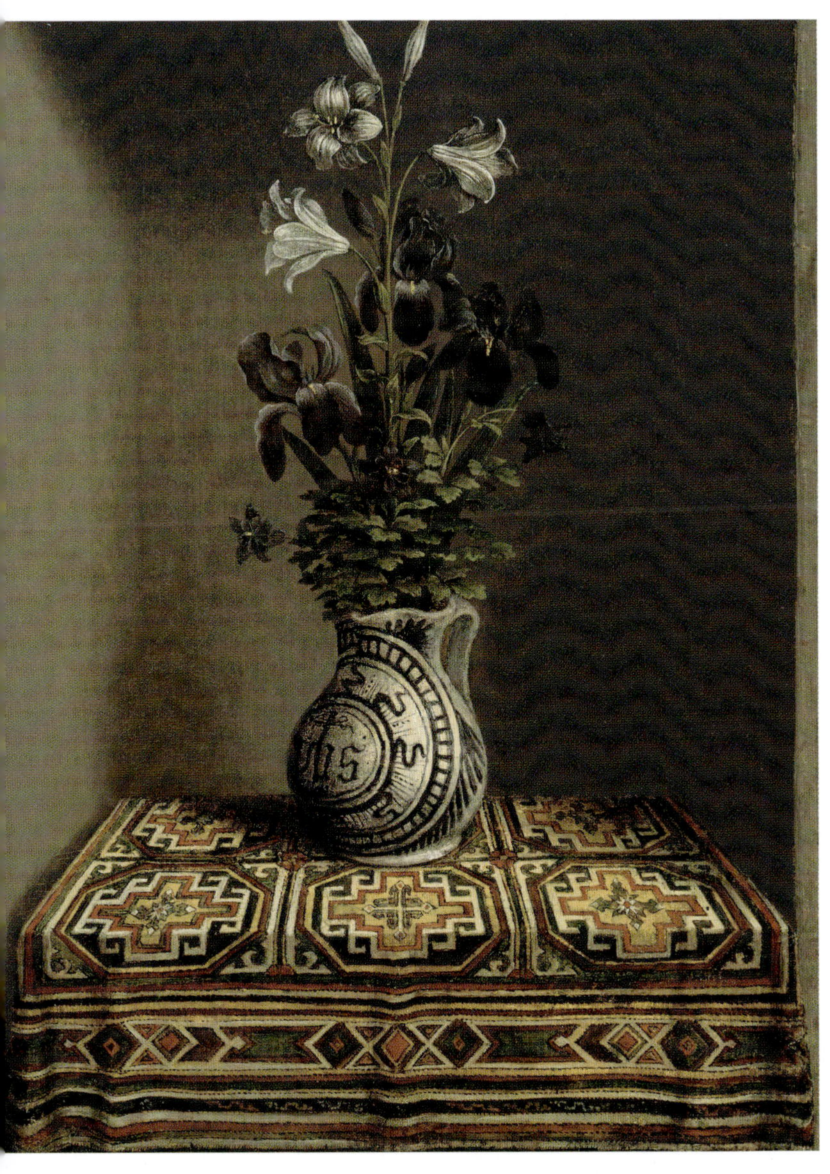

38 Hans Memling, *Flower Still-Life*, reverse of illus. 37, *c.* 1485–90, oil on oak.

or triptychs. The panel preserved in the Thyssen-Bornemisza museum in Madrid presents a fashionable young man who has been identified as Italian or Spanish based on his costume: a rumpled white blouse with decorative gold ties and ribbons along the length of the torso and sleeves, over which a dark fur garment is draped (illus. 37). Presented half-length, he gazes to the viewer's right with his hands clasped in a praying gesture, most likely facing a now lost Madonna and Child as one panel of a diptych (or a triptych with a third panel portraying a wife or patron saint, as seen in the triptych of Benedetto Portinari (see illus. 47)). Only hints of the loggia in which he sits remain, and behind him the edge of a richly marbled red column and its gold base frames a sliver of a carefully depicted landscape of trees. The balustrade on which the column rests stretches to the right, an Eastern carpet draped over it indicative of the international range of goods available in fifteenth-century Bruges. The reverse presents an appealing still-life – a genre that was itself still very rare in these years (illus. 38). An assortment of lilies, irises and columbines stands in a blue-and-white maiolica jug decorated with Christ's monogram in a sunburst pattern. The jug rests on another patterned Anatolian carpet in an otherwise unornamented architectural niche.[29]

Given the praying gesture and intensely directed gaze of the sitter, a panel that may depict a member of the Lespinette or de Visen families of Franche-Comté (based on a coat of arms found on the back of the panel) was likewise probably half of a devotional diptych paired with a Virgin and Child (illus. 39). The tightly cropped figure, wearing a black coat with white and brown fur trim over a loosely laced chestnut-coloured doublet, is adorned with one shiny ring just visible at the bottom corner of the panel, and a pearl-encrusted pendant on a gold necklace. He is set before a landscape with a low horizon, the pale sky gradually deepening into an intense, cloud-streaked blue, permitting only a glimpse of the church visible in the distance over his shoulder.[30]

The portrait *A Young Man at Prayer* in the National Gallery, London, is even more likely to have started its existence as a panel of a diptych or triptych, and the sitter's reverent gesture is emphasized by the prayer book open before him, in which a blue initial 'D' is clearly legible (illus. 40). Framed between two marbled columns in an otherwise featureless dark green space, his prayer book resting on a ledge in front of him, he serenely faces the figures that would have been depicted on the missing panel or panels. Although this is certainly a pious portrayal, the clasp, gilded edging and colourful binding of his prayer book speak to luxury, and his costume clearly marks him as belonging to an affluent family; he wears a black doublet with red velvet lining laced over a crisp white shirt, as well as two rings with gemstones and a necklace bearing an opulent pendant.[31]

Other portraits may have been conceived of as individual, self-contained 'secular' portraits, more purely intended to memorialize and simply record the likeness of an individual or married couple. Compared to the *Young Man* in London, the portrait of another young man preserved in the Met appears more inwardly focused, sitting with an undirected, placidly diffident gaze (illus. 41). Probably Italian, on account of the work's early influence on Florentine artists, the sitter wears a dark wine-coloured coat lined with fur and rests his hands one upon the other atop an unseen surface; while one half of the background is a grey stone wall, a window to the left is divided in two by a red marble column and permits a sweeping view of hilly countryside.[32]

Two portrait panels depicting an elderly couple – now surviving separately in Berlin and Paris – were originally one panel rather than pendants or separate wings, as is clear from the contiguous winding road and architectural details of the background setting (illus. 42). Both figures are treated with gentle sensitivity,

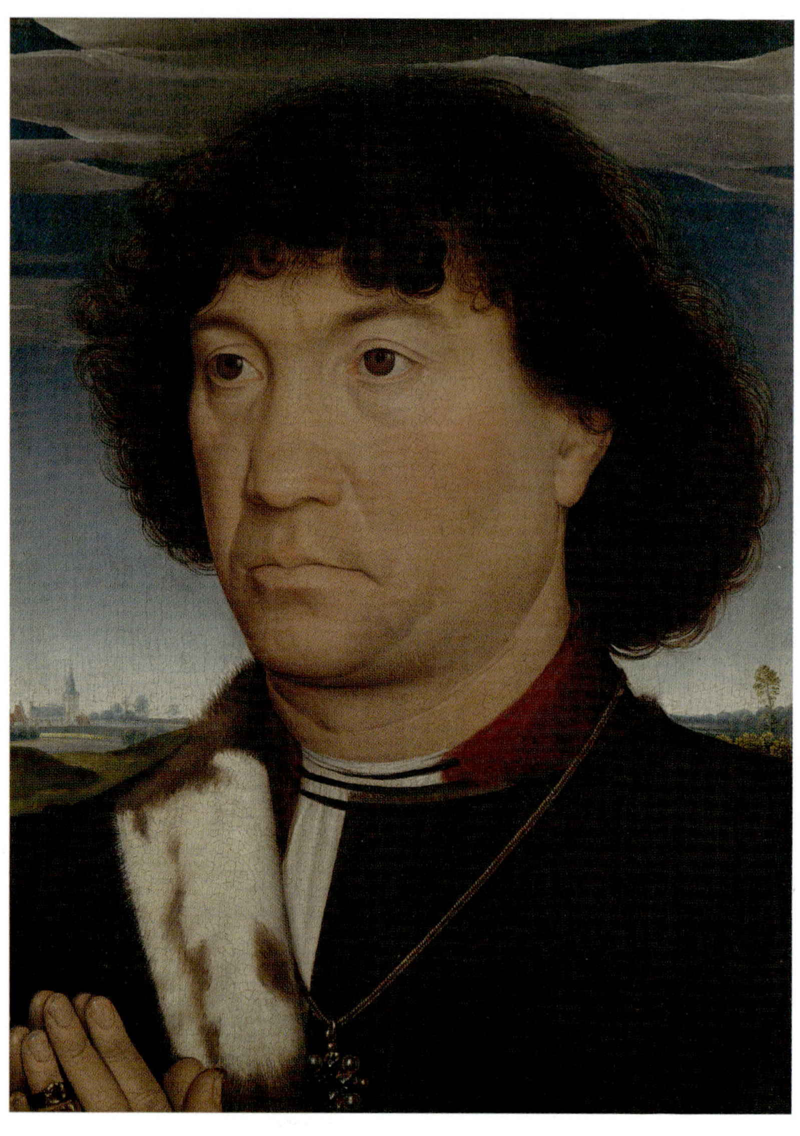

39 Hans Memling, *Man at Prayer before a Landscape*, c. 1485–90, oil on oak.

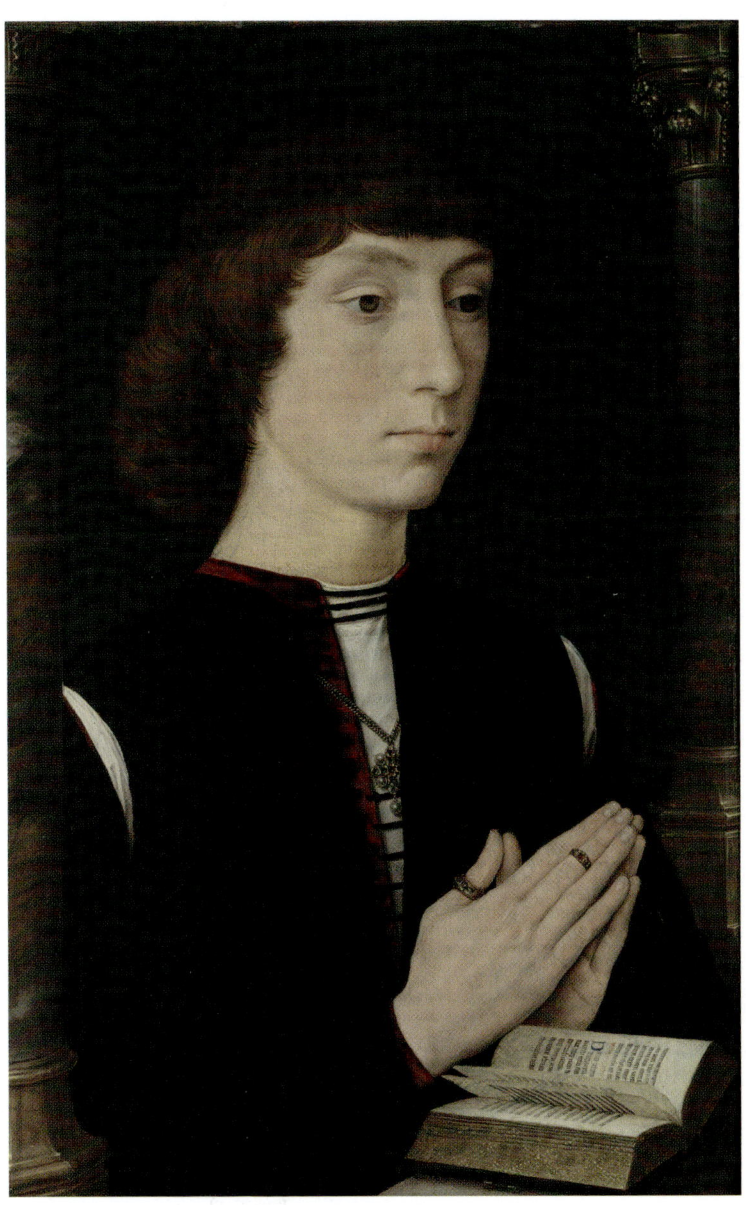

40 Hans Memling, *A Young Man at Prayer*, mid-1470s, oil on oak.

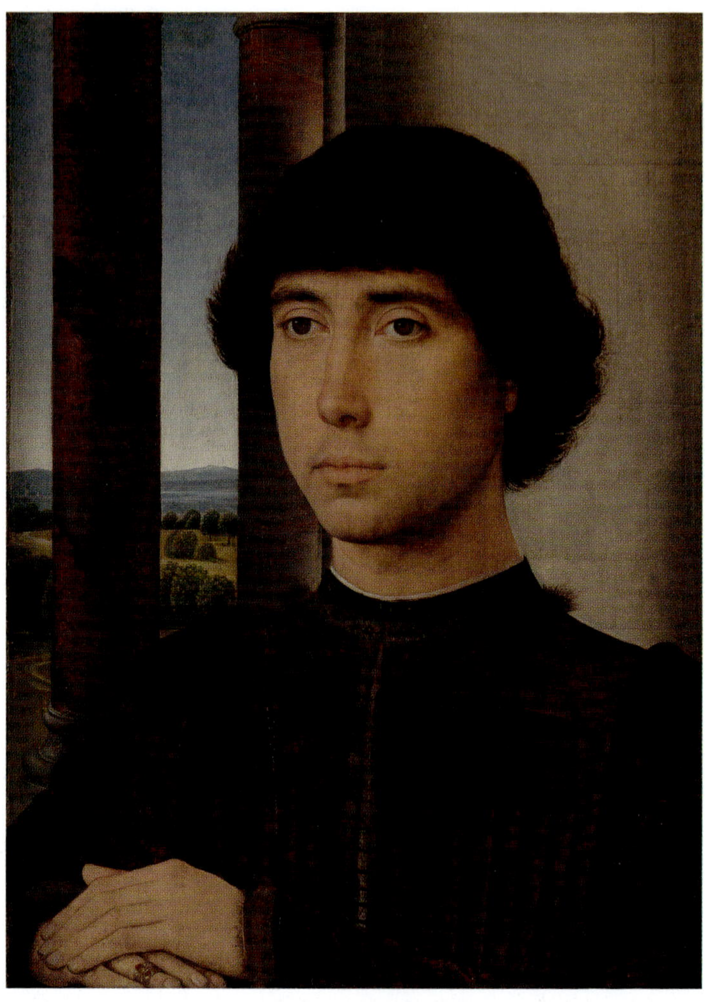

their mature features clearly and specifically rendered; the work perhaps marked a late remarriage or an anniversary of the sitters, who are well dressed in fur-lined coats – although the man's tall hat may in these years have been on the verge of going out of style. This sort of double portrait had been developed in

41 Hans Memling, *Man at a Loggia*, c. 1472–5, oil on oak.

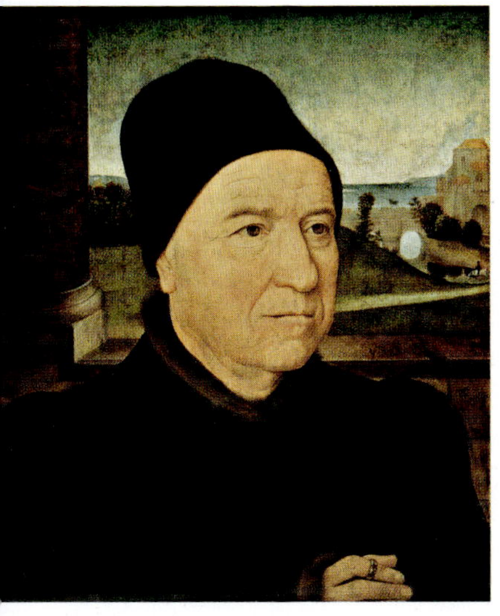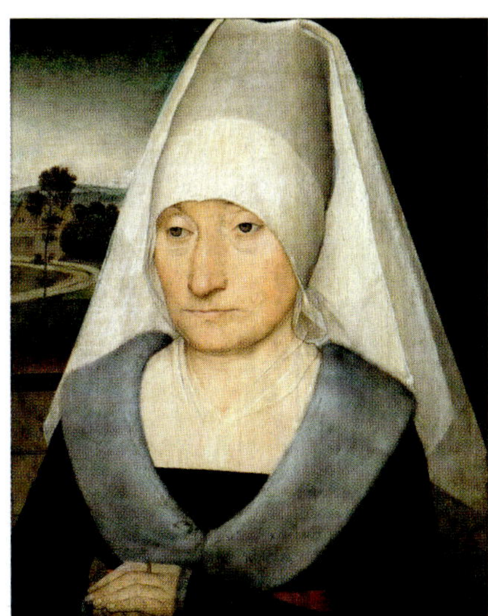

Germany, but these would be among the earliest such works in
the Low Countries, another indication of Memling's innovation
and response to the desires of his international clients.[33]

Complicating the question of portraits and their function
are those works intended as epitaphs, which, when divorced from
context and any original inscriptions, are impossible to differentiate from any other portrait. Many of the apparent portraits
and small devotional panels from Memling's workshop may have
served as public epitaphs and memorial paintings, reminding
the living to continue to pray for the deceased.[34] One probable
case is the portrait of Gilles Joye, a canon and musician at the
Sint-Donaaskerk in Bruges (illus. 43). Although wearing a
sumptuous auburn fur coat and two rings – one of which bears
his coat of arms – he appears in a featureless dark green space.
The painted treatment continues on to the original frame, which
is painted to simulate maroon marble. On the bottom and top
members of the frame, *trompe l'œil* engraved epigraphs declare his
current age of 47 and the year 1472; to the left and right appear

42 Hans Memling, *Diptych with an Elderly Couple*, c. 1470–75, oil on oak.

his coat of arms and personal device. In common with many of the sitters in devotional portraits, he lifts his hands in prayer and gazes unfocused to one side, but this panel does not appear to have been part of a diptych. It was probably installed above his tomb in the sacristy at Sint-Donaas alongside a text panel upon his death in 1483, if not earlier, by the executors of his will.[35]

While a large part of Memling's oeuvre remains undocumented in terms of original commissions and the identities of his clients, a number of works have been convincingly connected to known individuals, some of whom are very well recorded on account of their business and political activities. As case studies, these works help to illustrate the general demographic and functional trends described above: individual clients and their commissions, the destinations and purposes for which those works were intended and how their careers and activities fitted into the larger commercial and civic life of late fifteenth-century Bruges. These clients represent a range of groups, including international merchants and merchant bankers, their Bruges-native counterparts, foreign institutions and individuals who appear to have made use of travelling merchants as intermediaries, a handful of individuals whose careers were primarily political or diplomatic and the representatives of corporate institutions, including both the trade guilds and the religious foundations of Bruges, the last of which were as tightly interwoven as the others with the commercial life of the city.

As noted earlier, Memling seems to have been particularly popular among Italian patrons, and perhaps 20 per cent of his surviving work with identifiable patrons or strong suggestions of the nationality of the owner was intended for Italian clientele. While merchants from Lucca and Genoa had commissioned well-known paintings from such earlier fifteenth-century Bruges artists as Van Eyck and Christus, merchants of Florentine origin – in particular agents and allies of the Medici family – are represented

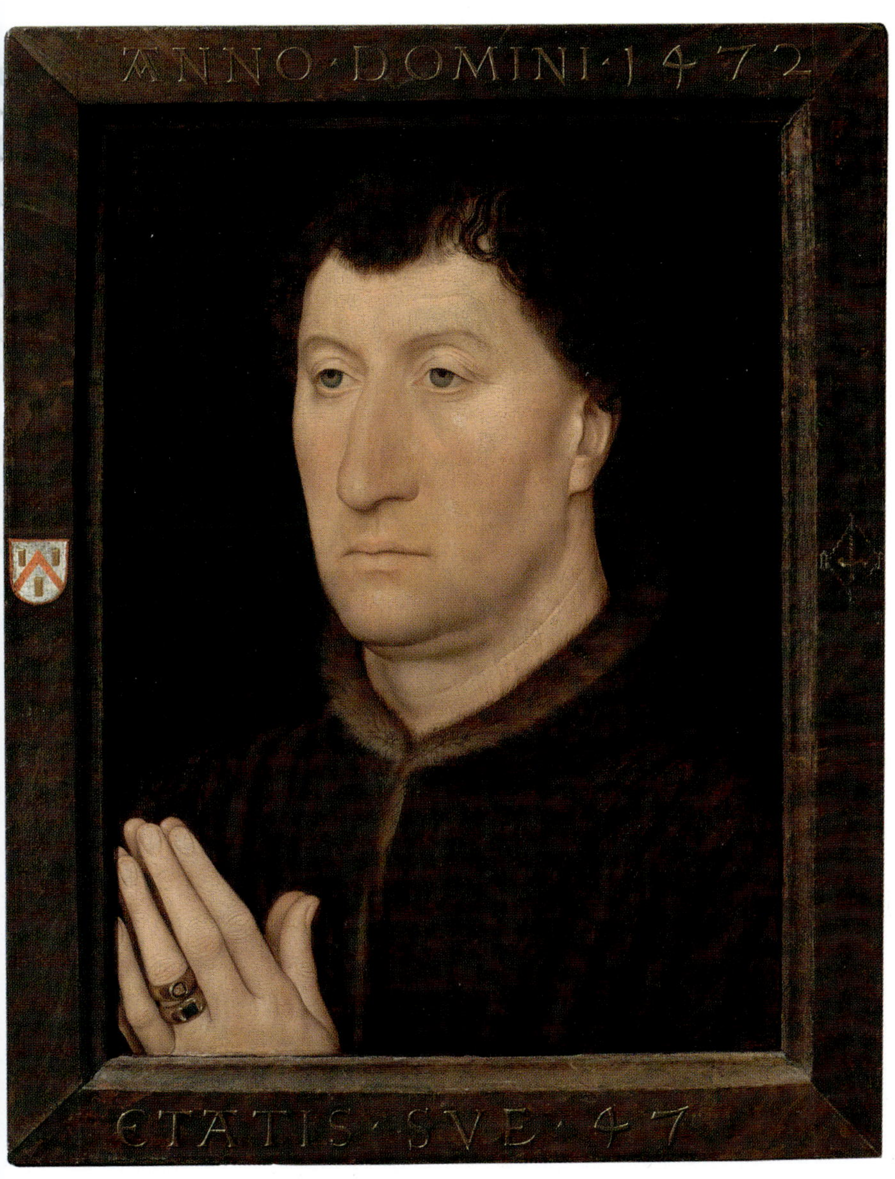

43 Hans Memling, *Gilles Joye*, 1472, tempera with oil on oak (in original painted frame).

particularly well in Memling's known oeuvre. Some of Memling's best-documented clients were Florentine, including the merchant banker Agnolo Tani, who, as we saw earlier, ordered the impressive *Last Judgement* triptych, one of the earliest commissions of Memling's career (see illus. 1 and 2).[36] In 1450 Tani was transferred from London and made chief of the recently established Bruges branch of the Medici, succeeding the first branch manager, Bernardo Portinari (manager 1439–48), and the second, who lasted for only a year. The Medici, seemingly unconvinced of the prospects of these northern branches, had Bruges correspondence signed 'Agnolo Tani e campagni di Bruggia', perhaps keeping some legal and financial distance.[37] Tani also seems to have served the Burgundian court as a purchasing agent in the late 1450s, perhaps adopting a taste for the trappings of nobility.[38]

During a period in 1464–5 in which Tani had travelled to Florence to have the Bruges contract renewed, another Medici agent, his assistant Tommaso Portinari, succeeded in having himself appointed as acting manager of the Bruges branch. It is unclear how precisely this occurred, but the two men continued to work together and have functional business contacts, and Tani continued to hold shares in the firm until 1481.[39] Perhaps marking his marriage to Caterina Tanagli, the *Last Judgement* triptych was probably intended for his chapel dedicated to St Michael at the church of the Badia Fiesolana monastery outside Florence (his coat of arms remains on the keystone).[40] This church was initially funded by Cosimo de' Medici and finished by Piero de' Medici in 1466, and chapels off the south side of the nave were in turn sponsored by various Medici officers and allies, including Tani, the Martelli family, the prominent Sassetti family and Pigello Portinari.[41] A puzzle surrounds the replacement portrait head – necessarily added before the triptych was shipped in 1473 – painted on foil and pasted on to the figure kneeling on Michael's scale, usually identified as Tommaso Portinari, Tani's successor as branch manager (and Pigello's brother).[42] Portinari's portrait on his altarpiece by Hugo van der Goes, now in the Uffizi, is similarly executed on a separate piece of material (in that instance vellum or paper) that was later glued to the panel. This feature may in both cases be a result of the absence of the sitter at the time the painting was made.[43]

While his involvement in the *Last Judgement* remains unclear, Tommaso Portinari himself commissioned works from Memling on at least two occasions. While Tani seems to have viewed his post in Bruges as a temporary affair, Portinari appears to have intended a lifelong career in Burgundy, and became more integrated within the community.[44] He had been present in Bruges since the age of twelve or thirteen, until 1448 working as an office boy and then factor for the Medici branch, first under his cousin Bernardo di Giovanni d'Adorado, who had been sent in 1436 to develop connections between Bruges and London. In time Portinari was also entrusted with the sale of silks and brocades and the arrangement of spice shipments with the Venice branch.[45] From 1455 he worked as an assistant to Tani, and in 1465 he finally became acting manager, with branch correspondence now signed 'Piero di Cosimo de Medici e compagni': some sign of confidence from the Florentines.[46] In 1466 Portinari convinced Piero de' Medici to purchase the Bladelinhof, one of the most luxurious mansions in Bruges, for use as offices, and there Portinari arranged the installation of a pair of bust-portrait relief roundels (by an anonymous artist) of Lorenzo de' Medici and his wife, Clara Orsini, in the courtyard.[47]

Portinari also represented the Medici at the court of Charles the Bold, having insinuated himself there as a purveyor of luxury textiles, but showing his usefulness in financing during the last years of Philip the Good's reign. Serving in an unofficial capacity as counsellor to Charles himself, he was present among the duke's contingent at the ducal wedding in 1468 and of the party that negotiated with Frederick III in Trier in 1473.[48] At the same time the finances of the duchy became increasingly entangled with Portinari's financing (and thus the Medici); a daring businessman, Portinari was involved in a number of high-risk ventures, including the galley enterprise in which Tani's triptych was lost, as described in Chapter One. His most spectacular overstep was arranging a loan to Charles's government for 9,500 Flemish pounds in the 1470s, a significant amount of money, far beyond what he was authorized to lend, and only part of which was ever repaid. While the Medici subsequently withdrew their shares from the partnership in 1480, essentially liquidating the Bruges branch, Portinari remained in the city until 1497, assuming the branch's assets and liabilities and continuing his career in finance and trade.[49] In 1483 he purchased citizen status in Bruges, perhaps finding the economic advantages it generated more crucial now that he was operating independently of the Medici.[50]

Portinari must have possessed substantial social skill, since by then his duties had become largely diplomatic. He was deployed by Maximilian on a mission to Milan, represented Florence in Spain and was sent by Lorenzo de' Medici to England to negotiate a Mediterranean wool staple in Pisa; he also served on the diplomatic team that affected the *Intercursus Magnus* treaty of 1496, which again normalized trade among Burgundy, England, the Hanseatic League and the Netherlands.[51]

While still in Bruges, Portinari integrated into the community in much the same way that other international merchants did, joining religious confraternities, such as Our Lady of the Dry Tree, and endowing chapels; he was named a representative of the Dry Tree – alongside Anselm Adornes, Jan van Nieuwenhove and Petrus Christus – in an agreement between the confraternity and the Franciscans for the use of a chapel at their old site.[52] He was also recognized in the accounts of his parish church in 1470 for his significant financial support of the ongoing church renovation, and in the following year he was granted the use of a family chapel there. In late 1474 he endowed that same chapel, probably intending it for his and his wife's burial (we know little about Maria Baroncelli, but her close relative Pierantonio Bandini-Baroncelli represented the Pazzi family interests in Bruges).[53] Even after the chapel was transferred to the furriers' guild as part of the endowment in 1474, Portinari was responsible for its maintenance, ornamentation and continuing masses, as he retained his burial privilege.[54] The Portinari family was also involved in similar activities in Florence, where the family endowed a daily mass at Santa Maria Nuova – a hospital founded in 1285 by Folco Portinari – and Tommaso endowed another mass at Santissima Annunziata in 1472: a campaign to elevate the family's reputation and his own status in Florence and in the eyes of those in the Medici orbit in Bruges.[55]

The first of Portinari's commissions with Memling are a surviving pair of portraits, probably commissioned to commemorate his wedding in 1470, when Maria would have been about 14 years old and Tommaso around 38 (illus. 44).[56] These portraits most likely served originally as the wings of a devotional triptych with a centre panel (now missing) depicting the Virgin and Child (a work in the National Gallery in London is a candidate).[57] The triptych was perhaps made for the altar of the family chapel at the Sint-Jakobskerk in Bruges, or for the Portinari family's Sant'Egidio chapel at Santa Maria Nuova, where the folding triptych format would still then have been a novelty for Florentine viewers.[58] Whatever the original intended destination for the small triptych, late in his life Portinari did return to Florence, where in 1501 he died. His will left several artworks to his son, a cleric in Florence, including 'a small, valuable panel painting, with an image of Our Lady in the middle and on the sides painted Tommaso and mona Maria his wife'.[59]

The second of Memling's paintings that appear to have been commissioned by Portinari is the panel 1 metre (3¼ ft) wide

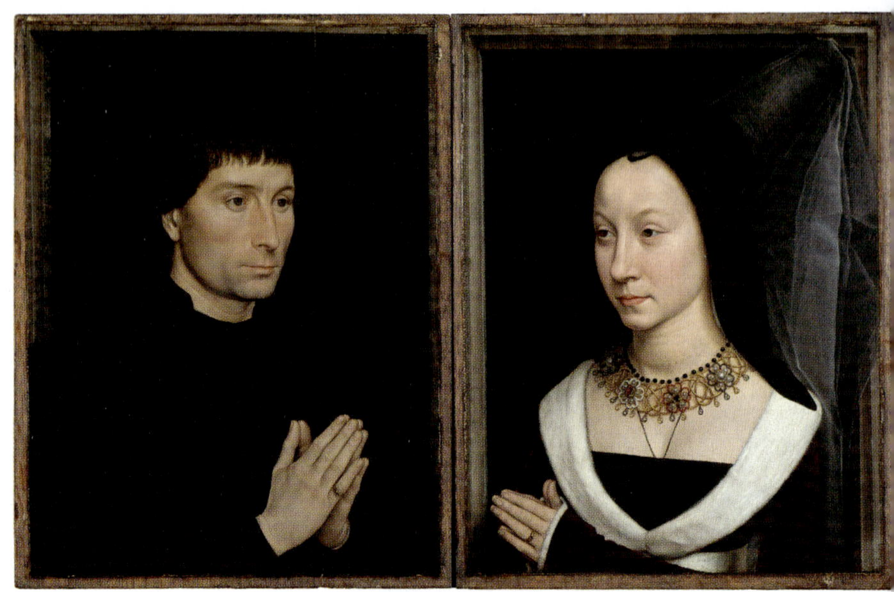

depicting scenes from the Passion of Christ, now preserved in the Galleria Sabauda in Turin and described above (see illus. 9).[60] It is perhaps the *Passion* panel that Giorgio Vasari claimed had been painted for Portinari but was then in Cosimo de' Medici's collection.[61] Like the portraits, the *Passion* may have been commissioned on the occasion of Tommaso and Maria's wedding, before the birth of a daughter in September 1471, but its original destination is, like that of the portraits, unclear; it is possible that it was first installed in Bruges, at the family chapel in the Sint-Jakobskerk, and only transported to the church of Santa Maria Nuova in Florence by his descendants.[62] Given its local artistic impact, it seems to have been present in Bruges for some time, but its size and subject matter may indicate that it was instead intended for the chancel in the church of the Observant Franciscans there, in whose *Obituarium* Portinari appears on account of his donations.[63] Considering the competitiveness of Portinari's career,

44 Hans Memling, *Tommaso Portinari and Maria Baroncelli*, c. 1472–4, oil on oak.

the potential indulgences available at the pilgrimage destinations
the work invokes – even through an imagined journey, as promised in fifteenth-century devotional works – may have spurred
him to encourage Memling to include as many potential 'sites'
for prayer as the size of the panel permitted.[64]

Other members of the Portinari family also appear to have
made use of Memling's skill: Tommaso's brother Pigello (a former
head of the branch in Bruges) and his sons Ludovico, Folco and
Benedetto – Tommaso's nephews.[65] Benedetto, the youngest,
worked as Tommaso's assistant, and upon Tommaso's retirement
from business in 1496, Benedetto and Folco appear to have
assumed his concerns and bought out his shares in Bruges.[66] Two
portraits of near-identical dimensions have been tentatively identified with Folco and Benedetto (illus. 45 and 46), commissions
perhaps arranged late in Tommaso's career as he looked ahead
to passing oversight of the family's business in Bruges to his

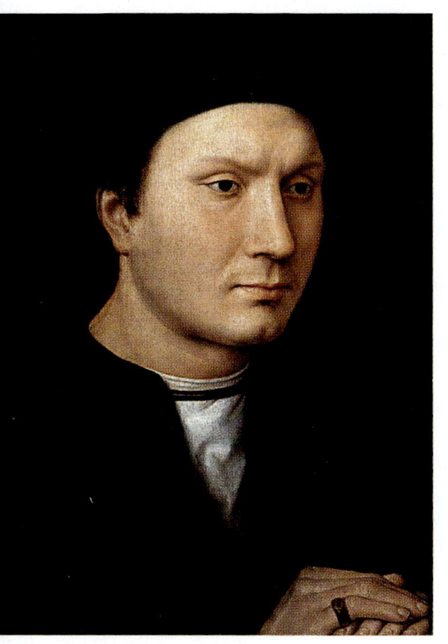
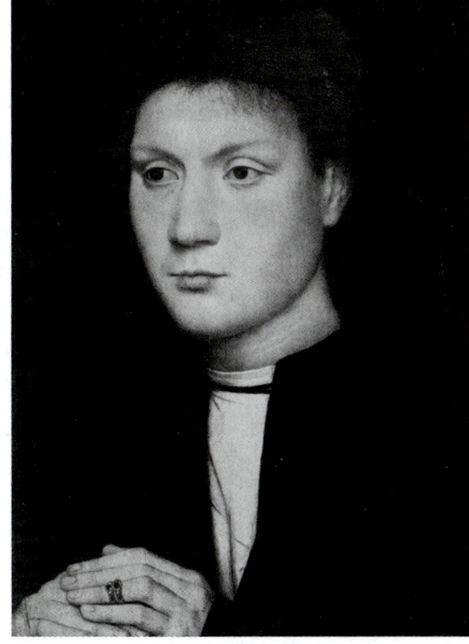

45 Hans Memling, *Folco Portinari* (?), *c*. 1490, oil on wood.
46 Hans Memling, *Benedetto Portinari* (?), *c*. 1490, oil on oak.

nephews. The portrait of Folco that survives in the Uffizi depicts an intense young man in a simple white shirt over which a thick fur coat with a broad collar is draped (see illus. 45). He rests his hands before him on an unseen parapet, a single ring bearing an unidentified motif; his hat is difficult to make out against the darkness of his featureless surroundings. While the treatment is almost aggressively simple, his face is smoothly rendered with great care. It is possible that the portrait was once matched by a pendant depicting a wife, or perhaps it accompanied the now lost portrait of his brother Benedetto, who faces left. Strikingly similar in conception, this work is recorded only in black-and-white photographs; it was stolen by the Nazis in 1944 and its whereabouts are unknown.[67]

Around this time Benedetto could have placed his own order for a triptych with Memling, the panels of which are now split between Berlin and Florence (illus. 47). The right-hand

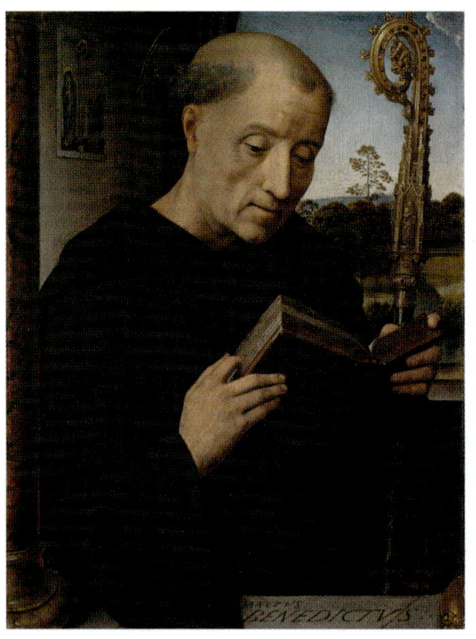
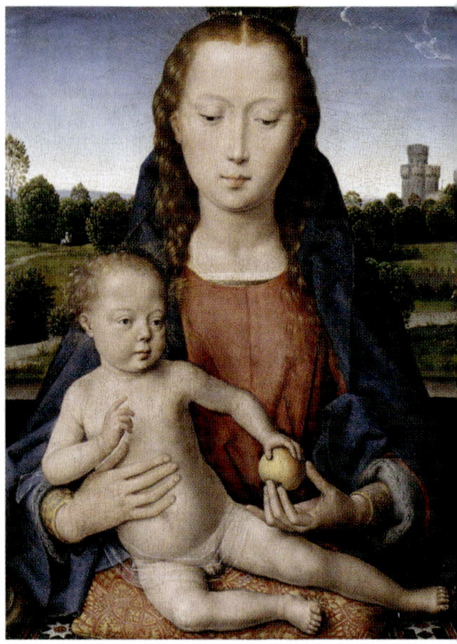

panel features the donor with his hands held in prayer, and a prayer book with a decorative clasp rests against the ornamented base of an unseen column. The broad fur lapels of his coat obscure a small device worn as a pendant on a beaded chain that hangs from the laces of his black doublet. On the parapet on which he rests his arm an inscription bears the date 1487, when he would have been 21 years old. In the centre panel the Virgin, wearing a blue mantle that covers a red dress and gold undergarment – the richness of their brocade and fur cuffs visible only at her wrists – props up the Christ Child. Dressed only in a diaphanous swatch of fabric draped across his waist, he grasps the apple held by his mother as he raises his other hand in an approximate blessing; the Eastern carpet underneath the red-and-gold brocade pillow on which he rests is scarcely visible.

The left wing features St Benedict, Benedetto's name saint, as indicated on the painted inscription on the surface before

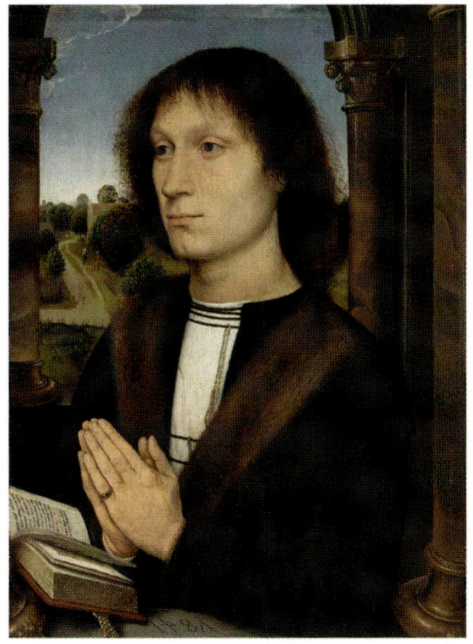

47 Hans Memling, *Triptych of Benedetto Portinari*, 1487, oil on wood.

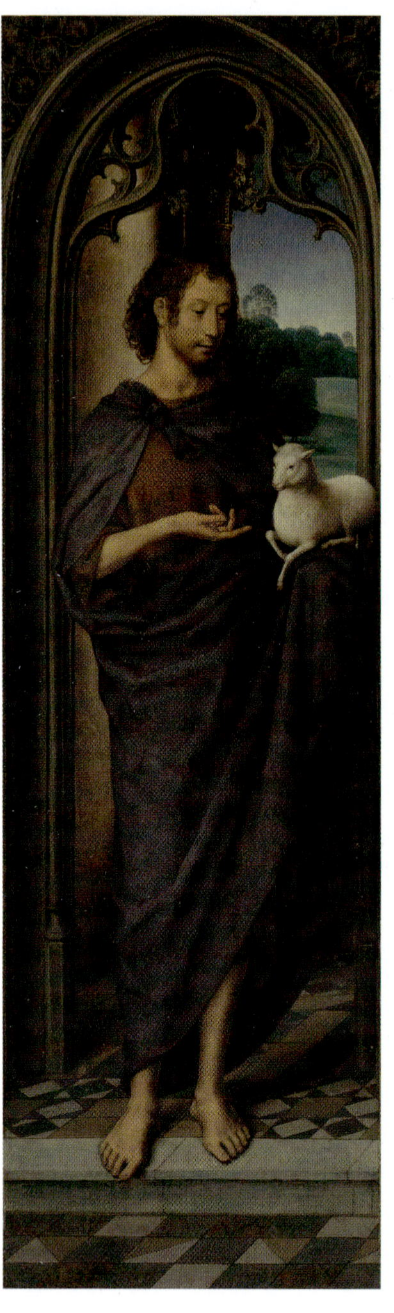

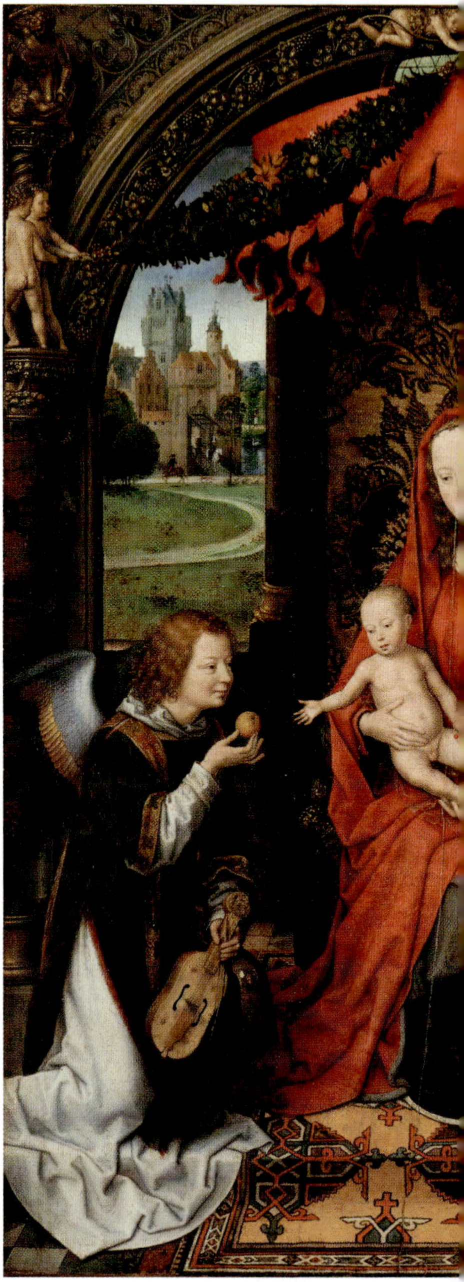

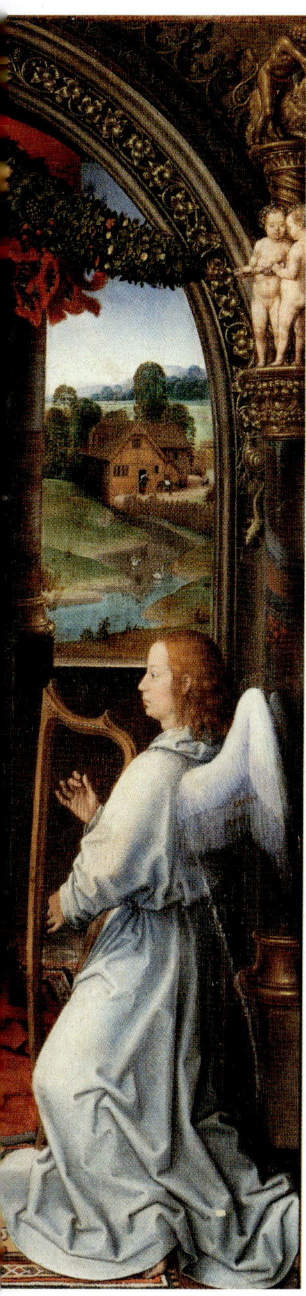
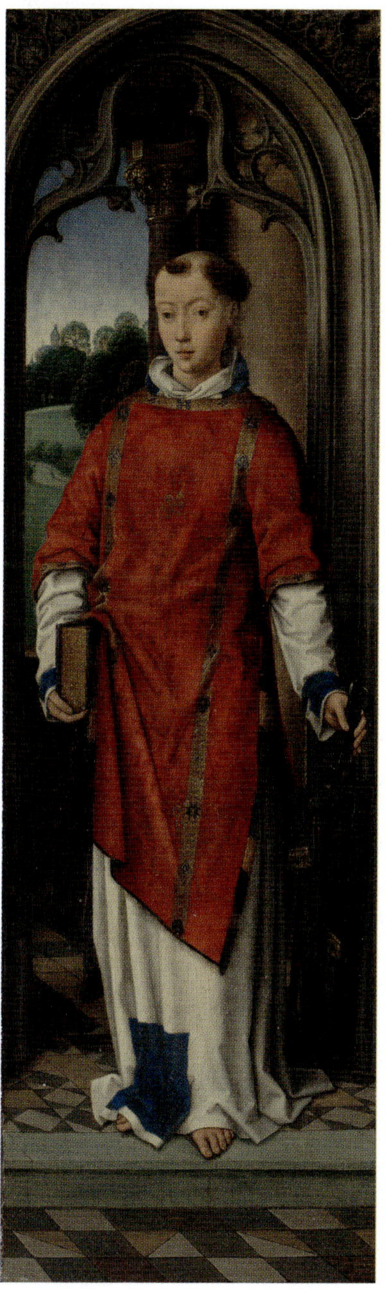

48 Hans Memling, Pagagnotti triptych, interior, *c.* 1478–82, oil on panel.

him. Studiously absorbed in the book he holds open – his right index finger marking an additional place in its gold-edged pages – he seems unaware of the others present. His crozier bears among its abundant ornamentation recognizable figures of John the Evangelist holding a chalice and, at its end, Samson and the lion, while behind him a small painting of a simple Crucifixion scene on parchment has been affixed to the wall. That these three panels once belonged together is made clear by their dimensions as well as the contiguous treatment of their appealing landscape backgrounds.[68]

The history of the wings can be traced back to the Hospital of Santa Maria Nuova, where the somewhat novel presentation of a half-length donor in a loggia before a landscape and the distinctively Northern treatment of that landscape itself would have been received well by its Florentine audience. With Memling's works, one by Hugo van der Goes and several other less well-documented paintings, the Portinari family chapel at Santa Maria Nuova served as a veritable gallery of examples of Netherlandish painting for an entire generation of Florentine artists and aficionados.[69]

A small triptych painted by Memling, now divided between London and Florence, was in the 1480s in the possession of the prominent Dominican bishop Benedetto Pagagnotti, who although himself not a merchant was another close ally of the Medici family (illus. 48).[70] Pagagnotti is not known to have travelled to Bruges, so this work was most likely commissioned either through an intermediary or as a gift; the arrangement with the Bruges workshop was possibly carried out via his nephew Paolo Ulivieri-Pagagnotti, a merchant known to have travelled and visited Bruges, or some other merchant or factor representing the Medici firm.[71] For this work Memling seems to have used a sort of stock composition, personalized for the absent recipient through the addition of Pagagnotti's coat of arms and the selection of saints on the triptych's wings; the idea of a Medici hand in the commissioning is perhaps supported by the inclusion of Laurence and John the Baptist, two of the family's favoured saints.[72] The fleur-de-lis motifs in the spandrels may refer to the Florentine lily, while other aspects of the iconography would have appealed to Pagagnotti's varied interests.[73] The nine cranes depicted on the exterior, for example, the foremost holding a stone, may relate to the watchful crane of folklore that would drop the stone if it fell asleep while on guard (the crane is also possibly a play on the Greek word for bishop: *episkopos* as 'watcher' or 'guardian'; illus. 49).[74] Rather Italianate garlands *all'antica* and the nude putti on the column capitals – this was the first Flemish painting to exhibit such details – were perhaps an appeal to his up-to-date central Italian taste.[75] The work was certainly on display in Florence by 1482, since Filippino Lippi and Fra Bartolommeo, among other artists, copied elements of the landscapes.[76]

A number of other portraits and devotional works from Memling's workshop can be tentatively connected to Florence on account of their influence on Tuscan painting trends, the sitters' attire and fashion, and other circumstantial evidence; many, although documented in Italian collections at tantalizingly early dates, remain difficult to identify in terms of commissioners and original destinations. Memling's *Portrait of a Man with a Letter* in the Uffizi, for example, is probably Italian (see illus. 13), and, as noted, the unidentified young man seated in a loggia (now in the Metropolitan Museum) was, judging by his attire, probably a Florentine visitor in the 1470s to Bruges, who would have returned home with the work or shipped it to family members there (see illus. 41). The presence of the latter portrait in Florence shortly after its completion is supported by its influence in workshops there by 1482, which may also explain the foreshortening of the overpainted halo that remained before its cleaning.[77] By the end of the century at least eleven of Memling's works would have been on view in Florence, as is clear from documentation but also from

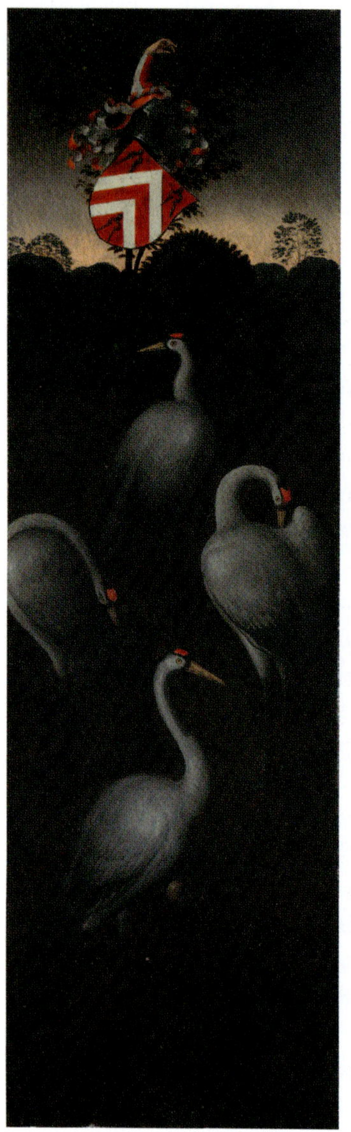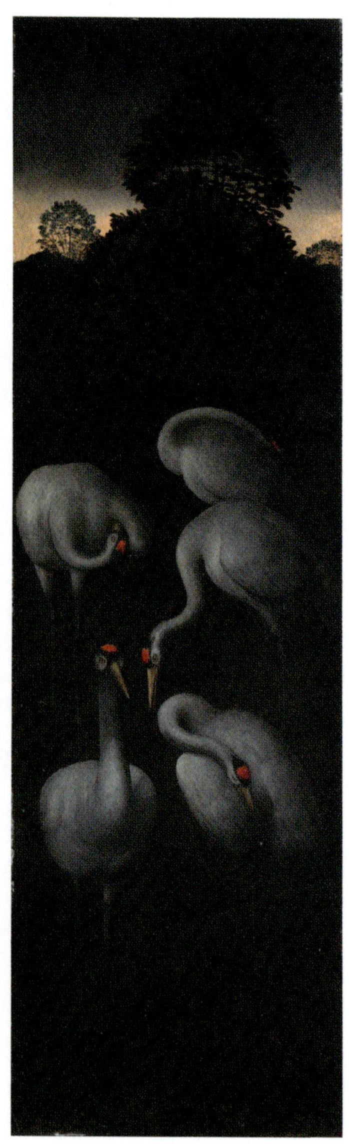

49 Hans Memling, Pagagnotti triptych, exterior, *c.* 1478–82, oil on panel.

their effect on Italian artists.[78] His compositional scheme of placing his sitters in loggias before landscapes had a clear influence on Italian painting (rather than the other way around) in the workshop of Verrocchio and his students – including Leonardo and Perugino – and on Raphael's work; while the format was not invented by Memling, his work for Italian merchants was the strongest mechanism for its dissemination to southern Europe.[79]

While Bruges did not host a large community of merchants from Bologna, members of at least one merchant family, the Loiani, commissioned a number of artworks in the area and may have been clients of Memling. Giacomo di Giovanni d'Antonio Loiani is documented in Bruges in the mid-1480s and his first wife appears to have been Flemish; he, his brother and his nephew also traded in Antwerp.[80] The surviving six sawn-apart panels of a once folding triptych now in the Museé des Beaux-Arts, Strasbourg, associated with Memling's workshop, present a moralizing allegory on the theme of vanity and salvation (illus. 50). The inventive original arrangement of the panels appears to have offered two diptych views, depending on how it was opened. One view depicts a demon dancing around various bodies that flail about in the jaws of a hell-mouth, placed opposite God the Father surrounded by four angels playing musical instruments. In a second view, an entirely nude woman, gazing at her reflection in a mirror as she stands in a landscape accompanied by various dogs, was paired with the figure of a decaying figure of Death posing before an opened grave with a carved stone slab; the closed object depicted a human skull in a niche and a panel with the Loiani owner's coat of arms. Given the unusual subject matter, this work is more likely to have been intended for private devotional contemplation than for the family chapel in the monastic church of Corpus Domini or at S. Giacomo Maggiore in Bologna.[81]

The presence of patrons from Venice among Memling's clientele is most clearly indicated by a diptych belonging to the diplomat and statesman Bernardo Bembo, which is now divided between the Alte Pinakothek in Munich and the National Gallery in Washington (illus. 51).[82] On the left panel John the Baptist sits on an outcrop of rock, gesturing towards the lamb that lies to his side; the view into landscape is blocked on one side by a dense grove of trees and on the other a steep wall of rocks. On the opposite panel Veronica sits in a landscape contiguous with that of the other panel, its rocky cliffs opening on to a gentler landscape and a walled city visible on the horizon. Draped in a voluminous blue mantle, she delicately lifts the *sudarium* bearing the miraculous visage of Christ. Bembo served the Florentine Medici and was also a Venetian ambassador to Duke Charles's Burgundian court in 1471 and 1474, spending a period in Bruges; he may have commissioned the work himself at that time.[83] The diptych is probably the work that was lent in 1502 to Isabella d'Este, marchioness of Mantua, by his son Carlo Bembo, since the inventory notes that it was 'painted by an artist from over the Alps'.[84]

The portrait of a *Man with a Roman Coin* in Antwerp has been identified as Bernardo Bembo himself, based on the inclusion of the palm tree and the laurel in the foreground – his personal device (illus. 52). The coin has been identified as a *sestertius* struck in Lyons, depicting the emperor Nero. As well as the palm tree, the background of the painting features a lake with two swans, perhaps another iconographic clue; such emblematic references would have appealed to Bembo's erudite humanist taste.[85] A number of artistic echoes suggest the work's early presence in Florence, most notably Botticelli's *Man with a Medal of Cosimo de' Medici* (1475); Leonardo's *Ginevra da Benci* – which also appears to have been made for Bembo, based on the emblem on the reverse – likewise reflects Memling's piece.[86] Bembo seems to have collected portraits of his friends and notables, so it is possible that this work represents not him but an ally, but the fact that he

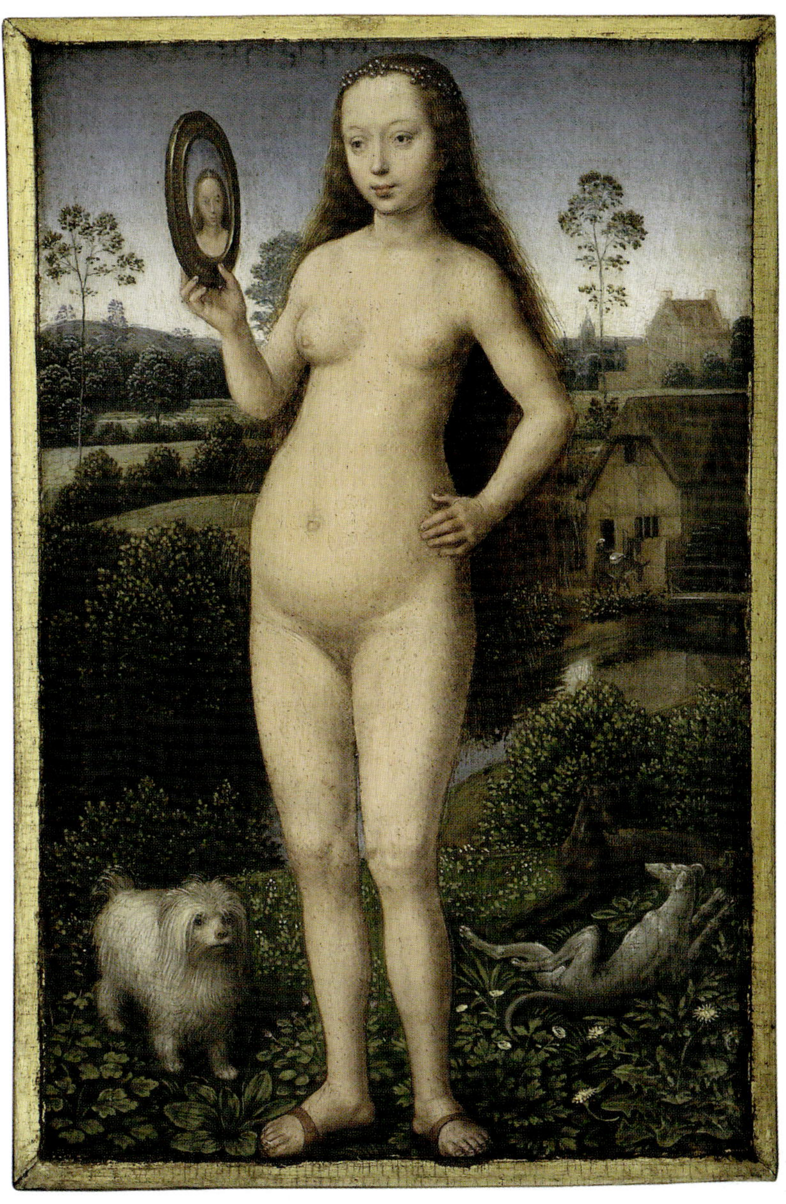

50 Hans Memling, *Vanity* panel from the *Polyptych of Earthly Vanity and Divine Salvation*, c. 1484, oil on oak.

collected it so soon after its creation does suggest that he had a hand in its commissioning.[87]

A number of works by Memling and his workshop have been linked to identified commissioners or their intermediaries from Spain, especially Castile, present in Bruges because of the thriving wool trade. A work that was probably arranged via Castilian merchants in Bruges would have been the now dismembered triptych from which two wing panels survive in Almazán in Soria, publicized only relatively recently (illus. 53 and 54).[88] These works – which depict standing figures in semi-grisaille of saints Peter, Francis of Assisi, Elizabeth of Hungary (dressed in her Franciscan tertiary habit) and Bernardino of Siena – are rendered on a fairly large scale, some 80 centimetres (31½ in.) high. These may have been ordered on behalf of Pedro IV Hurtado de Mendoza of Almazán, first count of Monteagudo, through intermediaries in Bruges – perhaps on the occasion of his marriage. Memling's

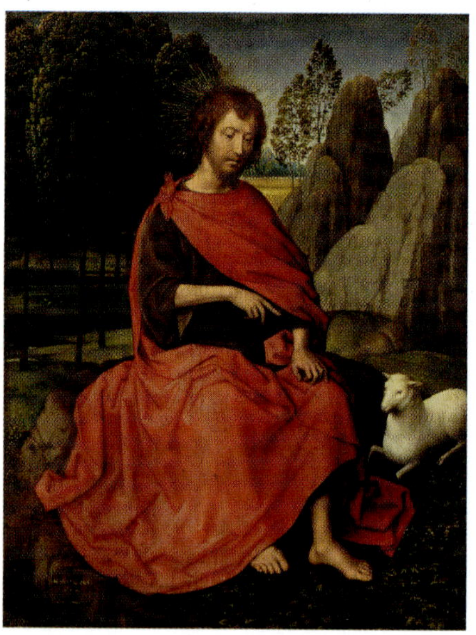
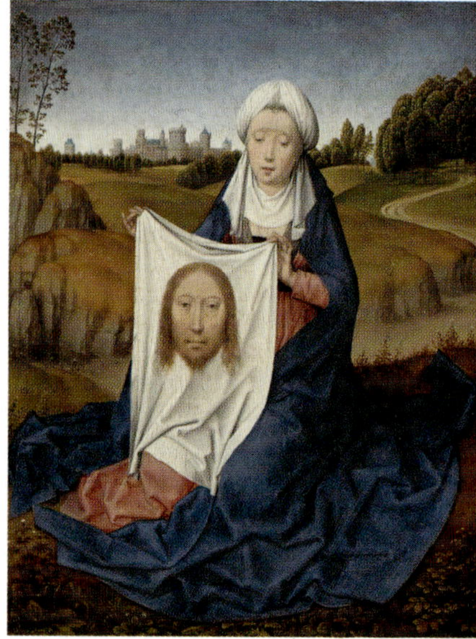

51 Hans Memling, St John and Veronica diptych (Bembo diptych), obverse, *c.* 1471–4, oil on wood.

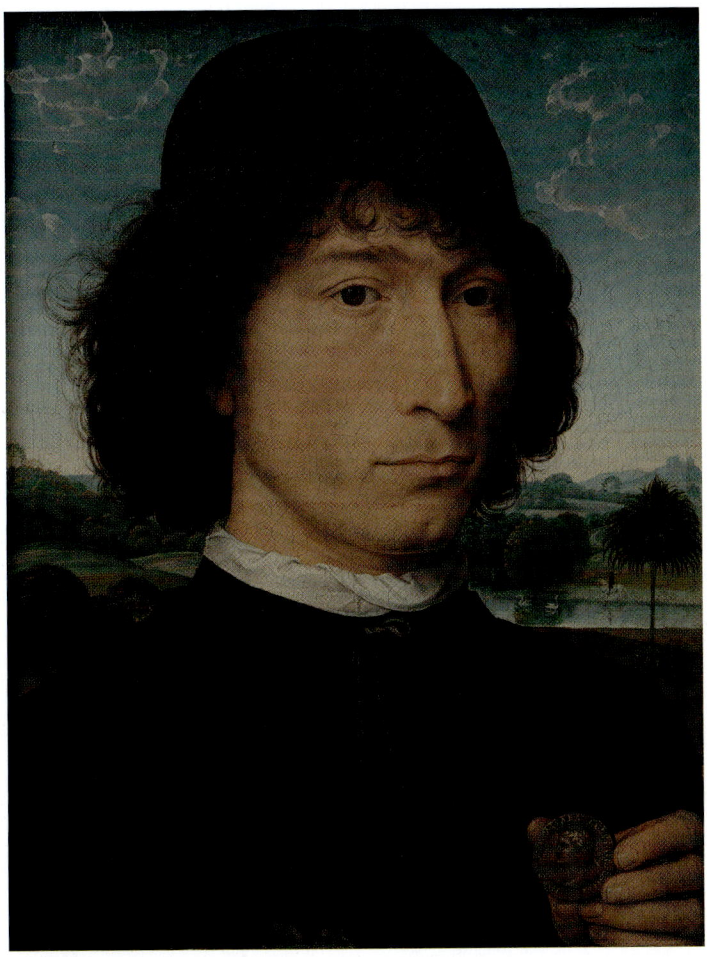

panels were probably destined for the Franciscan monastery in
Almazán, where an altar dedicated to St Bernardino served as the
site of the tombs where the Mendoza men, in accordance with
family tradition, would be buried dressed in Franciscan habit.
Three of the saints depicted, then, are specifically appropriate to
the site.[89] Under Pedro's tenure the castle in Almazán was rebuilt

52 Hans Memling, *Man with a Roman Coin* (Bernardo Bembo (?)), c. 1470–75,
oil on oak.

on the frontier between Castile and Aragon, close to Navarre, and it temporarily housed the court of the Catholic Monarchs Isabella of Castile and Ferdinand of Aragon, who then had no fixed court, seventeen times between 1474 and 1515; one could speculate that this is where Isabella who later employed Michael Sittow and Juan de Flandes, became aware of the Memling-influenced style.[90]

The large panels preserved in Antwerp that depict God the Father and singing and music-making angels likewise had a Castilian destination, as noted earlier.[91] The original arrangement of panels comprised several registers of images surrounding a lost Assumption of the Virgin (its appearance perhaps reflected in a composition by Sittow, now in Washington); as noted, such a retablo was a rare approach in Flanders and reflected its destination.[92] These works were ordered before 1483 by Gonzalo de Cabredo, the prior of the Cluniac Benedictine monastery of Santa María la Real at Nájera in Castile, probably through one of a number of merchants from Nájera known to have been active in Bruges in the wool trade; while Cabredo would serve as prior until 1486, the work would not be completed and delivered until the tenure of his successor.[93]

Several portraits of unidentified sitters can also be tentatively connected to Spain on the basis of costume or provenance. In a panel of uneven quality, not universally attributed to Memling himself, that has recently been installed in the Memling Museum at the Sint-Janshospitaal in Bruges, for example, the richly dressed client kneels with an open prayer book before a prie-dieu, set in a loggia before a landscape with a small figure of Joseph of Arimathea (suggesting the Crucifixion or Deposition as a theme for the lost centre panel of the probable original triptych; illus. 55). The work has been connected to the Rojas family on the basis of a painted coat of arms on the panel; it perhaps depicts Francisco de Rojas, who served as ambassador for the Castilian monarchs between

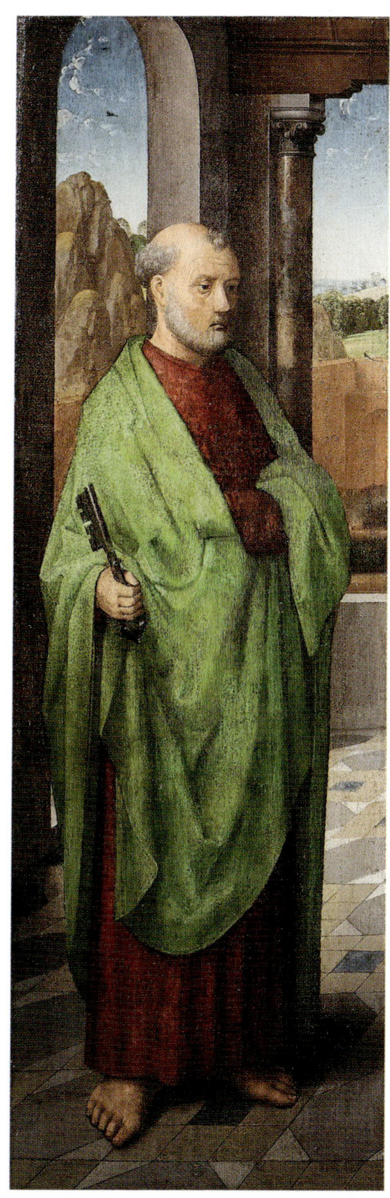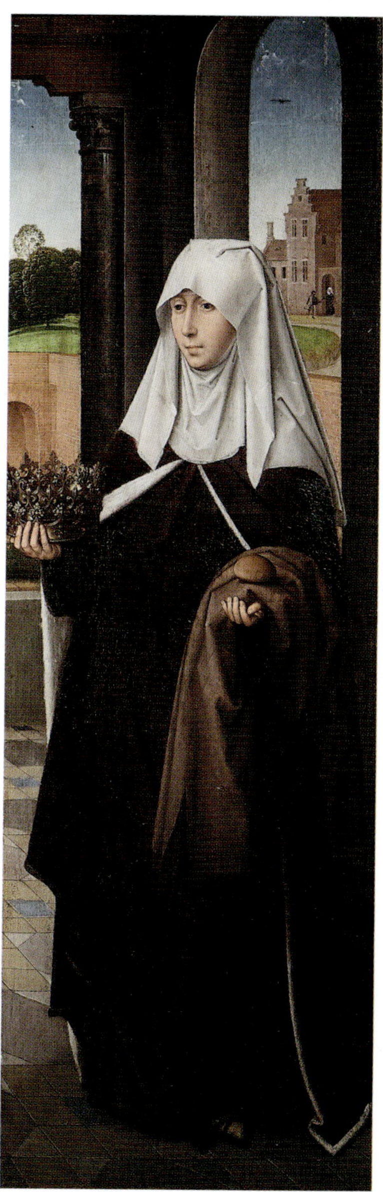

53 Hans Memling, Almazán triptych, interior wings: *SS Isabel of Hungary and Peter,* *c.* 1490–94, oil on wood.

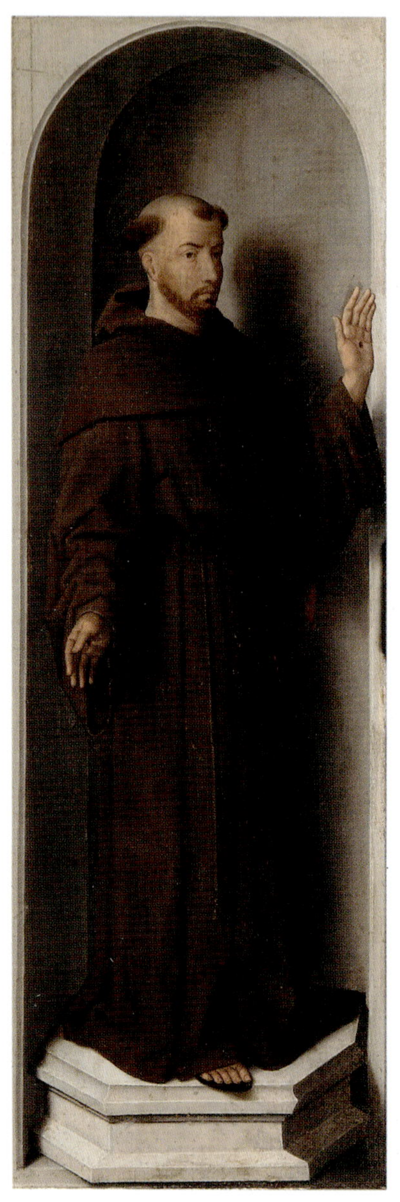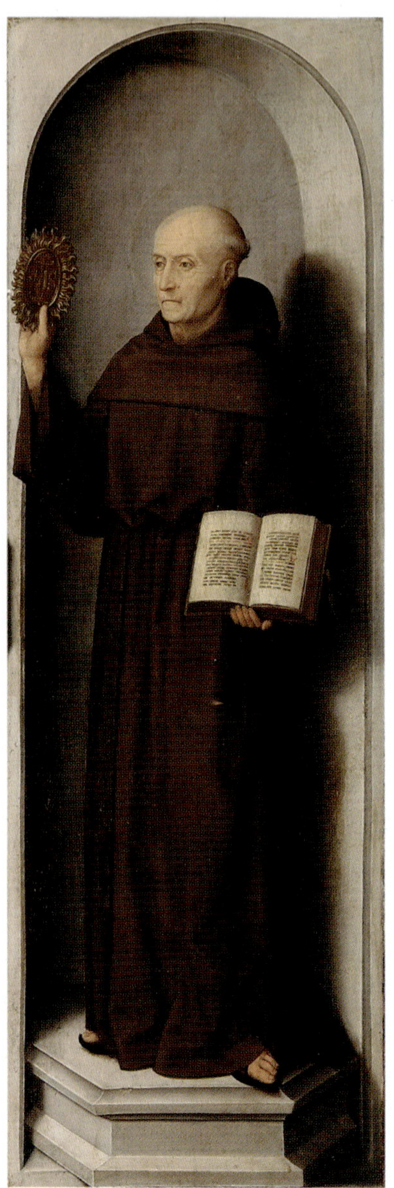

54 Hans Memling, Almazán triptych, exterior: *SS Bernardino of Siena and Francis of Assisi, c.* 1490–94, oil on wood.

1482 and 1492 and was intermittently resident in Flanders in these years.[94] Francisco was entrusted by the Spanish monarchs to negotiate the marriage of Prince Juan to Margaret, the daughter of Maximilian, as part of a strategic dual binding of these families – alongside the intended pairing of Princess Juana and Philip – that unified the two states against their common enemy, France.[95]

Only one of Memling's works has been tied with some certainty to a Hansa city patron, namely the large *Passion* triptych discussed previously, executed for one or both of the brothers Heinrich and Adolf Greverade of Lübeck (see illus. 16 and 17). Heinrich was a merchant and banker operating in Bruges, among other places, before his abrupt death in about 1500 while on pilgrimage to Rome, where he was buried.[96] Adolf, who was initially documented as a merchant burgher in 1493 and managing the currency exchange in Lübeck alongside Heinrich, later studied theology at the university in Leuven and became a canon in Lübeck in 1497.[97] As we have seen, the copious population of the Calvary scene suggests that the work was customized to suit the patrons' regional taste, and the work's relatively tall dimensions are also more typical of Germany than of the Low Countries. The polyptych double-winged arrangement with two closed positions is also a customary type in Germany, probably another adaptation for the work's destination of Lübeck.[98]

Another identifiable northern European client with ties to the merchant community but himself serving largely diplomatic and courtly roles was John Donne of Kidwelly, a Welshman born in Picardy, where his father served in the English military; he himself was knighted on the battlefield in 1471 during the Battle of Tewkesbury. Probably carried out in about 1478–80, the triptych Donne commissioned from Memling is very similar in composition and approach to the interior of the St Johns altarpiece (see illus. 11); Donne – who may have seen the larger triptych in an unfinished state and requested a similar work – probably found

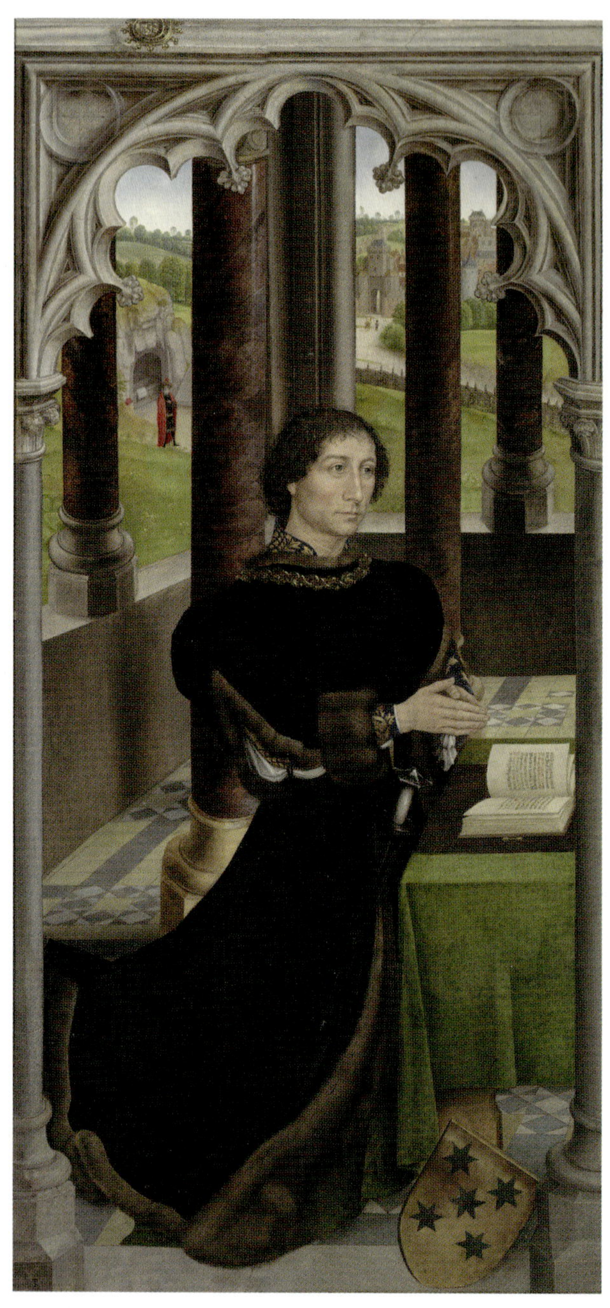

55 Hans Memling, *Francisco de Rojas* (?), *c.* 1470, oil on wood (marouflaged).

it appealing both for its beauty and for its focus on the two Johns (illus. 56).[99] Donne, his wife (Elizabeth Hastings) and one daughter are presented to the Virgin and Child by Catherine and Barbara and a pair of angels. Each sitter is indicated by heraldic arms displayed on the column capitals behind them in the centre panel, and Donne's coat of arms is rendered a second time on the window behind John the Evangelist on the right wing. The left wing features John the Baptist and an unidentified spectator, and the exteriors depict Anthony and Christopher, popular intercessory saints.

Donne spent his career in the service of the House of York, initially for Duke Richard, and was made usher of the chamber as Richard's son Edward IV became king.[100] In this role Donne had some financial responsibilities and seems to have been particularly useful in Anglo-Burgundian relations; he had been the guarantor of the Medici London branch's loans for the wedding of Charles the Bold and Margaret of York in Bruges in 1468, an event that he appears to have attended as part of Margaret's entourage. He may have been present in Flanders numerous times in the 1470s as part of Edward IV's retinue in exile at Bruges (during which it is thought that Memling painted a portrait, now lost, of Edward himself). When the prominent Bruges lord and merchant Lodewijk van Gruuthuse visited England in 1472, among those who received him was Donne, and they may already have been acquainted. Donne was on hand in 1475 for meetings between Edward and Charles of Burgundy, and he was sent to Ghent in 1477 to assist in negotiations surrounding the marriage of Mary of Burgundy and Maximilian; he would have had the opportunity to sit for Memling in this period.[101]

About one-fifth of the works that appear to be commissioned were executed by Memling for members of the affluent mercantile and professional classes of Bruges itself. Some of his works connected to identifiable local clients were executed for

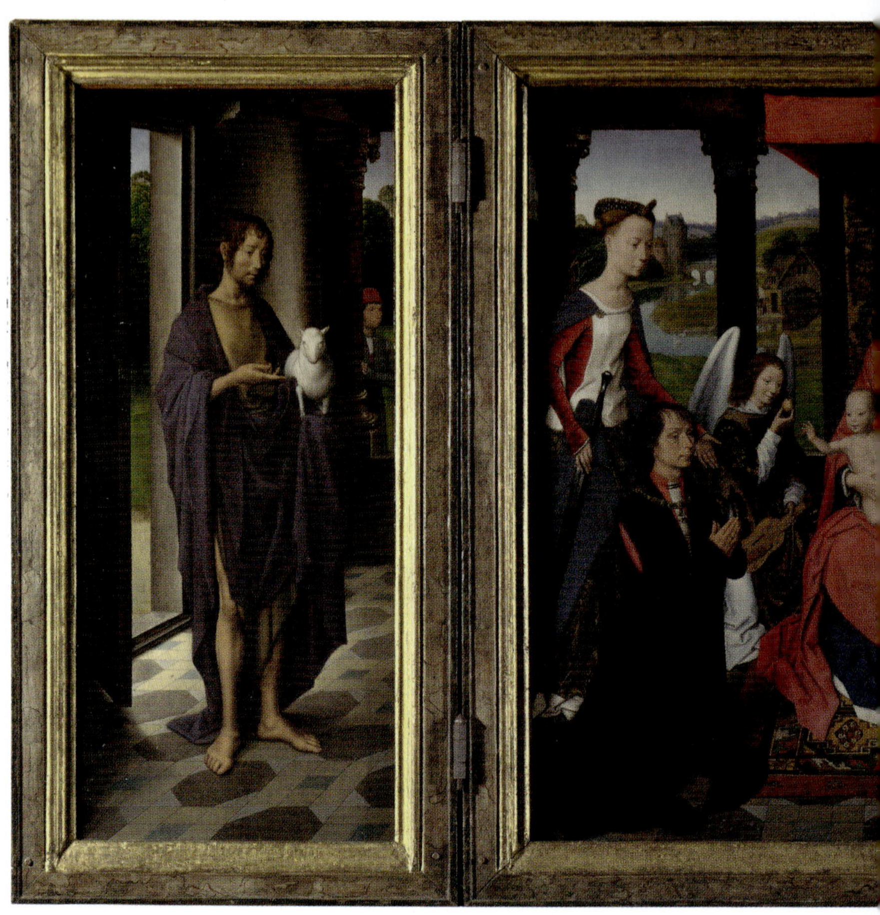

well-known residents of the city, the most prominent of whom
was the spice merchant and politician Willem Moreel. The Moreels
purchased from Memling both a small triptych and, some years
later, a larger altarpiece, discussed previously. The remains of the
earlier work are two panels, now separated and preserved in
Brussels, that depict the couple in shallow loggias before deep
landscapes. He wears a dark fur-lined coat, while she appears in

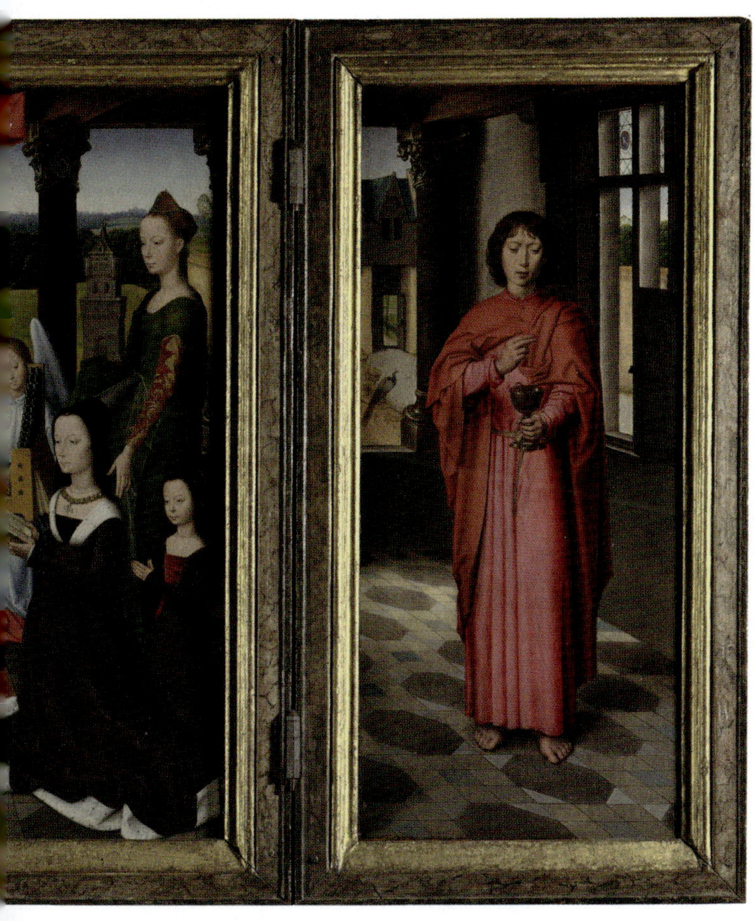

a short hennin (headdress) draped with translucent fabric, a dark
dress and a brooch with three gemstones suspended from a thick
golden necklace (illus. 57). These presumably once flanked a central panel showing a Virgin and Child, all sharing a continuous
landscape setting.[102] If this were a triptych, the two sitters' coats
of arms would have appeared on the outside of the closed work,
fitting for public view in support of a developing political career.[103]

56 Hans Memling, John Donne triptych, *c.* 1478, oil on oak.

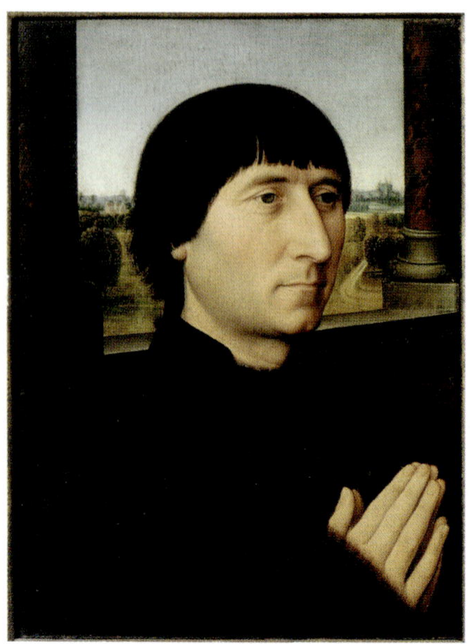
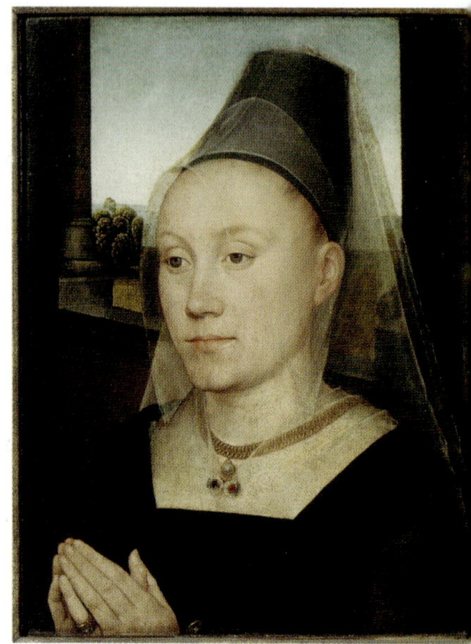

Another Bruges spice merchant to have employed Memling's services was Jan du Cellier, for whom a small diptych preserved in the Louvre was executed.[104] Less than 26 centimetres (10 in.) high, the left panel features a delicate *Virgo inter Virgines* – Mary accompanied by a number of female saints (illus. 58). These include, on one side, Catherine receiving a ring on to her finger, Agnes with her lamb and Cecilia playing a portative organ. On the other side Lucy holds a golden tray that bears a pair of eyes, a dog-headed dragon snarls at Margaret and Barbara sits before her attribute tower. The six women and Mary, who holds the Christ Child in both hands and wears a saturated blue robe and mantle, are separated from the deep, mountainous landscape by a line of trees and a low hedge of white and red roses, while three wispy angels at the top of the panel play trumpets. On the opposite panel the donor kneels with his hands clasped in prayer, accompanied by John the Baptist and the lamb. Diminutive

57 Hans Memling, *Willem Moreel and Barbara van Hertsvelde (Vlaenderberch)*, *c.* 1482, oil on oak.

narrative vignettes are found in the background landscape: George and the dragon – the composition perhaps copied from an engraving by Martin Schongauer – and John on Patmos, who appears on a small island, book open as he gazes towards an apocalyptic apparition in the sky.[105] James Weale, an early Memling scholar, linked the work to du Cellier and connected the presence of George to his brother Joris, a hat and textile merchant who held various civic offices (like his brother, he is found in the lists of those levied compulsory loans) and who – judging by his property activities and significant wine purchases – was possibly a hosteller and broker as well.[106]

In 1482 Jan married Anne de Woestijne, daughter of the nobleman Pieter van Woestijne and of Margarete van Gruuthuse. Margarete was the sister of Lodewijk van Gruuthuse, one of the

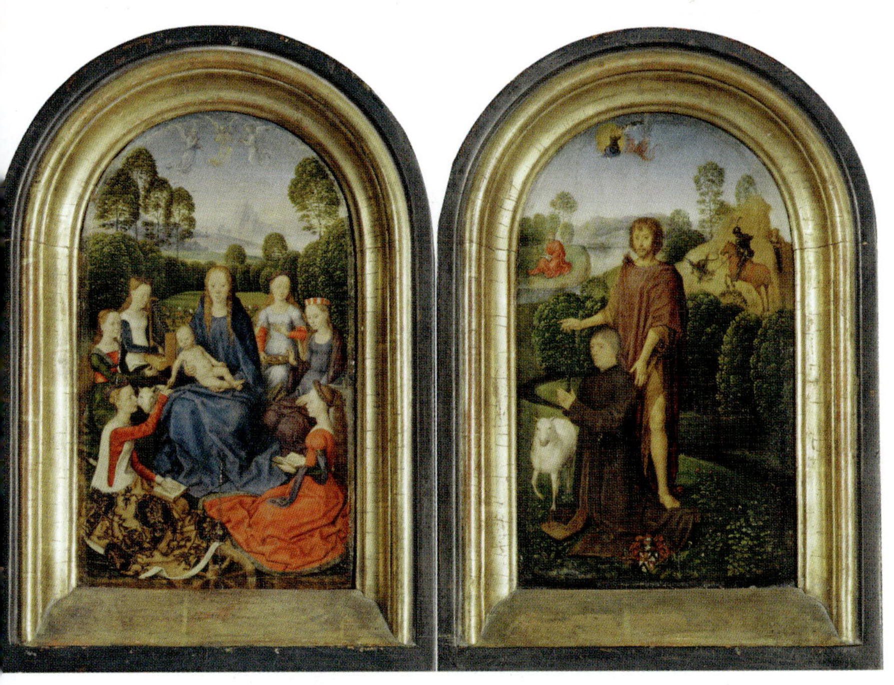

58 Hans Memling, *Diptych of Jan du Cellier*, c. 1488–91, oil on wood.

most prosperous residents of the city, part of whose considerable fortune was reaped from the tax levied on all imported and local beer until his political stance brought him into Maximilian's disfavour in the 1480s.[107] While du Cellier may have enjoyed some improvement in his social status as nephew-in-law to Gruuthuse, such political alliances may at times have been a liability, and while in those turbulent years du Cellier was elected director of the wholesalers' hall at the Hallen, he was also fined by the city.[108] In common with other guilds in Bruges, the operations of the community of the wholesale spice merchants and apothecaries were overseen by a dean and five *vinders*, and du Cellier served as a *vinder* several times. The account books of the prominent Bruges wholesaler Jacob Despars offer additional concrete ideas of Jan du Cellier's financial activities, and the fact that he appears there purchasing 59 Flemish pounds-worth of sugar in 1480 (a huge amount – more than 1,000 kilograms/2,200 lb) shows that he was not simply an apothecary dealing in small-weight goods, but a true wholesaler.[109] Jan and his wife were, like Memling, members of Our Lady of the Snow, and of the crossbowmen's Guild of St George; in 1482 the couple purchased a grave plot in the Onze-Lieve-Vrouwekerk, where the Marian subject matter of Memling's altarpiece would have been appropriate.[110]

Most scholars accept that Jacob Floreins, the younger brother of Jan Floreins introduced earlier, commissioned the large panel in the Louvre of unknown provenance depicting an even larger family than that of the Moreels (illus. 59). Seated in a church interior on a throne with a brocade cloth and canopy, the Virgin and Child are regarded by the male donor, presented by James, and his wife, presented by Dominic. Seven sons and twelve daughters are depicted – one daughter dressed as a Dominican nun – and slices of landscape background are visible to either side. Based on a small insignia in the carpet that has been identified as the commercial mark of the Floreins family, the patron has been identified as Jacob, like his brother an apothecary and spice merchant of Bruges.[111] Jacob Floreins's wife may have belonged to the Quintanadueñas family of Burgos, the centre of Castilian mercantile trade with Flanders, the union therefore an effort to strengthen commercial ties between Burgos and the Castilians in Bruges.[112] The woman pictured is dressed in mourning, so it is possible that the work was started during his lifetime (the portrait is very detailed) but completed after his death.[113] While the panel may eventually have been installed at the Quintanadueñas parish church of San Román in Burgos, on Jacob's widow's return to Spain after his death (or with a different family member), the original destination may have been as a memorial in the Floreins family chapel in Bruges.[114]

At the time that Maarten van Nieuwenhove commissioned his diptych from Memling, he was only 23 years old, but a member of a prominent Bruges family (illus. 60). The right-hand panel of his diptych shows the young man with his hands clasped in prayer, wearing a luxurious purple velvet doublet below a tan tabard with broad lapels of black fur, and his book of hours is similarly sumptuous, with gilded edges and a jewelled clasp. Behind him a stained-glass window displays his patron saint, Martin, with opened shutters that allow only a glimpse of a landscape in which figures are visible crossing a bridge or dam towards a tower set against a body of water. On the opposing wing, the Virgin wears underneath her red mantle a vivid blue dress with fur cuffs, a gold neckline edged with gems and pearls, and a brocade kirtle; her tiara is studded with clusters of pearls. She supports with one hand the nude Christ Child, who reaches towards the fruit she gingerly holds; his body rests on a brocade pillow set upon an Eastern carpet with simulated ornamental Kufic script visible along its edge. An open window behind her allows a view into a much deeper landscape, while the sashes above bear painted-glass roundels depicting George and the dragon, and

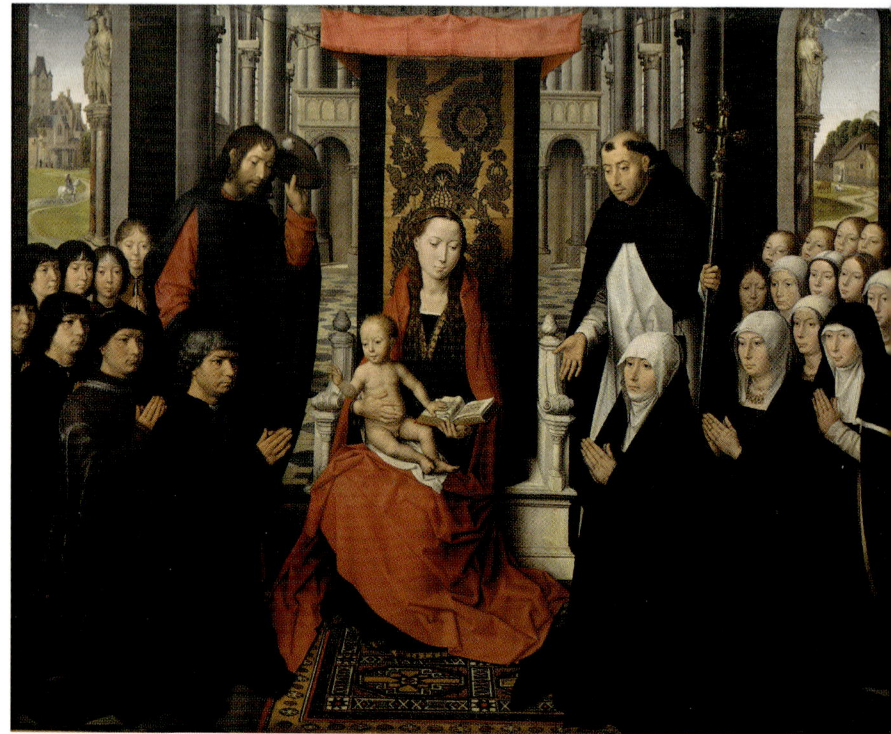

Christopher. Over her other shoulder the shutters remain largely closed; the arched upper portion of that window is filled with stained glass depicting the Nieuwenhove coat of arms, four roundels of the familial device (a hand sowing seeds for a 'new garden') and the family motto. A convex mirror portrays the contents of the painting from behind, including the backs of the Virgin and Maarten himself, thus revealed to be present in the same fictive room; indeed, her red mantle and the carpet both spread into the foreground of his panel.[115] Although devotional in character, such a precious work – and one so thoroughly branded with undeniable markers of ownership – clearly speaks to Maarten's ambition.[116]

59 Hans Memling, *Virgin and Child with ss James and Dominic* (Jacob Floreins altarpiece), *c.* 1490, oil on wood.

While members of the Van Nieuwenhove family had served as *burgemeesters*, aldermen and treasurers of the city, they, too, were merchants, making their fortune through exports to Baltic ports, principally olive oil and fruit.[117] Maarten's brother Jan was appointed *watergrave* in charge of all the waterways in Flanders, and was elected city alderman several times; striving for nobility, Jan was knighted by Maximilian in 1479 and subsequently spent a great deal of money on a seignory.[118] In 1487, then, Jan and his brother-in-law Pieter Lanchals – then the bailiff – were firmly at the top of the civic power structure, and this diptych perhaps publicly announced Maarten's intention of pursuing a similar career as a civic leader, carrying on the family tradition.[119] Probably through the intervention of his brother, the young Maarten was appointed in the late 1480s to be a collector of tolls for fish and *gruut* (preservative brewing spices) and the tax on hopped beer.[120] While Jan van Nieuwenhove and Pieter Lanchals were among those deposed and executed in the turnover of the government in 1488,

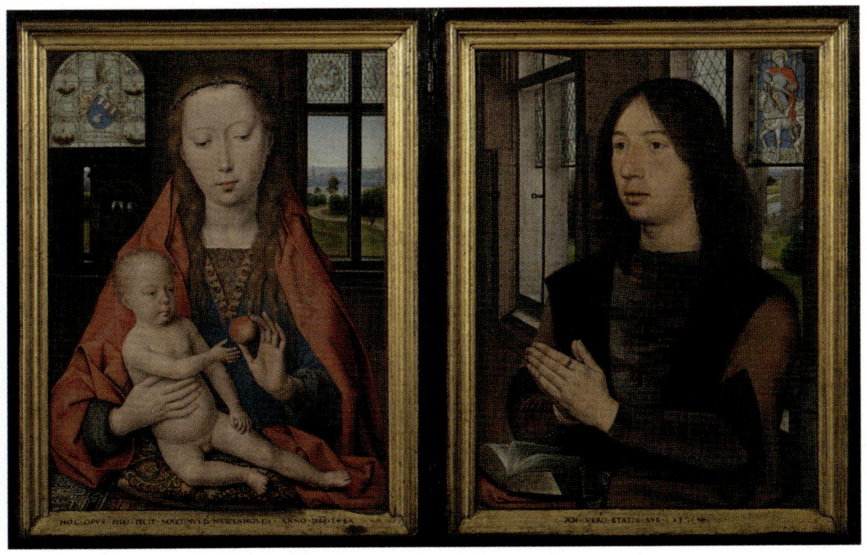

60 Hans Memling, *Diptych of Maarten van Nieuwenhove*, 1487, oil on oak.

Maarten appears to have thrived during the unrest and after peace was re-established.[121] In 1490 he was rewarded by Maximilian with an appointment to the post of receiver of 'extraordinary revenues' in Flanders, and later served as alderman and eventually mayor of the council (*burgemeester van de raadsleden*) in 1498.[122] While the family owned a chapel in the Onze-Lieve-Vrouwekerk, where Maarten would be buried alongside five other family members, he founded an additional chapel at the Sint-Donaaskerk – an institution more closely associated with counts and dukes – and had a window installed in St Martin's chapel there.[123]

A handful of Memling's works appear to have been intended for use in the chapels of artisanal guilds, another of the centres of economic and political power in Bruges. These commissions were spearheaded by prominent members of a guild, such as the deans, who would have wished, like the merchants, to reflect their social standing to the greater public through acts of magnificence. Pieter Bultinc served as dean of the tanners' guild for three terms between 1468 and 1476. The guild, affluent from shipping significant volumes of leather hides to Baltic destinations, purchased guild houses in the 1450s on the Huidenvettersplaats – the tanners' plaza – which featured their own corporate chapel. They also operated an altar at the Onze-Lieve-Vrouwekerk, for which Bultinc appears to have ordered an altarpiece from Memling (illus. 61).[124]

Compositionally and conceptually complex, this single broad panel, like the *Passion* ordered by Portinari, depicts a large number of episodes across its surface, no longer limited to the events of a few days but now encompassing scenes from before Christ's birth to the Virgin's death and Assumption. Often simplified as the *Advent and Triumph of Christ* (now in Munich), the contents centre on the Adoration of the Magi in the foreground, similar in treatment to other versions of the topic in Memling's work but here featuring an expanded cast of characters. The journey of the Magi begins in the distant background where they stand atop mountains viewing the miraculous star, and their retinue can be followed through the left-hand background to their rendezvous at a crossroads, their passage through an expansive city of Jerusalem and finally to the crumbling stable in the foreground; from there the cortège can be followed again through a mountain pass to their galleons waiting on the seashore in the distance. Along the left-hand side of the panel their story intersects with the infancy of Jesus: the Annunciation to Mary, the announcement to the shepherds and the Massacre of the Innocents, alongside associated legendary miracles. In the left foreground Pieter Bultinc and his son kneel near their coat of arms, witnessing the Nativity as the shepherds arrive in the archway nearby.

The right-hand quarter of the panel depicts scenes from much later: the Resurrection and several related episodes, and in the lower right corner the Pentecost – with Mary's presence highlighted – observed by Bultinc's wife, Katelyne van Ryebeke, kneeling near her family's arms. In the distance an appearance of Christ to his elderly mother (in which he announces her approaching death, its composition echoing the composition of the Annunciation on the left edge opposite) is paired with Mary's death surrounded by the disciples. At the top right Christ ascends from a mountaintop as his followers look on, while nearby Mary is herself bodily carried to heaven by angels.

In the late eighteenth century the panel still carried an original frame bearing an inscription, recorded then by a Bruges artist: 'In the year 1480 this work was given to the Tanners' Guild by Mr Pieter Bultinc son of Joos, tanner and merchant, and Miss Katelyne van Ryebeke his wife, Godevaert van Ryebeke's daughter; here must a priest for the guild after every mass read a *Miserere* and a *De profundus* for all souls.'[125] Calling for prayers for 'all souls' and invoking the tanners' guild collectively as a beneficiary of the work, the panel was intended to serve spiritual needs but

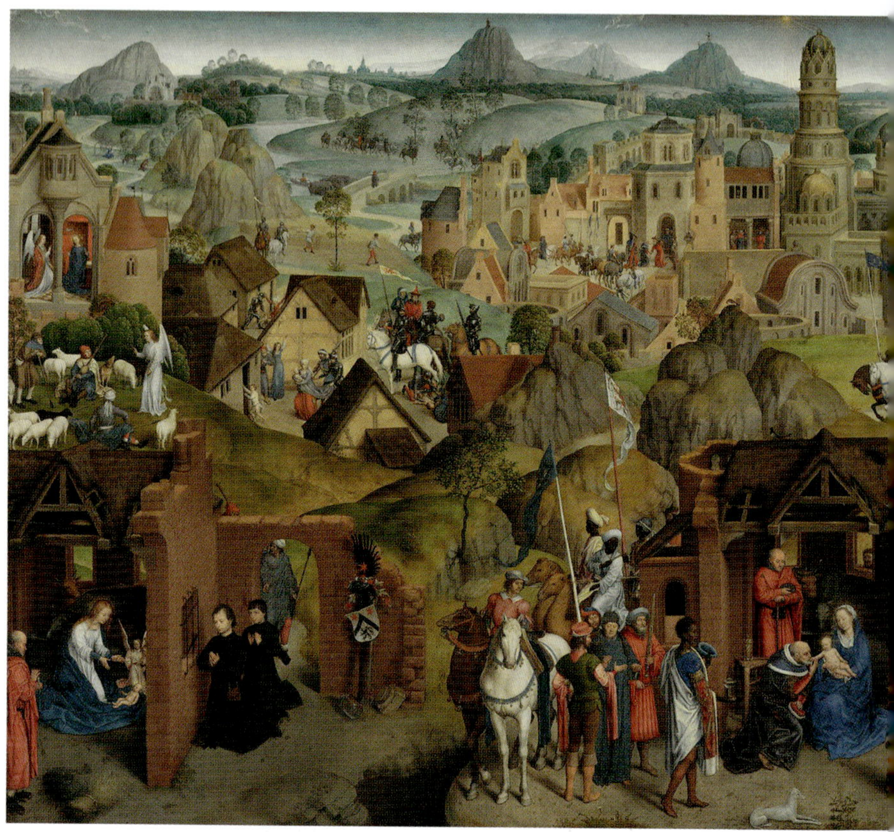

also, simultaneously, socio-political ones in elevating the public status of the donor.

Like Willem Moreel, Bultinc became involved in civic politics in the turbulent climate of the late 1470s; in 1477 he became an alderman in the new trade guild-dominated city board, and he would serve again in 1478 and 1480, so this work was installed when he was at the peak of his political career. Among the supporters of Moreel's pro-regency faction, Bultinc was named among the guarantors listed for the bond of Jan van Ryebeke (to whom

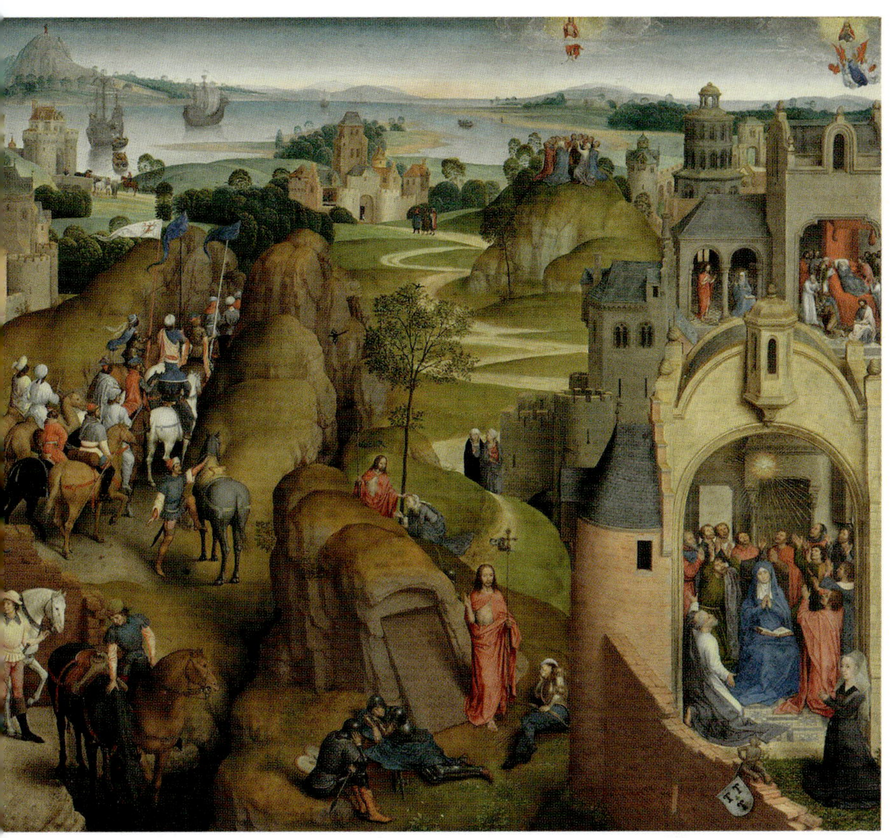

Bultinc was also related by marriage), who had been arrested
alongside Moreel in late 1481.[126]

Another trade-guild chapel commission executed by Memling
was that arranged by the prominent manuscript illuminator
Willem Vrelant for the librarians' guild chapel at Eeckhout Abbey
in 1478–9.[127] This carved wooden altarpiece, now lost and known
only from the archival documentation discussed earlier, seems
to have depicted John the Evangelist and Luke, the guild's patrons,
while Vrelant himself and his wife, Marie – herself perhaps an

61 Hans Memling, *Advent and Triumph of Christ*, 1480, oil on wood.

illuminator – were depicted on the wings.[128] Memling painted two of the four wings and was paid a total of four pounds and three shillings by the collective guild membership (apparently 21 members donated); Vrelant contributed a substantial portion of the cost.[129]

Memling also served a number of ecclesiastical clients: individuals and representatives of institutions whose careers were, like the merchants and tradespeople, tightly interwoven with the commercial and economic life of the city. One of his very first clients upon his arrival in Bruges, for example, was Jan Crabbe, the abbot of Ter Duinen, a Cistercian monastery on the coast west of Bruges (illus. 62 and 63). The triptych Crabbe commissioned from Memling is now split between the Museo Civico in Vicenza – the centre panel depicting the Crucifixion and the Cistercian donor with his patron saints – and the two wings preserved at the Morgan Library & Museum in New York; included on the wings are also a female and a male figure, who may be Crabbe's mother, Anne Willemszoon, and Willem de Winter, her son by her second husband.[130]

Crabbe was born into a respected bourgeois family in Zeeland, and his duties, like those of Jan Floreins, demonstrate how financially focused a religiously orientated career could be. His first important position was *dijkgraaf* (dyke warden) of a district to the west, responsible for the maintenance of dykes and water levels and the expansion of polders, that is, land reclaimed from the sea. He also served as *cellerar* of the abbey and secretary to the abbot, before his own politically contested election as abbot in 1457 (in which he was supported by the Medici but challenged by a Burgundian-backed candidate and briefly imprisoned). As abbot he oversaw the abbey's lucrative administration of waterways, and built a financial and banking network in Bruges; under his tenure Ter Duinen began to play a financial role within the Cistercian order as a whole, shrewdly investing English and Scottish abbey funds en route to Cîteaux.[131] Although it may have been painted in 1472 for the abbey, the work seems to have been ultimately installed in a chapel consecrated in 1478–9 at the refuge house in Bruges that served as Crabbe's frequent residence, where he seems to have expressed his luxurious and humanistic taste.[132] There a priest from the nearby Carmelite abbey performed a daily mass dedicated to the Virgin, both saints John and Bernard, all of whom already appear on the triptych.[133]

Among Memling's patrons, a number of other ecclesiastical clients – despite their insecure identification – remain prominent in the literature owing to their connections to Memling's most famous works, namely the pieces executed for the Sint-Janshospitaal in Bruges. The community of this institution in the fifteenth century comprised perhaps eight brothers and twelve sisters at any given time, who cared for between 100 and 150 patients. In the late fifteenth century, under the authority of the Bruges civic government and the bishop, the hospice was administered by a male master and a female superior, a bursar, a chief sister who oversaw the care of the sick and impoverished and at times financial receivers. The aldermen would select the master of a hospital from among its brethren to maintain day-to-day operations, and one or two guardians from among the city's aldermen to oversee the finances; the individuals appointed tended to be selected from the most prominent families in Bruges. The activities these officers administered were in large part economic: the Sint-Janshospitaal reaped rents and annuities from significant property holdings, held rights for wine-measuring in the city and sole eel-fishing rights in the city's waters, and in 1470 was granted a privilege to gauge weights and measures in the city, all of which provided it with reliable and continuous funding.[134]

The 'donors' of the St Johns altarpiece, for example, suggested by their patron saints on the wings (see illus. 10 and 11), have been tentatively identified as Antheunis Seghers (master of the hospice for much of the 1460s and '70s), Agnes Casembroodt (mother superior during several periods), Jacob de Ceunic (bursar/ treasurer in the late 1480s) and Clara van Hulsen (a sister until her death in 1478). The work preserves its original frame bearing a date of 1479, probably the year in which it was completed and installed in the hospital's chapel.[135] Amid the small slice of urban landscape on the left edge of the panel, past John the Baptist, one of the brothers is found measuring wine from casks on the Kraanplein, a citation of one of the hospice's sources of income and perhaps an additional quasi-portrait of Brother Josse Willems, who oversaw wine-measuring in the years 1467–88 and was the hospital's master when the work was installed in 1479.[136] Since the patients at the hospital would have been encouraged to pray for the souls of their benefactors – that is, the staff of the hospital and its administrators – the inclusion of the donors in the

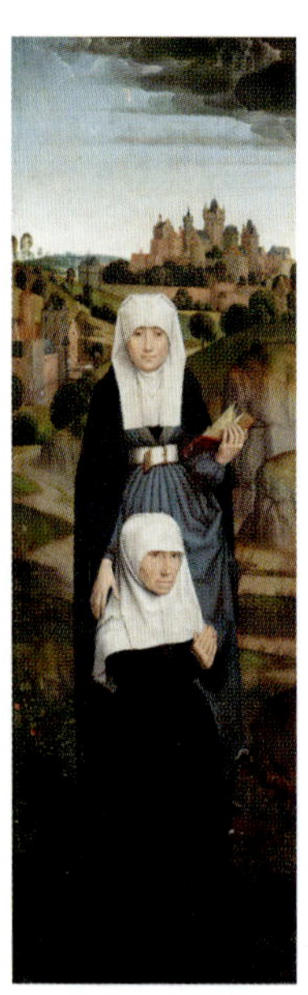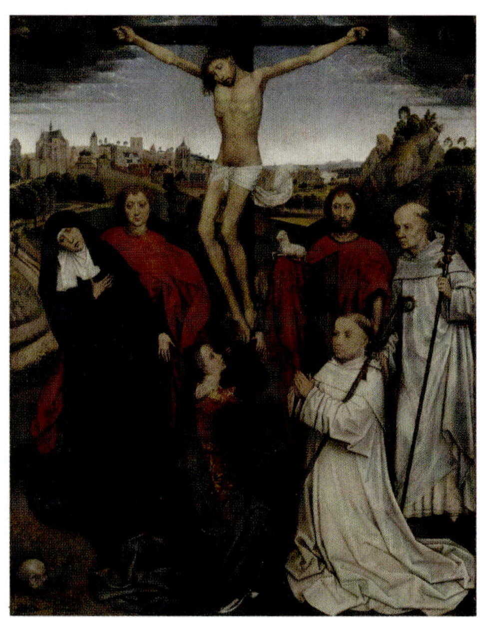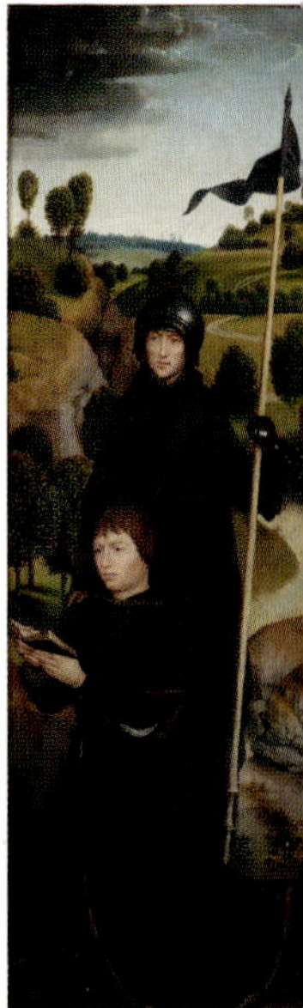

62 Hans Memling, *Triptych of Jan Crabbe*, interior, *c.* 1468–70, oil on oak.

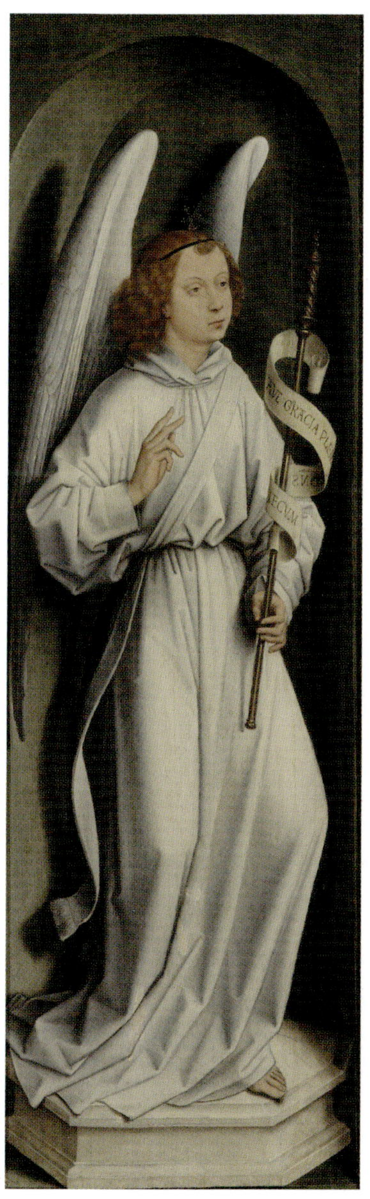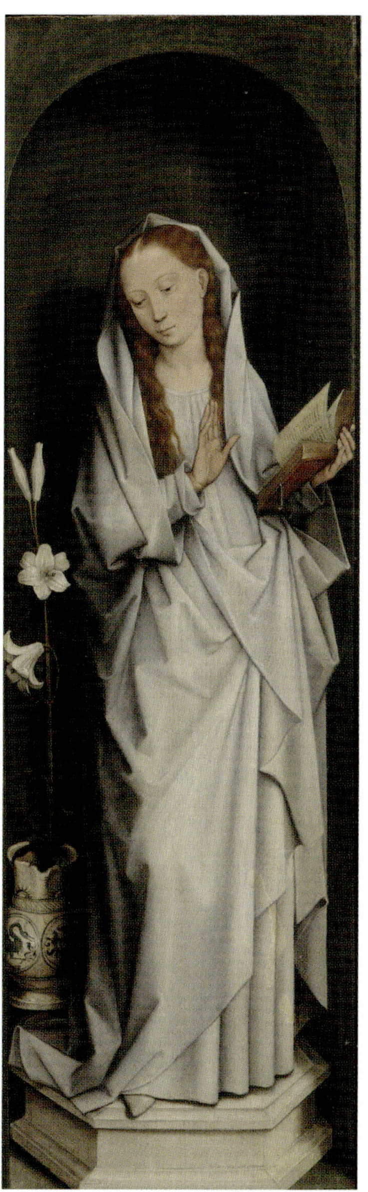

63 Hans Memling, *Triptych of Jan Crabbe*, exterior, c. 1468–70, oil on oak.

paintings that served as the focus for these prayers would have benefited the commissioners spiritually.[137]

Also painted for a side chapel of the hospital was the triptych of Jan Floreins, already described (see illus. 4 and 5); the young man standing behind him in the centre panel has been identified as his youngest brother, Jacob, the spice merchant considered earlier who may have commissioned a panel in the Louvre (see illus. 59).[138] The Floreins family, which stemmed from Hainault, was related to the noble de Silly and Brabantine Van der Rijst families and to the Bishop of Cambrai; a social climber, Jan appears not to have been shy to invoke these aristocratic connections when to do so might be advantageous.[139] The brethren of the hospital being beholden to the Augustinian rule and dwelling in common dormitories, however, his work would not have been understood as 'private property' nor intended for strictly personal devotion by Floreins, and would have become the property of the institution at his death.[140]

As a professional seeking to make a space for his business in this busy commercial city, taking advantage of the diversity of potential customers and the opportunities available in this dynamic trading centre, Memling was much like the individuals for whom he worked. His clientele was largely composed of this new class of merchants, bankers and financiers that emerged in late medieval Europe, whose livelihoods centred on local and international trade. Others depended on activities peripheral to this commercial environment – diplomats, clerics, members of the artisanal guilds – but an inspection of their careers reveals how they, too, were occupied with the economic life of the city, drawing income from trade itself, the regulation of that trade – levies or the measuring of goods – or other responsibilities that centred on institutional revenues and expenses.

Memling's clients included individuals from across Europe – representing, especially, the various states of the Italian and

Iberian peninsulas and the Hanseatic League – and institutions that operated through intermediaries that represented them in Bruges. The purposes to which the works they commissioned were put were varied, at times privately or communally devotional, personal and domestic, and at times public: for the community's liturgical use, commemorating financial and political success, and publicly communicating ambition, power, wealth and good taste. While Memling's artistic predecessors in fifteenth-century Bruges, too, served this class of patron at times, it is clear – especially considering the many commissions and clients on whom we have little information save their apparent social status and occupation – that his career remains distinctive in working above all as a painter for merchants.

Conclusion

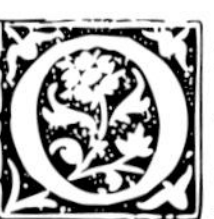

On 3 July 1468 Memling would have witnessed a spectacle. Early that morning, as part of the celebration of her marriage to Duke Charles the Bold of Burgundy, Margaret of York, the daughter of Richard Plantagenet, was met at the Kruispoort of Bruges by the Beguines of the Wijngaard, who presented her with a rose chaplet. Also in attendance were perhaps two hundred representatives of Charles, all clothed in black and mounted on horses, followed by ten bishops, including delegations from Rome, Salisbury and Utrecht (illus. 64). Margaret entered the city carried in a sedan drawn by black horses and richly appointed with red and golden cloths, accompanied by twelve knights on foot and twenty archers; she was followed by thirteen hackneys carrying ladies-in-waiting.[1] The cortège was announced by the sound of trumpets and clarions, the blazons of England and the duke and heralds bearing the coats of arms of neighbouring states. At the gate were gathered the clerics of all the city's mendicant churches and abbeys, the members of the Brotherhood of the Holy Blood (the city's most precious relic), courtiers of the duke, members of the noble families and other elites.

All the houses on the streets through which the cortège would pass displayed flaming torches and were draped with tapestries of gold and silver thread, and other silk and wool textiles decorated 'with every fantasy and detail'; the houses operated by the Catalonian, Lucchese and Portuguese merchants were particularly richly decorated. Installed at intersections and upon squares were ten 'histories': ephemeral decorations featuring triumphal arches and *tableaux vivants* erected by the various trade guilds of the city. Outside the bailiff's house, for example, the butchers' guild had produced a magnificent gate-like structure decorated with Margaret's family coat of arms and a depiction of Ptolemy giving Cleopatra in marriage to Alexander, through which Margaret would pass as white doves and other small birds were let loose. The 'seventeen trades' had erected a presentation on the Wedding at Cana with paintings and other ornamentation, and on the market square nearby, in front of the mansion called the Moor's Head, the collective of smaller artisanal guilds had erected a stage depicting the story of Ahasuerus and Esther.

Margaret was met on the Burg by the provost, deacons, canons and chaplains of the collegiate church of Sint-Donaas, assembled for procession and bearing incense and holy water.[2] Musical instruments played and young girls showered the bride with grain and rose petals. She reached the courtyard of the Prinsenhof – a frequent residence of the dukes of Burgundy – which was decorated with a golden tree that housed a sculpted pelican from whose pierced breast a fine red hippocras (spiced wine) flowed.

Contributing to this spectacle was the substantial presence of the merchants of the international trade community of Bruges. At the wedding celebration, the delegations of the trading nations present in the city appeared with great pageantry. The cities of the north German Hansa, for example, were represented by 108 merchants on horseback, preceded by 72 torch-bearers in violet and each accompanied by 6 pages dressed in satin pourpoints and damask robes. The 34 Castilian merchants appeared in violet damask with footmen in black satin and crimson velour jackets, with 60 torch-bearers clad in purple and green. The eighteen

Genoese and their pages brought with them a representation of a maiden in white damask protected from the dragon by St George, her horse in a crimson velvet caparison while George's horse was decorated with a large crimson cross. The Florentine merchants – dressed in blue – carried torches, their pages in red pourpoint doublets and silver cloth mantles, and their horses covered with white satin embroidered with blue. The Florentines were led by Tommaso Portinari, then chief of the Bruges branch of the Medici bank, but here dressed in his role as adviser to the Duke of Burgundy and accompanied by eleven factors in crimson and black satin doublets and at last 24 servants dressed in blue. Likewise reported in the surviving documents as present were the merchants

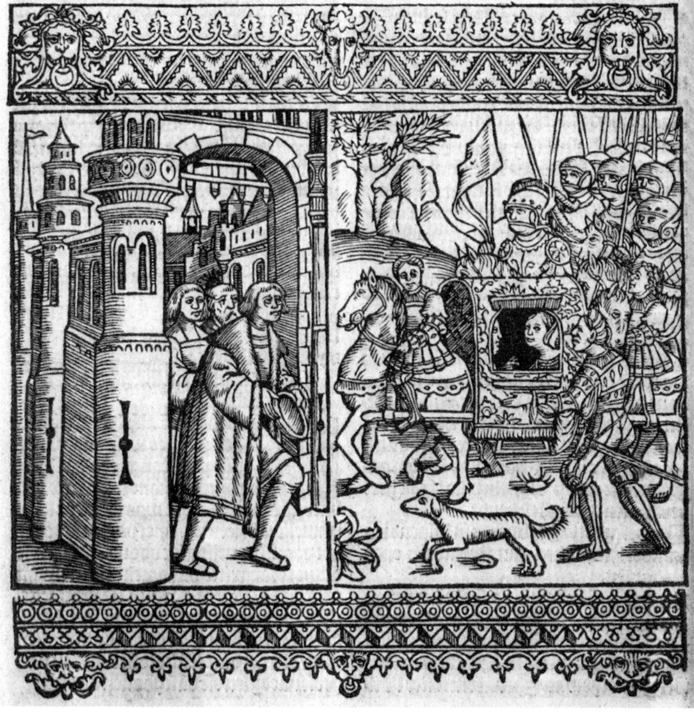

64 Officials of Bruges greeting Margaret of York at the Cruispoort, 1468, woodcut from Anthonis de Roovere, *Dits die excellente cronike van Vlaenderen* (1531).

of Lucca, Venice, Portugal, Sicily, Aragon and Catalonia, appearing just as opulently as the others.[3]

Although not mentioned in the written accounts of the event – preoccupied as they were with the pomp of the nobility and foreigners – also undoubtedly present was another collective arm representing the city: the membership of Bruges' 54 trade and artisanal guilds, perhaps led by their officers in livery and carrying their standards (as they were at similar events, such as the annual procession of the Holy Blood). Among the membership of the guild of the painters and saddlers would have been Hans Memling. As a relative newcomer to Flanders, he would have witnessed this Burgundian and international spectacle with a sense of both wonder and entrepreneurial promise. While many painters working in the surrounding cities had been employed to work on the decorations for the wedding celebrations, Memling does not appear among their ranks in the lists of payments pre-served in the city account books; nor, however, do other prominent Bruges painters, such as Petrus Christus. They may already have been collectively occupied with civic decoration commissions from earlier activities in the year – such as Charles's triumphal entry in April or the Holy Blood procession in May – or it could be that at this early point in his career Memling was, perhaps, fully occupied with individual commissions as he strived to estab-lish his workshop and reputation in his adopted city. He was, after all, already at work on Agnolo Tani's *Last Judgement*, and the same Tommaso Portinari who led the contingent of Florentine merchants would soon commission at least two works from him.

Almost twenty years later the monarch would again encounter the trade guilds of Bruges on the main square of the city, but in a very different light and with different consequences for the commercial life of Bruges.[4] In the early morning of 1 February 1488 Maximilian and his soldiers were prevented from leaving Bruges by the new city militia, made up largely of members of the masons' and carpenters' guilds.[5] Later that day, the membership of the trade and artisanal guilds arrived at the market square with their banners and tore down the execution scaffold, a despised symbol of the previous civic regime. Among the first to arrive on the square were the members of the so-called seventeen trades, a group of crafts including not only the masons, carpenters and other construction-sector guilds but the sculptors' and the painters' guilds.[6] Perhaps Memling – the most prominent painter in the city and by then well into his fifties – stood among his fellow guild members on the Grote Markt 'as a *Bruggeling* among *Bruggelingen*'.[7] Attempts to placate the guilds – through negotiators representing the city council, international merchants and the ducal court – all failed.[8] The insurgents reclaimed the severed heads of some of the civilian factional leaders who had opposed Archduke Maximilian in an earlier uprising of 1485, and which still adorned the side towers of the Hallen.[9] They installed a new city council dominated by guild members, and carried out a number of their own trials and executions over the months that followed.

The new city leaders' most remarkable action, however, was to imprison Maximilian – the future Holy Roman Emperor – for three and a half months, initially in the old jail on the Burg square.[10] The cities of Flanders paid dearly for this act, and by 1492, after several years of warfare, sieges and hunger, Bruges was depopulated and demoralized. Its community of foreign merchants had been compelled to relocate as part of Maximilian's campaign to disempower the city, and those few who returned after the armistice did so slowly. In this troubled environment, Memling – even as he worked to finish a number of high-profile works for international clients – seems to have turned, perhaps out of necessity, to a greater number of small, local commissions in these later years of his life.

Hans Memling's almost thirty-year career in Bruges, from 1465 to 1494, coincided with the climax and end of Burgundian

Flanders as the duchy was absorbed into the Holy Roman Empire. He arrived in the city just two years before the death of Philip the Good, and his own death occurred only months before the inauguration of Philip the Handsome in 1494. Memling also witnessed the last years of the dominance of Bruges as a commercial capital of northern Europe. While its fortunes as a commercial centre may have begun to slip by the middle of the fifteenth century – with a tumultuous political environment resulting in periodic slumps in trade, the temporary absences of one or more of the various communities of international merchants, the disruption of embargoes and state-sanctioned piracy – in large part the city remained resilient; the engineering efforts and expense needed to mitigate the silting of the Zwin and keep the waterways navigable, for example, were seen as simply the cost of doing business. The city enjoyed a sense of opportunity for the wealthy mercantile class and the prosperous professional and artisanal class that had emerged over the course of the late Middle Ages, to whom unprecedented social mobility appeared possible. The traditional nobility had now to vie with these new power blocs joining the de facto patriciate: striving individuals eager to apply their new economic pull, and the collective political and economic power of the artisanal and trade corporations.

It was a moment of change, and by the end of the century Bruges' fate had begun its gradual turn. While the conflict between Maximilian and the city may have been the deciding event in the city's destiny, trade in Bruges had already begun to suffer in earlier decades, with intermittent departures and dwindling numbers of merchants from the middle of the century.[11] Wages remained stagnant; while in the first half of the fifteenth century labourers in Bruges had earned significantly more than their counterparts in other cities of the region, by the end of the century wages in Ghent, Damme and Geraardsbergen had nearly caught up.[12] Years of state-sanctioned piracy and naval blockades likewise compelled the Flemish to organize protected convoys, at great cost.[13]

Antwerp, the alternative centre that benefited the most from the intermittent disruptions to trade in Bruges, had meanwhile promised various privileges to the international communities and secured the vital alum staple.[14] Attempts by Bruges to entice the merchants to return were expensive and only marginally successful, and many offers were countered by Antwerp.[15] After painful negotiations, for example, in 1493 Bruges granted to the merchants from Aragon and Catalan a charter, two buildings and a substantial cash incentive; the Castilian wool staple was also assigned to Bruges. The return of the English cloth trade in fits and starts and the addition of a second annual fair likewise could not resuscitate the city.[16] The merchants of Lübeck remained attached to Bruges and the Castilians maintained the city as the centre of their northern wool trade into the sixteenth century, but Bruges no longer dominated commercial life in the North. Surviving shipping records from Sluis testify to the situation: in 1486 some 75 ships had docked in Sluis carrying a total of 8,300 tonnes of cargo; in 1489, at the height of the conflict, only 33 ships arrived with 3,500 tonnes of goods, and several years after the end of hostilities trade had improved little, with 42 ships carrying 4,200 tonnes in 1500.[17] In 1493 Maximilian suspended taxes from Bruges, citing the depopulation of the city and the absence of mercantile activity, and in 1494 he even acknowledged the role of his taxation in the city's parlous state.[18]

The situation was certainly apparent to foreigners, as Hieronymus Monetarius, a physician and humanist from Nuremberg, noted in 1495: 'Twenty years ago, Bruges was the largest market and the largest warehouse in the world. The merchants of all lands flocked there, and greatly enriched the city.'[19] With the end of the Valois line itself at the death of Charles the Bold at Nancy in 1477, Mary of Burgundy's death and the Treaty of Arras had ensured that the bulk of the Burgundian territories would be absorbed by the Holy Roman Empire under the house of Habsburg. Philip the Handsome would, in his relatively short life, further bind that monarchy to Castile and Aragon through his marriage to Juana, the daughter of Ferdinand and Isabella; the economic and political epicentre thus shifted away from Bruges and towards their courts in Antwerp, Brussels and Mechelen.

Flanders, now part of the Spanish Netherlands, did continue to serve as a cultural hub for these monarchs, however. Although commercially subdued, Bruges endured for some time into the sixteenth century as a centre for artistic production for the remaining merchants: the same community (albeit depleted in Bruges itself) that had been served by Memling.[20] The remaining merchant community of Bruges – the Castilians and Portuguese who maintained trade there, as well as those of ascendant Antwerp – continued to seek out the remaining artists in Bruges.

The workshop of Memling's contemporary Gerard David, who had arrived in 1484, in the middle of Memling's career, attracted the last of the successful artists who immigrated to Bruges from outside the Low Countries, Ambrosius Benson of Lombardy (perhaps from Milan), whose sons would in turn be painters in Bruges. They and artists including Adriaen Isenbrant, Jan Provost, Pieter Pourbus and Lancelot Blondeel continued to produce works that built on the traditions developed by Jan van Eyck, Petrus Christus and Memling.[21] In such paintings as the portraits of *Jan van Eyewerve and Jacquemyne Buuck* (1551) by Pourbus, for example, we find a presentation reminiscent of Memling's work (illus. 65). The proud, wealthy sitters pose before background insets of a Bruges cityscape that illustrates the sources of their wealth: the old city crane – with the barrels and porters so similar to its treatment in Memling's St Johns altarpiece – and a shop facade.

In the later sixteenth century some artists departed Bruges as trade continued to drift towards Antwerp and new political and religious unrest unfolded; some indeed left for Antwerp, among them Frans Pourbus I, Pieter's son. Marcus Gheeraerts the Elder, whose plan of Bruges provided a sense of place for scholars of the city's history, was for his religious convictions driven to England, where he made his own mark. Both Jan van der Straet (known in the south as Stradanus) and Pieter de Witte (Pietro Candido), natives of Bruges, found their way to Florence; the former, who had trained in Antwerp, spent his career working for the Florentine Grand Duchy under Giorgio Vasari's oversight, and in Rome for the Vatican. De Witte likewise apprenticed under Vasari, and worked for Francesco de' Medici, at the Vatican, on the Florentine Duomo, and for Wilhelm V and Maximilian I in Munich.[22]

In the late fifteenth century, however, the fate of Bruges and the full extent of the economic challenges it would face were impossible to foretell, and the city still enjoyed a reputation as the commercial centre of northern Europe. In the years of Memling's early career the city's economy appeared, at least on the surface, to be vibrant and active, and it still reigned as the most prosperous of the Flemish cities. Memling himself, like many other residents of Bruges at the time, was an immigrant seeking a career in its thriving economy, emblematic of his moment as one of many merchants and craftsmen drawn there. He and the artisanal class he represented interacted with a local and international community of merchants, commodity bankers and brokers in the economic, social and built environment of the city. Bruges as a commercial centre – its patterns of trade and economic opportunity – shaped the lives of the members of this artisanal and emerging merchant class as they gathered in its marketplaces, hostels and churches.

Memling lived and worked in the city as a burgher and a professional artisan, integrated into the community through membership of his trade guild, his parish and the city's religious confraternities, where he would have encountered potential clients from the merchant and artisanal classes. His workshop and assistants operated both according to the artistic traditions of the era and under the oversight of the civic government and the guild system. The greater economic and commercial patterns of Bruges and European trade further intersected with his activities through their effects on wages, workshop techniques and methods, and the availability and expense of the required materials. During his career Memling successfully adapted to the marketplace and the artistic conventions of his time to become the most prominent painter in the city. His workshop was sought out by the merchant class in particular for the portraiture that had so recently become available to them, and it furnished many of the altarpieces and smaller personal devotional works with which they and their corporate organizations would adorn their environments, memorialize their families, announce their social

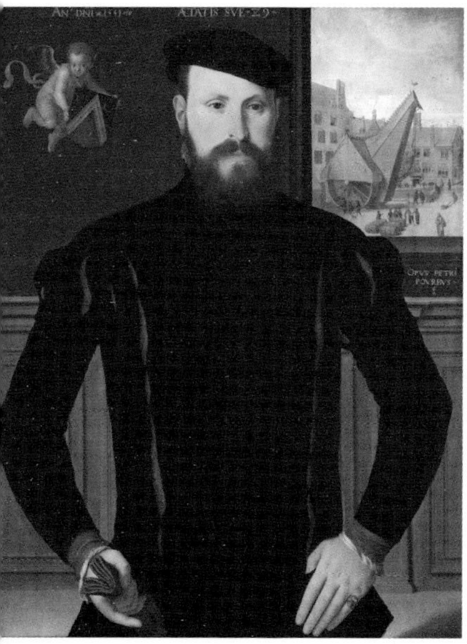
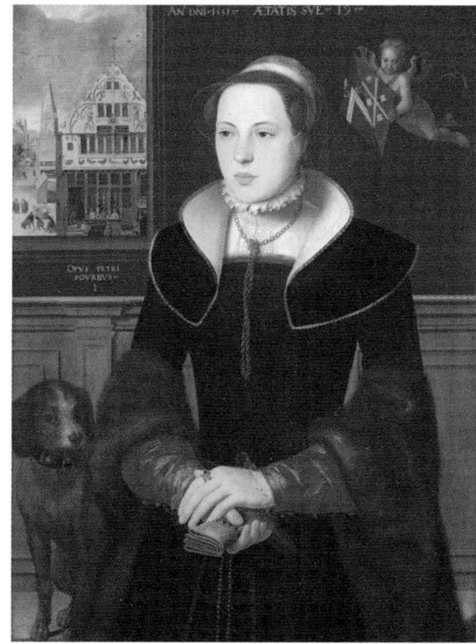

65 Pieter Pourbus, *Jan van Eyewerve and Jacquemyne Buuck*, 1551, oil on oak.

ambitions, elevate their status, express their devotion and tend their salvation. To a greater extent than even his artistic contemporaries, this community was at the centre of Memling's clientele. These intersections between place, commerce and craft in late fifteenth-century Bruges reveal the distinctiveness of both this cultural milieu and Memling's life.

CHRONOLOGY

1134	Storm surge expands navigation in Zwin district
1252	Hansa Federation cities granted trading privileges in Bruges. Reorganization of Bruges' trade guild system and statutes
1290	Port of Sluis established
1297	Franco-Flemish War
1302	'Bruges Matins' revolt against French occupation. Battle of the Golden Spurs
1323–8	Flemish Peasant Revolt
1332	Venetians establish consulate in Bruges
1359	Scots granted trading privileges in Bruges
1369	Marriage of Margaret of Male, Countess of Flanders, to Philip the Bold, Duke of Burgundy: Flanders will become part of the duchy of Burgundy. Lucca granted trading privileges in Bruges
1376	Construction of Bruges City Hall
1397	Organization of the Genoese association in Bruges. Venetians begin use of the house ter Ouder Beurze
1404	Death of Duke Philip the Bold
1419	Death of Duke John the Fearless
1427	Florentines establish consulate in Bruges
1430–40	Birth of Hans Memling near Seligenstadt
1436–8	Bruges Rebellion
1440	'Joyous Entry' of Duke Philip the Good into Bruges
1441–2	Revision of the Bruges trade guilds' charters
1444	Petrus Christus, painter, arrives in Bruges
1450	Death of Memling's parents in Seligenstadt. Death of Stephan Lochner, painter, in Cologne

1454	Marriage of Duke Charles the Bold and Isabella of Bourbon
1455	Biscayne merchant organization splits from Castilians
1457	Hansa returns staple to Bruges
1464	Death of Rogier van der Weyden, painter
1465	Memling's registration as a citizen in Bruges. Death of Isabella of Bourbon
1467	Death of Duke Philip the Good
1468	Wedding of Duke Charles the Bold and Margaret of York in Bruges
1472	Medici purchase the Bladelinhof
1473	Memling joins Bruges Confraternity of Our Lady of the Snow. Hansa pirates seize shipment to Florence with Memling's *Last Judgement* altarpiece, which is subsequently installed in Gdansk. Colard Mansion in Bruges publishes the first book printed in English
1475/6	Death of Petrus Christus, painter
1476	Betrothal of Mary of Burgundy to Maximilian of Austria
1477	Death of Charles the Bold at the Battle of Nancy. Issuance of 'Grand Privilege' by Mary of Burgundy. Uprising of trade guilds in Bruges, and new city charters
1478	Construction of Oosterlingenhuis, the Hansa headquarters in Bruges
1479	Memling's St Johns altarpiece and Jan Floreins altarpiece. Willem Vrelant orders from Memling an altarpiece for the librarians' guild chapel
1480	Memling's panel for Pieter Bultinc. Memling's workshop registers an apprentice, Hannekin Verhanneman. Medici family withdraws from Bruges partnership with Tommaso Portinari
1481	Food crisis in Bruges. Arrest of Willem Moreel; pro-Maximilian civic government is installed
1482	Death of Mary of Burgundy and start of the regency of Philip the Handsome
1483	Castilians establish consulate house. Memling's workshop registers an apprentice, Passchier van der Meersch
1484	Temporary relocation of foreign merchants to Antwerp. Memling's triptych for the Moreel family. Gerard David, painter, arrives in Bruges
1485	Uprising in Bruges against Archduke Maximilian quashed. Blockade of Sluis

1486	Maximilian made King of the Romans
1487	Death of Tanne, Hans Memling's wife
1488	February: Bruges guilds uprising; anti-Maximilian civic government installed. Imprisonment (February) and release (May) of Maximilian in Bruges. Foreign merchants expelled from Bruges
1490	Bruges capitulates to Maximilian
1491	Date on Memling's Greverade altarpiece
1492	Defeat of Ghent and Peace of Cadzand
1493	Peace of Senlis ends hostilities with France
1494	Delivery of Memling's Nájera altarpiece to Castile. Memling's death (11 August). Castilian and Portuguese merchants return to Bruges. Inauguration of Duke Philip the Handsome
1496	*Intercursus Magnus* treaty renormalizes trade between Burgundy, England, the Hanseatic League and the Netherlands
1500	Birth of Charles, son of Duke Philip the Handsome, future Holy Roman Emperor
1503	Death of Margaret of York
1504	Delivery of Greverade altarpiece to Lübeck
1506	Death of Duke Philip the Handsome
1508	Maximilian made Holy Roman Emperor

REFERENCES

Introduction

1 Barbara G. Lane, 'The Patron and the Pirate: The Mystery
   of Memling's Gdansk Last Judgment', *Art Bulletin*, LXXIII/4
   (1991), p. 629; Paula Nuttall, *From Flanders to Florence: The Impact
   of Netherlandish Painting, 1400–1500* (New Haven, CT, and London,
   2004), pp. 55–6.

2 Lane, 'Patron and the Pirate', pp. 626–7; Dirk De Vos, *Hans Memling:
   The Complete Works*, trans. Ted Alkins (Antwerp, Ghent and New
   York, 1994), p. 87.

3 De Vos, *Complete Works*, pp. 87, 88 n. 20; Paula Nuttall suggests
   that the portrait of Caterina is based on drawings sent from
   Florence, since Italian women in Netherlandish portraits were
   often depicted in Burgundian-style clothing. Paula Nuttall,
   'Memlinc's Last Judgement, Angelo Tani and the Florentine
   Colony at Bruges', in *Polish and English Responses to French Art and
   Architecture: Contrasts and Similarities,* ed. Francis Ames-Lewis
   (London, 1995), pp. 160–61.

4 Till-Holger Borchert, 'Memling – Life and Work', in *Memling's
   Portraits*, ed. Till-Holger Borchert et al. (Ghent and Amsterdam,
   2005), pp. 24–6; Nuttall, *From Flanders to Florence*, pp. 54–5.

5 Nuttall, *From Flanders to Florence*, pp. 54–60; Lane, 'Patron and the
   Pirate', pp. 623–7; Grzybkowska's argument that it was originally
   a Gdansk merchant's commission and not Tani has received little
   traction. Teresa Grzybkowska, 'The Last Judgement by Hans
   Memling: Looted or Commissioned for Gdansk', *Polish Art Studies*,
   XII (1991), pp. 15–25; De Vos, *Complete Works*, pp. 82–9. For the
   suggestion that the altarpiece was commissioned jointly by a
   number of Florentines in Bruges, perhaps spearheaded by Tani, see
   Beata Purc-Stępniak, 'Portraits in Hans Memling's Last Judgement;

or, How Prudence and Fame Were Portrayed: A Contribution to the Research on the History of the Portrait and Its Commemorative Role in 15th Century European Art', *Brvkenthal Acta Mvsei*, XII/2 (2017), pp. 356–9.

6 Raymond de Roover, *The Rise and Decline of the Medici Bank, 1397–1494* (Cambridge, MA, and London, 1963), pp. 341–3, 347.

7 Nothing further is known of the second altarpiece. Borchert, 'Life and Work', p. 22; De Vos, *Complete Works*, p. 89 n. 24.

8 Borchert, 'Life and Work', p. 22.

9 For this event, see especially Lane, 'Patron and the Pirate', pp. 623–40; Marc Boone, 'Apologie d'un banquier médiéval: Tommaso Portinari et l'état Bourguignon', *Le Moyen âge*, CV/1 (1999), p. 37; De Roover, *Rise and Decline*, pp. 374–8; Tobias Daniels and Arnold Esch, 'A Donatello for Rome, a Memling for Florence: The Maritime Transports of the Sermattei of Florence', *Renaissance Studies*, XXXV/4 (2021), pp. 669–73.

10 Peter Stabel, 'De gewenste vreemdeling: Italiaanse kooplieden en stedelijke maatschappij in het laat-middeleeuws Brugge', *Jaarboek voor middeleeuwse Geschiedenis*, IV (2001), pp. 194–5.

11 Pero Tafur, ed., *Pero Tafur, Travels and Adventures, 1435–1439*, Broadway Travellers series (New York and London, 1926; reprinted Abingdon, 2005), pp. 198–200.

1 Memling's Life: A Biographical Sketch

1 Dirk De Vos, *Hans Memling: The Complete Works*, trans. Ted Alkins (Antwerp, Ghent and New York, 1994), p. 158.

2 Memling had depicted an African magus in the earlier *Prado Adoration* and would maintain this practice subsequently. An African magus appears in an *Adoration* on canvas attributed to Justus van Ghent (1475) in the Metropolitan Museum of Art, and in works by Hugo van der Goes, including the Monforte altarpiece from around 1470, now in Berlin. A magus probably intended as African or Moorish appears in Rogier van der Weyden's earlier Bladelin triptych of the late 1440s.

3 Barbara G. Lane, *Hans Memling: Master Painter in Fifteenth-Century Bruges* (London and Turnhout, 2009), pp. 186–90; De Vos, *Complete Works*, pp. 158–61.

4 Jacques Mertens, 'Jan Floreins: Enkele gegevens over zijn beheer in het laat-middeleeuws Sint-Janshospitaal te Brugge', *Handelingen van*

het Genootschap voor Geschiedenis 'Société d'Émulation' te Brugge, CL/1 (2013), pp. 101–9.

5 This privileging of Memling among Jan van Eyck and Rogier by these Italians may stem from their perception of his connection to commissions held by the Medici family. Lodovico Guicciardini, *Descrittione di m. Lodouico Guicciardini patritio fiorentino, di tutti i Paesi Bassi . . . Con piu carte di geographia del paese, & col ritratto naturale di piu terre principali* (Antwerp, 1567), p. 98; Giorgio Vasari, *Le vite de' piv eccellenti pittori, scvltori, et architettori* (Florence, 1568), vol. III, p. 857.

6 Carel van Mander, *Het Schilder-Boeck: Waerin voor eerst de leerlustighe iueght den grondt der edel vry schilderconst in verscheyden deelen wort voorghedraghen*, vol. II: *Het Leven der Doorluchtighe Nederlandtsche en Hoogh-duytsche Schilders* (Amsterdam, 1618), p. 127v.

7 R. A. Parmentier, *Indices op de Brugsche Poorterboeken*, vol. II: *Poorterboeken over 1450–1794, Geschiedkundige Publicatiën der Stad Brugge 2* (Bruges, 1938), pp. 630–31.

8 André Vandewalle, 'A propos du lieu de naissance de Memling', in *Memling Studies: Proceedings of the International Colloquium (Bruges, 10–12 November 1994)*, ed. Roger van Schoute, Maurits Smeyers and Hélène Verougstraete (Leuven, 1997), p. 19, for discussion.

9 H. W. Strasser, 'Hans Memling te Seligenstadt', *Handelingen Genootschap 'Société d'Émulation' Brugge*, XCVIII/1–2 (1961), pp. 97–8; Till-Holger Borchert, 'Memling – Life and Work', in *Memling's Portraits*, ed. Till-Holger Borchert et al. (Ghent and Amsterdam, 2005), p. 12.

10 Strasser, 'Hans Memling', p. 98; Hilde Lobelle-Caluwé, 'Hans Memling, het succes van een kunstenaar', *Openbaar Kunstbezit in Vlaanderen*, II (1994), p. 45; De Vos, *Complete Works*, p. 16.

11 Strasser, 'Hans Memling', pp. 98–9; De Vos, *Complete Works*, pp. 58–9.

12 *Fragments inédits de Romboudt De Doppere découverts dans un manuscrit de Jacques De Meyere: Chronique brugeoise de 1491 à 1498* (Bruges, 1892), p. 49; De Vos, *Complete Works*, pp. 52, 58–60.

13 Lobelle-Caluwé, 'Succes', p. 46.

14 Friedrich Battenberg, 'Zeit und Umwelt des Malers Hans Memling aus Seligenstadt: Zur Situation des Reichs und Flanderns im Spätmittelalter', *Archiv für hessische Geschichte und Altertumskunde* NF, XLVI (1988), pp. 21, 24, 27–8.

15 Strasser, 'Hans Memling', p. 97; Michael Wolfson, 'Den Duytschen Hans: Memling and German Panel Painting of the Mid-Fifteenth Century', in *Hans Memling: Essays*, ed. Dirk De Vos and Maryan W. Ainsworth (Ghent, 1994), p. 10.

16 Strasser, 'Hans Memling', p. 98; Lobelle-Caluwé, 'Succes', p. 45.

17 Dirk De Vos's suggestion. See De Vos, *Complete Works*, pp. 217–18.

18 Battenberg, 'Zeit', pp. 28–9.

19 Lobelle-Caluwé, 'Succes', p. 46; Wilfred Brulez, 'Bruges and Antwerp in the 15th and 16th Centuries: An Antithesis?', in *Acta Historiae Neerlandicae/Studies on the History of the Netherlands* VI, ed. Wilfred Brulez et al. (Dordrecht, 1973), p. 20.

20 Wolfson, 'Den Duytschen Hans', pp. 10–11.

21 For a concise summary, see ibid., pp. 11–13. Brigitte Corley has presented a critique of the evidence for the *Dombild* master's identification as Lochner and noted the documented Hans von Memmingen. Brigitte Corley, *Painting and Patronage in Cologne, 1300–1500* (London, 2000), pp. 133–67, 174–6, 285 n. 20. See also J. J. Merlo, *Die Meister der altkölnischen Malerschule. Mit Rücksichtnahme auf die verwandten Kunstzweige der Kalligraphen, Rubricatoren, Illuminatoren, Glasmaler, Emailmaler und Kunststicker* (Cologne, 1852), pp. 134–5; Frank Günther Zehnder, *Gotische Malerei in Köln: Altkölner Bilder von 1300 bis 1550 (Bildhefte zur Sammlung, 3)*, 2nd edn (Cologne, 1993), pp. 24–5.

22 Noted as early as James Weale. William Henry James Weale, *Hans Memlinc* (London, 1901), p. 49.

23 Rainer Budde, *Köln und seine Maler 1300–1500* (Cologne, 1986), p. 99; Hans Martin Schmidt, *Der Meister des Marienlebens und Sein Kreis: Studien zur Spätgotischen Malerei in Köln* (Düsseldorf, 1978), vol. XXII, pp. 36, 98, 186–7, 189.

24 On this installation, see Corley, *Painting and Patronage*, pp. 44, 176.

25 Maryan W. Ainsworth, 'Memling's Preliminary Working Stages: The Nájera Panels in Context', in *Harmony in Bright Colours: Memling's God the Father with Singing and Music-Making Angels Restored*, ed. Lizet Klaassen and Dieter Lampens (Brussels, 2021), p. 144; Bernhard Ridderbos and Molly Faries, 'Hans Memling's Last Judgement in Gdańsk', *Oud Holland*, CXXX/3–4 (2017), p. 61.

26 Ainsworth, 'Memling's Preliminary Working Stages', pp. 147–8; see also Maryan W. Ainsworth and Keith Christiansen, eds, *From Van Eyck to Bruegel: Early Netherlandish Painting in the Metropolitan Museum of Art* (New York, 1998), p. 114; Borchert, 'Life and Work', p. 19; and Maximiliaan P. J. Martens, 'Patronage and Politics: Hans Memling's St John Altarpiece and the Process of Burgundization', in *Le dessin sous-jacent dans le processus de création*, ed. Hélène Verougstraete and Roger van Schoute (Louvain-la-Neuve, 1995),

p. 169. Barbara Lane offers a brief critique of these propositions
and offers alternative readings of the situation. Lane, *Hans Memling*,
p. 33.

27 Lane, *Hans Memling*, pp. 63–77, 79–91.

28 Parmentier, *Indices II*, pp. 630–31; Alfred Jamees, *Brugse Poorters:
Optekend uit de Stadsrekeningen*, vol. II: *1418–78* (Handzame, 1980),
p. 324.

29 Noël Geirnaert, 'Commentary: Some Experiences of an Archivist
in Bruges', in *Early Netherlandish Painting at the Crossroads: A Critical Look
at Current Methodologies*, ed. Maryan W. Ainsworth (New York, 2001),
pp. 41–2; Wim Blockmans, 'The Creative Environment: Incentives
to and Functions of Bruges Art Production', in *Petrus Christus in
Renaissance Bruges: An Interdisciplinary Approach*, ed. Maryan W. Ainsworth
(New York and Turnhout, 1995), pp. 12–13.

30 Noël Geirnaert, 'Hans Memling, lid van het schildersambacht en
poorter van Brugge, 1465', in *Bedenkingen vanuit het Stadsarchief van Brugge*
(Bruges, 2017), pp. 12–17. While earlier statutes indicate that
residents who had lived in Bruges for a year could register as citizens
free of charge, this rule had most likely been abandoned before the
middle of the fifteenth century. Jan Dumolyn et al., 'Margaret van
Eyck, a House Called "The Wild Sea" and Jan van Eyck's
Posthumous Workshop', *Burlington Magazine*, CLXIV/1427 (February
2022), p. 129 n. 62.

31 Blockmans, 'Creative Environment', pp. 13–14. Between the first
year of the surviving records (1453) and the year 1499–1500, a total
of 245 new masters were registered.

32 Geirnaert, 'Memling, lid', pp. 15–16; Albert Schouteet, *De vlaamse
primitieven te Brugge: Bronnen voor de schilderkunst te Brugge tot de dood van
Gerard David*, vol. I: *(A–K)* (1989), p. 168.

33 That Tanne's identity as a de Valkenaere was uncertain was
acknowledged by Weale in 1871 and by Borchert in 2021; in 1942
Ludwig von Baldass reported the fact without any such caveat.
William Henry James Weale, *Hans Memling. Zijn leven en zijne schilder-
werken. Eene schets* (Bruges, 1871), p. 26; Till-Holger Borchert,
'Memling's Workshop', in *Harmony in Bright Colours*, ed. Klaassen and
Lampens, p. 190 n. 19; Ludwig von Baldass, *Hans Memling* (Vienna,
1942), p. 8.

34 De Vos, *Complete Works*, pp. 411, 413; James M. Murray, *Bruges, Cradle of
Capitalism, 1280–1390* (Cambridge, 2005), p. 135; Albert Janssens, 'De
schilder Hans Memling: Als Brugs poorter financieel, sociaal en

politiek doorgelicht', *Handelingen van het Genootschap voor Geschiedenis 'Société d'Émulation' te Brugge*, CXXXIV (1997), p. 80.

35 Janssens, 'Schilder', p. 80.

36 Some scholars see this work as being too far outside Memling's norms to include in his oeuvre.

37 De Vos, *Complete Works*, p. 76.

38 Lane, *Hans Memling*, pp. 147–55; Vida Hull, 'Spiritual Pilgrimage in the Paintings of Hans Memling', in *Art and Architecture of Late Medieval Pilgrimage in Northern Europe and the British Isles*, ed. Sarah Blick and Rita Tekippe, 2 vols (Leiden and Boston, MA, 2005), vol. I, pp. 29–50; Mitzi Kirkland-Ives, *In the Footsteps of Christ: Hans Memling's Passion Narratives and the Devotional Imagination in the Early Modern Netherlands* (Turnhout, 2013), esp. pp. 1–18.

39 Borchert, 'Life and Work', pp. 39–40.

40 Maryan W. Ainsworth, 'The Business of Art: Patrons, Clients, and Art Markets', in *From Van Eyck to Bruegel*, ed. Ainsworth and Christiansen, p. 35; Paula Nuttall, 'Memling and the European Renaissance Portrait', in *Memling's Portraits*, ed. Borchert et al., pp. 74–5.

41 Borchert, 'Life and Work', p. 34; Ainsworth, 'Business of Art', p. 35.

42 Maximiliaan P. J. Martens, 'Hans Memling and His Patrons: A Cliometrical Approach', in *Memling Studies*, ed. Van Schoute, Smeyers and Verougstraete, pp. 38–40.

43 Namely Willem Moreel and Pieter Bultinc, and, on the other wing, Maarten van Nieuwenhove. Jan du Cellier was tied to Lodewijk van Gruuthuse, who had a complex relationship with Maximilian.

44 Borchert, 'Life and Work', p. 40; Martens, 'Hans Memling', pp. 38–40.

45 Dirk De Vos, D. Marechal and Willy Le Loup, *Hans Memling: Catalogue* (Brussels, 1994), p. 225; Peter Stabel, 'De gewenste vreemdeling: Italiaanse kooplieden en stedelijke maatschappij in het laat-middeleeuws Brugge', *Jaarboek voor middeleeuwse Geschiedenis*, IV (2001), pp. 190, 207–9.

46 Charles Louis Carton, 'Obituaire de la Société de St-Luc', *Annales de la Société d'Émulation de Bruges*, XVI (1862–3), pp. 1–38.

47 De Vos, *Complete Works*, p. 408; Albert Schouteet, 'Nieuwe teksten betreffende Hans Memling', *Revue belge d'archéologie et d'histoire de l'art*, XXIV (1955), pp. 81–3.

48 Borchert, 'Life and Work', p. 16.

49 Schouteet, 'Nieuwe teksten', p. 82.

50 Ibid., p. 83.

51 William Henry James Weale, 'Documents authentiques concernant la vie, la famille et la position sociale de Jean Memlinc découverts à Bruges', *Journal des Beaux-Arts et de la littérature*, III (1861), pp. 23–8, 46–9.

52 'Die XI. augusti, obiit magister Johannes Memmlinc, quem praedicabant pertissimum fuisse et excellentissimum pictorem totius tunc orbis christiani. Ordinus erat Magunciaco, sepultus Brugis ad Aegidii.' Rombout de Doppere also served as the notary at the act of translation of the relics of Ursula's shrine, and indirectly as the notary signing the agreement between the librarians' guild and Eeckhout Abbey. *Fragments inédits*, p. 49; Hugo Loersch, 'Hans Memling's Heimath und Todestag', *Zeitschrift für christliche Kunst*, II (1889), pp. 301–2; De Vos, *Complete Works*, p. 413.

53 Charles Vanden Haute, *La corporation des peintres de Bruges* (Kortrijk, 1913), p. 198; Carton, 'Obituaire', p. 181.

54 Schouteet, 'Nieuwe teksten', pp. 82–3.

55 Strasser, 'Hans Memling', pp. 98–9.

56 Till-Holger Borchert, 'The Discovery of Bruges Painting', in *Bruges and the Renaissance: Memling to Pourbus*, ed. Maximiliaan P. J. Martens, Paul Huvenne and Maryan Wynn Ainsworth (Brussels, 1998), p. 19.

57 Jean-Baptiste Descamps, *La vie des peintres flamands, allemands et hollandois, avec des portraits gravés en taille-douce, une indication de leurs principaux ouvrages, & des réflexions sur leurs différentes manieres, tome premier* (Paris, 1753), p. 8.

58 Frederick von Schlegel, 'Description of Paintings in Paris and the Netherlands in the Years 1802–1804. Letter IV', in *The Aesthetic and Miscellaneous Works of Frederick von Schlegel*, trans. Ellen J. Millington (London, 1860), pp. 124–5.

2 Memling's Bruges

1 Dirk De Vos, *Hans Memling: The Complete Works*, trans. Ted Alkins (Antwerp, Ghent and New York, 1994), p. 54.

2 Nöel Geirnaert, 'Universitas mercature: Kooplieden, cultuur en religie in het middeleeuwse Brugge', in *Hanzekooplui en medicibankiers: Brugge, wisselmarkt van culturen*, ed. André Vandewalle (Bruges, 2002), pp. 151–2; Patricia Carson, 'Bruges and the British Isles', in *Bruges and Europe*, ed. Valentin Vermeersch (Antwerp, 1992), pp. 132–4.

3 Peter Spufford, *Power and Profit: The Merchant in Medieval Europe* (New York, 2003), pp. 34, 48–50.

4 These fairs lay along a route between Lille, Mesen, Ypres and Torhout. David Nicholas, *Medieval Flanders* (London and New York,

1992), p. 112; James M. Murray, *Bruges, Cradle of Capitalism, 1280–1390* (Cambridge, 2005), pp. 44–5; Peter Stabel, Jerome Puttevils and Jan Dumolyn, 'Production: Markets and Socio-Economic Structures I: *c.* 1100–*c.* 1300', in *Medieval Bruges, c. 850–1550*, ed. Andrew Brown and Jan Dumolyn (Cambridge and New York, 2018), pp. 104–5; Galbert of Bruges and Jeff Rider, *The Murder, Betrayal, and Slaughter of the Glorious Charles, Count of Flanders* (New Haven, CT, 2013), p. 32.

5 Murray, *Cradle*, pp. 44–5.

6 J. A. Van Houtte, *De Geschiedenis van Brugge* (Tielt and Bussum, 1982), p. 30; Murray, *Cradle*, pp. 28–9; Jan Dumolyn et al., 'Origins and Early History', in *Medieval Bruges*, ed. Brown and Dumolyn, p. 33; English translation here from *Encomium Emmae Reginae*, trans. Alistair Campbell (London, 1949), p. 7.

7 Murray, *Cradle*, pp. 31–4, 44–50; Marc Ryckaert, *Brugge: Historische Stedenatlas van België*, ed. Adriaan Verhust and Jean-Marie Duvosquel (Brussels, 1991), pp. 15–49, 66–7; Jan Trachet et al., 'Turning Back the Tide: The Zwin Debate in Perspective. A Historiographical Review of the Medieval Port System Northeast of Bruges', *Revue du Nord*, XCVII/413 (2015), pp. 305–7; Marc Ryckaert et al., *Brugge: De geschiedenis van een Europese stad* (Tielt, 1999), p. 65; Jan Dumolyn et al., 'The Urban Landscape I: *c.* 1100–*c.* 1275', in *Medieval Bruges*, ed. Brown and Dumolyn, pp. 77–9; Jan Dumolyn and Ward Leloup, 'The Zwin Estuary: A Medieval Portuary Network', in *Las Sociedades Portuarias de la Europa Atlántica en la Edad Media*, ed. Jesús Ángel Solórzano Bolumburu Telechea, Beatriz Arízaga and Michel Bochaca (Logroño, 2016), pp. 197–212; Kristiaan Dillen, 'A Paradox of Maritime Access. Origins and Consequences of Subaltern Relations in a Medieval Portuary System in Flanders: The Case of Hoeke', *International Journal of Maritime History*, XXX/3 (2018), pp. 414–15.

8 Trachet et al., 'Turning Back', pp. 311–15; Roger Degryse, 'Van koggen en koggeschepen in Vlaanderen en elders (12de–15de eeuw)', *Handelingen van het Genootschap voor Geschiedenis 'Société d'Émulation' te Brugge*, CXXIX/1–2 (1992), pp. 65–93; Van Houtte, *Geschiedenis*, pp. 40, 185; Walter Prevenier, Willem Pieter Blockmans and An Blockmans-Delva, *The Burgundian Netherlands* (Cambridge and New York, 1986), p. 17.

9 Murray, *Cradle*, pp. 31–6, 39–40; Nicholas, *Medieval Flanders*, p. 129; Wim Blockmans and Walter Prevenier, *The Promised Lands: The Low Countries under Burgundian Rule, 1369–1530*, trans. Elizabeth Fackelman

and Edward Peters (Philadelphia, PA, 1999), pp. 157–8; Dillen, 'Paradox', pp. 411–42.

10 Blockmans and Prevenier, *Promised Lands*, pp. 151–4.

11 Stabel, Puttevils and Dumolyn, 'Production, I', p. 108.

12 Blockmans and Prevenier, *Promised Lands*, pp. 159–63; Stabel, Puttevils and Dumolyn, 'Production, I', pp. 106–7; Peter Stabel et al., 'Production, Markets and Socio-Economic Structures II: *c.* 1320– *c.* 1500', in *Medieval Bruges*, ed. Brown and Dumolyn, pp. 199–203; Wilfred Brulez, 'Bruges and Antwerp in the 15th and 16th Centuries: An Antithesis?', in *Acta Historiae Neerlandicae/Studies on the History of the Netherlands* VI, ed. Wilfred Brulez et al. (Dordrecht, 1973), pp. 15–16.

13 Lodovico Guicciardini, *Descrittione di m. Lodouico Guicciardini patritio fiorentino, di tutti i Paesi Bassi . . . Con piu carte di geographia del paese, & col ritratto naturale di piu terre principali* (Antwerp, 1567), p. 179.

14 J. A. Van Houtte, 'The Rise and Decline of the Market of Bruges', *Economic History Review*, XIX/1 (1966), p. 34.

15 On the alum trade, see Hugo Soly, *Capital at Work in Antwerp's Golden Age* (Turnhout, 2021), pp. 124–38; Spufford, *Power and Profit*, pp. 246, 334.

16 Peter Stabel, 'A Taste for the Orient? Cosmopolitan Demand for "Exotic" Durable Consumables in Late Medieval Bruges', in *London and Beyond: Essays in Honour of Derek Keene*, ed. Matthew Davies and James A. Galloway (London, 2012), pp. 89–97.

17 Spufford, *Power and Profit*, pp. 29–30; Alison Hanham, 'A Medieval Scots Merchant's Handbook', *Scottish Historical Review*, L/150, part 2 (1971), pp. 107–20; Stuart Jenks, 'Werkzeug des spätmittelalterlichen Kaufmans: Hansen und Engländer im Wandel von *memoria* zur Akte (mit einer Edition von *The Noumbre of Weyghtys*)', *Jahrbuch für fränkische Landesforschung*, LII (1992), pp. 283–319.

18 Double-entry bookkeeping had appeared by the end of the thirteenth century and spread throughout Italy, but publication of the technique was only in 1494 with Luca Pacioli's *Summa de Arithmetica* in Venice. Raymond de Roover, 'The Account Books of Collard de Marke', *Bulletin of the Business Historical Society*, XII/3 (1938), pp. 44–7; Spufford, *Power and Profit*, p. 29.

19 Called *jetons, worpghelt* or *rekenpfennige*. Bert van Beek, 'Jetons: Their Use and History', in *Perspectives in Numismatics: Studies Presented to the Chicago Coin Club*, ed. Saul Ben Needleman and Richard S. Yeoman (Chicago, IL, 1986), pp. 196–7, 201–2; David Eugene Smith, *Computing Jetons*, Numismatic Notes and Monographs (New York, 1921), pp. 17–33, 68.

20 English modernized. Jenks, 'Werkzeug', p. 307; Hanham, 'Scots Merchant's Handbook', pp. 109–10.

21 John F. Padgett, 'The Emergence of Corporate Merchant-Banks in Dugento Tuscany', in *The Emergence of Organizations and Markets*, ed. John F. Padgett and Walter W. Powell (Princeton, NJ, 2012), pp. 121–3; Raymond de Roover, *Money, Banking and Credit in Medieval Bruges: Italian Merchant-Bankers, Lombards, and Money-Changers: A Study in the Origins of Banking* (London and New York, 1999), pp. 29–42, esp. 32–5.

22 De Roover, *Money*, pp. 12, 52–4; Spufford, *Power and Profit*, pp. 22–5, 35; John Munro, 'The Medieval Origins of the Financial Revolution: Usury, *Rentes*, and Negotiability', *International History Review*, XXV/3 (2003), p. 542.

23 Spufford, *Power and Profit*, pp. 38–40.

24 Ibid., pp. 25, 27; De Roover, *Money*, p. 30.

25 Phillipe Dollinger, *The Emergence of International Business, 1200–1800*, vol. 1: *The German Hansa*, intro. Mark Casson (London and New York, 1999), p. 157; Wim Blockmans, 'Bruges and France', in *Bruges and Europe*, ed. Vermeersch, p. 219.

26 Tobias Daniels and Arnold Esch, 'A Donatello for Rome, a Memling for Florence: The Maritime Transports of the Sermattei of Florence', *Renaissance Studies*, XXXV/4 (2021), pp. 664–5.

27 Spufford, *Power and Profit*, pp. 30–33; André Vandewalle and Noël Geirnaert, 'Bruges and Italy', in *Bruges and Europe*, ed. Vermeersch, p. 186.

28 Daniels and Esch, 'Donatello', pp. 669–73; Barbara G. Lane, 'The Patron and the Pirate: The Mystery of Memling's Gdansk Last Judgment', *Art Bulletin*, LXXIII/4 (1991), p. 623.

29 Ryckaert, *Brugge: Historische Stedenatlas*, pp. 96–102; Albert Janssens, 'Het Brugse Bevolkingsaantal in 1477', in *Van Middeleeuwen tot Heden: Bladeren door Brugse Kunst en Geschiedenis*, ed. Mieke de Jonghe and Jan van Brugghe (Bruges and Beernem, 1983) pp. 29–35.

30 Ryckaert, *Brugge: Historische Stedenatlas*, pp. 60–66, 91–103; Murray, *Cradle*, pp. 55–6; Jan Dumolyn et al., 'The Urban Landscape II: c. 1275–c. 1500', in *Medieval Bruges*, ed. Brown and Dumolyn, pp. 158–9. On the twelfth-century fortifications, see Dumolyn et al., 'Urban Landscape I', pp. 66–7.

31 Murray, *Cradle*, pp. 59–61.

32 Initially modelled on the Palatine Chapel at Aachen, built under Arnulf I and perhaps invoking his great-grandfather Charles the

Bald. Van Houtte, *Geschiedenis*, pp. 40–43; Luc Devliegher, 'Enkele nota's over de burcht en de oudste stadsomwalling van Brugge', *Handelingen van het Genootschap voor Geschiedenis 'Société d'Émulation' te Brugge*, CXXXIV/I (1997), pp. 7–12.

33   Dumolyn et al., 'Urban Landscape II', p. 181; Ryckaert, *Brugge: Historische Stedenatlas*, pp. 167–70; Murray, *Cradle*, p. 68.

34   Murray, *Cradle*, p. 71; Paul Trio, 'Ambacht, nering or neringilde? De identiteit van het corporatieve karakter van het Brugse librariërsgilde in de vijftiende eeuw', in *Boeken uit Brugge: Studies over Brugse boekgeschiedenis*, ed. Ludo Vandamme (Bruges, 2021), p. 40.

35   Dumolyn et al., 'Origins', p. 37.

36   Murray, *Cradle*, pp. 64–5.

37   Ibid., pp. 63–4, 63 n. 166; Wilfried Carlier, 'Het Brugse Belfort en Hallen', in *Brugge Belfort en Beiaard*, ed. Hedwig Daquin and Martin Formesyn (Bruges, 1984), pp. 17–27.

38   Thomas A. Boogaardt, 'Evolution of a Communal Milieu: An Ethnogeography of Late Medieval Bruges, 1280–1349 (Belgium)', PhD diss., University of Wisconsin-Madison, 2000, pp. 285–8, 304.

39   Dumolyn et al., 'Urban Landscape II', pp. 164–5; Ryckaert, *Brugge: Historische Stedenatlas*, pp. 170–71; Murray, *Cradle*, p. 67.

40   Ryckaert, *Brugge: Historische Stedenatlas*, pp. 106–7; Murray, *Cradle*, p. 72; Ryckaert et al., *Brugge: De geschiedenis*, p. 68.

41   Maurice Vandermaesen, Bertrand Soens and André De Bock, *Van Poortersloge tot Rijksarchief: Een gebouw met inhoud te Brugge (15de eeuw–1995)* (Brussels, 1995), pp. 10–16.

42   Ryckaert, *Brugge: Historische Stedenatlas*, pp. 164–5; Murray, *Cradle*, p. 73; *Medieval Bruges*, ed. Brown and Dumolyn, p. 165 n. 21; Luc Devliegher, *Von Waterhalle tot Provinciaal Hof* (Bruges, 1994), pp. 9–38.

43   Geert de Clercq, 'In Brugge is er een Plein: Brugge als financiële markt in de 14de – 15de eeuw', in *Ter Beurze: Geschiedenis van de aandelenhandel in België, 1330–1900*, ed. de Clercq (Antwerp, 1992), p. 18.

44   Joseph Marechal, 'Het international karakter van de Brugse Handelsbeurs', in *Europese aanwezigheid te Brugge: De vreemde kolonies (XIVde–XIXde eeuw)* (Bruges, 1985), pp. 172–9.

45   'Supra plateam Bursi, ubi mercatores soliti sunt congregari', Laura Galoppini, *Mercanti Toscani e Bruges nel Tardo Medievo* (Pisa, 2014), pp. 236–7; Guicciardini, *Descrittione*, p. 67.

46   Murray, *Cradle*, p. 54.

47 Ibid., p. 48; Dumolyn et al., 'Urban Landscape I', pp. 73–4; one of
    the earliest hospital rules, and which inspired other hospital rules
    established shortly afterwards in Ghent and Ypres, and possibly
    influencing hospitals in northern Germany.

48 Murray, *Cradle*, p. 73.

49 Ibid., p. 54; Maximiliaan P. J. Martens, 'Artistic Patronage in Bruges
    Institutions, ca. 1440–1482', PhD diss., University of California,
    Santa Barbara, 1992, pp. 316–21.

50 Ibid., p. 314.

51 De Roover, *Money*, p. 21.

52 Andrew Brown, 'Cities, Nations and Divine Service: Identifying
    Spanish Merchants in Late Medieval Bruges', *Urban History*, XLIV/2
    (2016), pp. 167–71.

53 Peter Stabel, 'De gewenste vreemdeling: Italiaanse kooplieden en
    stedelijke maatschappij in het laat-middeleeuws Brugge', *Jaarboek voor
    middeleeuwse Geschiedenis*, IV (2001), p. 198; Murray, *Cradle*, pp. 73–4.
    On the financial benefits of property ownership and annuities, Jan
    Verheyen, 'The Residences of the Lucchese Merchants in Bruges
    (1390–1430): Their Social Network, the Locations of Their Real
    Estate, and the Financial Drivers for Their Properties', *Medieval Low
    Countries*, VIX/1 (2022), pp. 67–70.

54 De Roover, *Money*, pp. 13–16.

55 Nicolaas Despars, *Cronijcke van den Lande ende Graefscepe van Vlaenderen*,
    2nd edn, ed. J. de Jonghe (Bruges and Rotterdam, 1840), vol. IV,
    pp. 431–2.

56 Van Houtte, *Geschiedenis*, p. 96; Wim Blockmans, 'Bruges, a European
    Trading Centre', in *Bruges and Europe*, ed. Vermeersch, p. 52.

57 Stabel, 'Gewenste vreemdeling', pp. 190, 207–9; Brown, 'Cities,
    Nations', p. 167 n. 2.

58 Reneé Rössner, *Hansische Memoria in Flandern: Alltagsleben und
    Totengedenken der Osterlinge in Brügge und Antwerpen (13. bis 16. Jahrhundert)*,
    vol. V: *Hansekaufleute in Brügge* (Frankfurt am Main and Bern, 2001),
    p. 107.

59 To Aardenburg and Dordrecht in the thirteenth and fourteenth
    centuries, and to Antwerp, Deventer and Utrecht in the mid-
    fifteenth. Werner Paravicini, 'Bruges and Germany', in *Bruges and
    Europe*, ed. Vermeersch, pp. 102–3.

60 Ibid., pp. 106–9; Anke Greve, *Hansische Kaufleute, Hosteliers und
    Herbergen im Brügge des 14. und 15. Jahrhunderts*, vol. VI: *Hansekaufleute in
    Brügge* (Frankfurt am Main and Bern, 2011), pp. 98–102.

61 Rössner, *Hansische*, pp. 72, 125–34; Firmin de Smidt, *Het Oosterlingenhuis te Brugge en zijn ontwerper Jan vanden Poele* (Antwerp, 1948), p. 8; Joseph Marechal, 'De betrekkingen tussen Karmeliten en Hanzeaten te Brugge van 1347 tot 1523', *Handelingen van het Genootschap voor Geschiedenis 'Société d'Émulation' te Brugge*, C/1–3 (1963), p. 206.

62 Paravicini, 'Bruges and Germany', pp. 102, 105.

63 'genannt des coepmans huys . . . daer de clercke pleghen te wonen'. Designed by the Bruges architect-mason Jan vanden Poele, who would also design the new ambulatory at Sint-Salvators and buildings of the Bruges Vrije on the Burg. Rössner, *Hansische*, pp. 72–4; Ryckaert, *Brugge: Historische Stedenatlas*, p. 105; Wim de Baker, 'Het Oosterlingenhuis te Brugge', *Brugse Gidsenkroniek*, XXXI (1998), pp. 117–22; de Smidt, *Oosterlingenhuis*, pp. 10, 25–43.

64 Paravicini, 'Bruges and Germany', p. 108; Rössner, *Hansische*, pp. 79–82. On individual ownership of homes in Bruges, see Rössner, *Hansische*, pp. 109–10.

65 Marechal, 'Betrekkingen', pp. 211–12. Members were also buried at the Austin Friars and at the Onze-Lieve-Vrouwekerk, where the Hansa installed a coat of arms representing the Holy Roman Emperor and imperial electors. Paravicini, 'Bruges and Germany', pp. 110, 210.

66 Paravicini, 'Bruges and Germany', pp. 112–13. Attempts of the Hansa to leverage favourable trading conditions led to such conflict as that on Trinity Sunday in 1436, when a bar brawl in Sluis escalated into a massacre in which perhaps as many as eighty people were killed, effectively including the entire Hansa presence in Sluis. Rössner, *Hansische*, pp. 71, 211.

67 Brulez, 'Bruges and Antwerp', p. 20.

68 Paravicini, 'Bruges and Germany', pp. 114–15.

69 Rössner, *Hansische*, pp. 256–9; Martens, 'Artistic Patronage', p. 316.

70 Blockmans and Prevenier, *Promised Lands*, p. 165.

71 Vandewalle and Geirnaert, 'Bruges and Italy', p. 191. The merchants from Milan are not well documented, and they were among the first merchants to abandon Bruges when the political situation deteriorated, before 1494. On Sienese and Aretino merchants in Bruges and London, see Galoppini, *Mercanti*, pp. 256–67, 279–82.

72 Rössner, *Hansische*, p. 249.

73 Stabel, 'Gewenste vreemdeling', pp. 190, 207–9.

74 Rössner, *Hansische*, p. 250; Vandewalle and Geirnaert, 'Bruges and Italy', p. 185; Soly, *Capital*, p. 123.

75 De Clercq, 'Ter Beurze', p. 16.

76 Stabel, 'Gewenste vreemdeling', p. 211; Alfons Dewitte, 'Brugge en Venetie, 1430–1460: Een vlotte koopmanschap', *Biekorf*, CI (2001), p. 314; Vandewalle and Geirnaert, 'Bruges and Italy', pp. 183–5.

77 Stabel, 'Gewenste vreemdeling', pp. 195–6; Vandewalle and Geirnaert, 'Bruges and Italy', pp. 183–4; Dewitte, 'Brugge en Venetie', pp. 314–15.

78 Vandewalle and Geirnaert, 'Bruges and Italy', pp. 184–5, 190–91; Rössner, *Hansische*, p. 251; Martens, 'Artistic Patronage', p. 316.

79 Verheyen, 'Residences', pp. 56–62.

80 Vandewalle and Geirnaert, 'Bruges and Italy', pp. 188–9; Verheyen, 'Residences', pp. 45, 62–5.

81 Eugenio Lazzareschi, ed., *Libro della Comunità dei mercanti lucchesi in Bruges* (Milan, 1947), p. 272.

82 Lori van Biervliet, 'De Brugse Volto Santo', *Handelingen van het Genootschap voor Geschiedenis*, CXXX/3–4 (1994), p. 60; Vandewalle and Geirnaert, 'Bruges and Italy', p. 189; Lazzareschi, *Libro*, pp. 272–6.

83 Paula Nuttall, *From Flanders to Florence: The Impact of Netherlandish Painting, 1400–1500* (New Haven, CT, and London, 2004), pp. 43–5.

84 E. Z. Gabriëlle Claeys, *Het Hof Bladelin te Brugge* (Bruges, 1988), pp. 27, 36–40.

85 Marc Boone, 'Apologie d'un banquier médiéval: Tommaso Portinari et l'état Bourguignon', *Le Moyen âge*, CV/1 (1999), pp. 31–55; Claeys, *Hof Bladelin*, pp. 39–40.

86 Martens, 'Artistic Patronage', pp. 308, 314; Nuttall, *From Flanders*, pp. 45–6. Other decorations donated to the Observants included an altarpiece of the Adoration painted by Gerard David (now lost), left to the friars by a Florentine merchant.

87 Nuttall, *From Flanders*, pp. 47–50, 72–3.

88 Patricia Carson, 'Bruges and the British Isles', in *Bruges and Europe*, ed. Vermeersch, pp. 130–31; Anne F. Sutton, 'The Merchant Adventurers of England: Their Origins and the Mercers' Company of London', *Historical Research*, LXXV/187 (2002), p. 32.

89 John H. A. Munro, 'Bruges and the Abortive Staple in English Cloth', in *Textiles, Towns and Trade: Essays in the Economic History of Late-Medieval England and the Low Countries* (Aldershot and Brookfield, VT, 1994), pp. 1140–47.

90 Carson, 'British', pp. 131–5; Ryckaert, *Brugge: Historische Stedenatlas*, p. 107.

91 Carson, 'British', pp. 132–5; Van Houtte, 'Rise and Decline', p. 35.

92 Joseph Marechal, 'De Kapel van de Engelsen te Brugge, 1344–1563', in *Europese aanwezigheid te Brugge*, pp. 41–2; Sutton, 'Merchant Adventurers', p. 30; Marechal, 'Betrekkingen', pp. 206–7; Carson, 'British', pp. 134–5; Ryckaert, *Brugge: Historische Stedenatlas*, p. 107; Joseph Marechal, 'De Devotie te Brugge tot Sint-Niniaan, biscop van Whithorn in Schotland, 1366–1548', in *Europese aanwezigheid te Brugge*, p. 51.

93 Brown, 'Cities, Nations', p. 171.

94 Joseph Marechal, 'Le colonie espagnole de Bruges, du XIVe au XVIe siècle', in *Europese aanwezigheid te Brugge*, p. 115; de Clercq, 'Ter Beurze', p. 18; André Vandewalle, 'Bruges and the Iberian Peninsula', in *Bruges and Europe*, ed Vermeersch, p. 171.

95 Marechal, 'Colonie espagnole', pp. 94–7, 114; Brown, 'Cities, Nations', p. 172 n. 40.

96 William D. Phillips Jr, 'Local Integration and Long-Distance Ties: The Castilian Community in Sixteenth-Century Bruges', *Sixteenth Century Journal*, XVII/1 (1986), p. 34; Ovide Laleman, 'De Biskajers in Brugge', *Brugse Gidsenkroniek*, XXXI (1998), pp. 45–9; Marechal, 'Colonie espagnole', pp. 90–94.

97 Brown, 'Cities, Nations', p. 172; Carla Rahn Phillips, 'Spanish Merchants and the Wool Trade in the Sixteenth Century', *Sixteenth Century Journal*, XIV/3 (Autumn 1983), p. 266. On Flemish and German artists drawn to work and sell in Castile itself, see Mari-Tere Alvarez, 'Artistic Enterprise and Spanish Patronage: The Art Market during the Reign of Isabel of Castile (1474–1504)', in *Art Markets in Europe, 1400–1800*, ed. Michael North and David Ormrod (Aldershot and Brookfield, 1998), pp. 45–59.

98 Phillips, 'Spanish Merchants', pp. 259–63; Brown, 'Cities, Nations', pp. 171–2; Blockmans and Prevenier, *Promised Lands*, pp. 162–3; Vandewalle, 'Iberian Peninsula', p. 170.

99 Marechal, 'Colonie espagnole', pp. 91, 109–12.

100 The Universidad de los Mercaderes y maestres de Bilbao represented Biscay and other northern coastal towns in Asturias, Galicia and Navarre, and the Universidad de la Contratación de los Mercaderes de Burgos represented Burgos and other inland cities, including Nájera and Soria. Hilario Casado Alonso, 'La Nation et le quartier des Castillans de Bruges (XVe et XVIe siècles)', *Handelingen van het Genootschap voor Geschiedenis 'Société d'Émulation' te Brugge*, CXXXIII/1–3 (1996), p. 64; Brown, 'Cities, Nations', pp. 166–7,

173 n. 45; Marechal, 'Colonie espagnole', p. 99; Phillips, 'Local Integration', p. 35.

101 Casado Alonso, 'Castillans de Bruges', p. 64; Brown, 'Cities, Nations', p. 172 n. 41, 173; Marechal, 'Colonie espagnole', pp. 94–7, 114.

102 Brown, 'Cities, Nations', p. 172; Casado Alonso, 'Castillans de Bruges', pp. 68–9; Ryckaert, *Brugge: Historische Stedenatlas*, p. 107; Marechal, 'Colonie espagnole', p. 115; Dumolyn et al., 'Urban Landscape II', p. 167.

103 Marechal, 'Colonie espagnole', p. 91; Vandewalle, 'Iberian Peninsula', pp. 170–72; Marechal, 'Colonie espagnole', p. 115.

104 Vandewalle, 'Iberian Peninsula', pp. 159–63. Bruges became the chief trading house for sugar in the 1470s, the primary source of the fortunes of the Despars family and Maarten Lem. See Brulez, 'Bruges and Antwerp', pp. 17–18.

105 Rössner, *Hansische*, p. 248; Vandewalle, 'Iberian Peninsula', pp. 164–5.

106 Vandewalle, 'Iberian Peninsula', pp. 162–4.

107 Raymond van Uytven, 'Stages of Economic Decline: Late Medieval Bruges', in *Peasants and Townsmen in Medieval Europe: Studia in honorem Adriaan Verhulst*, ed. Jean-Marie Duvosquel and Erik Thoen (Ghent, 1995), pp. 260–61; Ryckaert, *Brugge: Historische Stedenatlas*, pp. 106–7; Vandewalle, 'Iberian Peninsula', pp. 164–5.

108 Established in 1293, the so-called *compagnie des courtiers* or *makelaars*. Stabel, Puttevils and Dumolyn, 'Production, II', p. 205; Greve, *Hansische Kaufleute*, p. 83.

109 De Roover, *Money*, p. 16; Stabel, Puttevils and Dumolyn, 'Production, I', pp. 115, 205–6; Greve, *Hansische Kaufleute*, pp. 87–95; de Clercq, 'Ter Beurze', pp. 17–18; Ryckaert, *Brugge: Historische Stedenatlas*, p. 73; Andries van den Abeele and Michaël Catry, *Makelaars en Handelaars: Van neering der makelaars naar kamer van koophandel in her XVIIde-eeuwse Brugge* (Bruges, 1992), p. 23.

110 Stabel, Puttevils and Dumolyn, 'Production, II', pp. 207–8; Jan Dumolyn et al., 'Social Groups: Political Power and Institutions II, c. 1300–c. 1500', in *Medieval Bruges*, ed. Brown and Dumolyn, p. 312; Spufford, *Power and Profit*, p. 206.

111 Greve, *Hansische Kaufleute*, p. 71; Van den Abeele and Catry, *Makelaars*, pp. 20–22, 25–6.

112 Murray, *Cradle*, pp. 124–5, 163–4; Spufford, *Power and Profit*, p. 37.

113 Many pawnbrokers were from Piedmont, or from northern France and Francophone cities of southern Flanders, such as Tournai and Lille. Murray, *Cradle*, pp. 37–8, 130, 136–53.

114 Krisa De Jonge, '1384–1477 Het Prinsenhof als "Bourgondische"
    residentie', in *Het Prinsenhof in Brugge*, ed. Bieke Hillewaert and
    Elisabeth Van Besien (Bruges, 2007), pp. 40–49.

115 Dumolyn et al., 'Origins', pp. 45–6; Jan Dumolyn, Georges Declerq
    and Jelle Haemers, 'Social Groups: Political Power and Institutions I,
    c. 1100–*c.* 1300', in *Medieval Bruges*, ed. Brown and Dumolyn,
    pp. 137–8.

116 Bruges itself was divided into six administrative districts, the so-
    called *Zestendeelen*; each had a number of officials serving under a
    hoofdman and contributed a share of militiamen to the city's defence.
    Ryckaert, *Brugge: Historische Stedenatlas*, p. 90.

117 Stabel, Puttevils and Dumolyn, 'Production, II', p. 205;
    Vandermaesen, Soens and De Bock, *Poortersloge*, p. 9; Greve,
    Hansische Kaufleute, pp. 40–41; Jan Dumolyn et al., 'Social Groups, II',
    p. 311.

118 Greve, *Hansische Kaufleute*, pp. 40–41.

119 Wim Blockmans, 'The Creative Environment: Incentives to and
    Functions of Bruges Art Production', in *Petrus Christus in Renaissance
    Bruges: An Interdisciplinary Approach*, ed. Maryan W. Ainsworth
    (New York and Turnhout, 1995), pp. 16–17; Wim Blockmans,
    'The Burgundian Court and the Urban Milieu as Patrons in
    15th-Century Bruges', in *Economic History and the Arts*, ed. Michael
    North (Cologne and Vienna, 1996), pp. 23–4.

120 Paul de Win, 'The Lesser Nobility of the Burgundian Netherlands',
    in *Gentry and Lesser Nobility in Late Medieval Europe*, ed. Michael Jones
    (New York, 1986), p. 105; Frederik Buylaert, 'The Late Medieval
    "Crisis of the Nobility" Reconsidered: The Case of Flanders',
    Journal of Social History, XLV/4 (Summer 2012), pp. 1126–7. For
    a study of social differentiation and mobility within the lesser
    nobility, see de Win, 'Lesser Nobility', pp. 99–104, and Buylaert,
    'Late Medieval', pp. 1122–6. Because of the absorption of Flanders
    into Burgundy and the Empire, knightly titles became less
    accessible for urban strivers owing to decreased proximity to
    monarchs. Frederik Buylaert, 'Lordship, Urbanization and Social
    Change in Late Medieval Flanders', *Past and Present*, CXXVII/1 (May
    2015), pp. 63–6.

121 Jean C. Wilson, *Painting in Bruges at the Close of the Middle Ages: Studies in
    Society and Visual Culture* (University Park, PA, 1998), pp. 16–84; de
    Win, 'Lesser Nobility', p. 97.

122 Boogaardt, 'Evolution', pp. 334, 346–9.

123 Charles Louis Carton, ed., *Het boeck van al 't gene datter gheschiedt is binnen Brugghe, sichtent jaer 1477, 14 februarii, tot 1491* (Ghent, 1859), pp. 116–27.

124 Jan Dumolyn, '"Our Land Is Only Founded on Trade and Industry": Economic Discourses in Fifteenth-Century Bruges', *Journal of Medieval History*, XXXVI/4 (2010), p. 375.

125 Jan Dumolyn, 'The "Terrible Wednesday" of Pentecost: Confronting Urban and Princely Discourses in the Bruges Rebellion of 1436–1438', *History*, XCII/305 (2007), pp. 3–20.

126 Blockmans and Prevenier, *Promised Lands*, pp. 141–53.

127 Nicholas, *Medieval Flanders*, pp. 168–9, 392; Blockmans and Prevenier, *Promised Lands*, pp. 142–50, 164–7, 174–85.

128 Jelle Haemers, *For the Common Good: State Power and Urban Revolts in the Reign of Mary of Burgundy (1477–1482)* (Turnhout, 2009), pp. 168–87; Nicholas, *Medieval Flanders*, pp. 394–5.

129 Haemers, *Common Good*, pp. 187–93; Jelle Haemers, 'Factionalism and State Power in the Flemish Revolt (1482–1492)', *Journal of Social History*, XLII/4 (Summer 2009), pp. 1009–14.

130 Oscar Gelderblom, 'The Decline of Fairs and Merchant Guilds in the Low Countries, 1250–1650', *Jaarboek voor middeleeuwse Geschiedenis*, VII (2004), p. 21; Nicholas, *Medieval Flanders*, pp. 396–7; Haemers, 'Factionalism', p. 1014; Munro, 'Abortive Staple', p. 1148.

131 Nicholas, *Medieval Flanders*, pp. 397–8; Haemers, 'Factionalism', p. 1015.

132 *Dits die Excellente Chronijcke van Vlaenderen* (Antwerp, 1531), p. 244.

133 Ibid., p. 246.

134 Van Houtte, 'Rise and Decline', pp. 44–5.

135 Nicholas, *Medieval Flanders*, p. 398.

136 Joseph Marechal, 'Le Départ de Bruges des marchands étrangers', *Handelingen van het Genootschap voor Geschiedenis*, LXXXVIII (1951), pp. 27–8; Van Uytven, 'Stages', p. 262.

3 Memling's Career in Bruges: The Painter's Workshop

1 Dirk De Vos, *Hans Memling: The Complete Works*, trans. Ted Alkins (Antwerp, Ghent and New York, 1994), pp. 56–7.

2 Bart Fransen and Louise Longneaux, 'Hans Memling's Altarpiece of the Benedictine Abbey Church of Nájera', in *Harmony in Bright Colours: Memling's God the Father with Singing and Music-Making Angels Restored*, ed. Lizet Klaassen and Dieter Lampens (Brussels, 2021), pp. 39, 51 n. 48;

Barbara G. Lane, *Hans Memling: Master Painter in Fifteenth-Century Bruges* (London and Turnhout, 2009), pp. 102–3; Marie Postec and Lizet Klaassen, 'The Frames and Framing of Memling's Nájera Panels', in *Harmony in Bright Colours*, ed. Klaassen and Lampens, pp. 134–5.

3 Bart Fransen, 'Hans Memling's Nájera Altarpiece: New Documentary Evidence', *Burlington Magazine*, CLX/1379 (February 2018), pp. 101–5; Fransen and Longneaux, 'Hans Memling's Altarpiece', p. 35; Maximiliaan P. J. Martens, 'Artistic Patronage in Bruges Institutions, ca. 1440–1482', PhD diss., University of California, Santa Barbara, 1992, p. 38 n. 11.

4 De Vos, *Complete Works*, p. 56; Fransen and Longneaux, 'Hans Memling's Altarpiece', pp. 36–7.

5 Joel M. Upton, *Petrus Christus: His Place in Fifteenth-Century Flemish Painting* (University Park, PA, and London, 1990), p. 7; Maximiliaan P. J. Martens, 'Petrus Christus, A Cultural Biography', in *Petrus Christus: Renaissance Master of Bruges*, ed. Maryan W. Ainsworth (New York, 1994), pp. 15, 19.

6 Martens, 'Petrus Christus', pp. 16–19.

7 Maryan W. Ainsworth, *Gerard David: Purity of Vision in an Age of Transition* (New York, 1998), p. 2.

8 Anne Hagopian van Buren, 'Willem Vrelant: Questions and Issues', *Belgisch Tijdscrift voor Oudheidkunde en Kunstgeschiedenis*, LXVIII (1999), p. 8.

9 Marc Goetinck, 'De ontluikende boekdrukkunst in Brugge (ca. 1474–1484): William Caxton, Colard Masion en Jan Brito', *Vlaanderen Kunsttijdscrift*, XLIII (1994), pp. 125–49; Noël Geirnaert, 'Boeken in het middeleeuwse Brugge: Een verhaal van eeuwen', *Vlaanderen Kunsttijdscrift*, XLIII (1994), pp. 120–35.

10 Marc Ryckaert et al., *Brugge: De geschiedenis van een Europese stad* (Tielt, 1999), p. 108.

11 Guy Delmarcel, *Het Vlaamse wandtapijt van de 15de tot de 18de eeuw* (Tielt, 1999), pp. 180–84.

12 William Henry James Weale, 'Documents authentiques concernant la vie, la famille et la position sociale de Jean Memlinc découverts à Bruges', *Journal des Beaux-Arts et de la littérature*, III (1861), pp. 53–4; Martens, 'Artistic Patronage', pp. 330–33; M. Goetinck and Marc Ryckaert, 'Hans Memling (°ca. 1433–†1494): Brugse archivalia betreffende Hans Memling', in *Sint-Janshospitaal Brugge 1188/1976* (Bruges, 1976), p. 495; Albert Schouteet, 'Inventaris van het archief van het voormalige gild van de librariers en van de verening van

schoolmeesters te Brugge', *Handelingen van het Genootschap voor Geschiedenis 'Société d'Émulation' te Brugge*, C/1–3 (1963), p. 244.

13 Albert Janssens, 'De schilder Hans Memling: Als Brugs poorter financieel, sociaal en politiek doorgelicht', *Handelingen van het Genootschap voor Geschiedenis 'Société d'Émulation' te Brugge*, CXXXIV/1 (1997), pp. 65–89.

14 Till-Holger Borchert, 'Memling – Life and Work', in *Memling's Portraits*, ed. Till-Holger Borchert et al. (Ghent and Amsterdam, 2005), p. 14.

15 Albert Janssens, 'Willem Moreel en Hans Memling: Bijdrage tot het onderzoek naar de schilderijen van Memling in opdracht van de familie Moreel', *Handelingen van het Genootschap voor Geschiedenis 'Société d'Émulation' te Brugge*, CXL/1–2 (2003), pp. 68–70.

16 Janssens, 'Schilder', pp. 75–8; Borchert, 'Life and Work', p. 18.

17 Wim Blockmans, 'The Creative Environment: Incentives to and Functions of Bruges Art Production', in *Petrus Christus in Renaissance Bruges: An Interdisciplinary Approach*, ed. Maryan W. Ainsworth (New York and Turnhout, 1995), pp. 16–17; see also Wim Blockmans, 'The Burgundian Court and the Urban Milieu as Patrons in 15th-Century Bruges', in *Economic History and the Arts*, ed. Michael North (Cologne and Vienna, 1996), pp. 17–18. For the similar situation in Ghent, see Els Cornelius, 'De Kunstenaar in het laat-middeleeuwse Gent (1)', *Handelingen der Maatschappij voor Geschiedenis en Oudheidkunde te Gent*, XLI (1987), pp. 107–8; and Els Cornelius, 'De Kunstenaar in het laat-middeleeuwse Gent (II)', *Handelingen der Maatschappij voor Geschiedenis en Oudheidkunde te Gent*, XLII (1988), pp. 97–101.

18 Noël Geirnaert, 'Hans Memling, lid van het schildersambacht en poorter van Brugge, 1465', in *Bedenkingen vanuit het Stadsarchief van Brugge* (Bruges, 2017), p. 16; James M. Murray, *Bruges, Cradle of Capitalism, 1280–1390* (Cambridge, 2005), pp. 16–17. Flemish literature tends to describe the trade and craft guilds as *ambachten*, while the term *gild* is reserved for religiously focused organizations.

19 Albert Schouteet, *De vlaamse primitieven te Brugge: Bronnen voor de schilderkunst te Brugge tot de dood van Gerard David*, vol. 1: *(A–K)* (Brussels, 1989), pp. 8, 15.

20 Jean Jacques Gailliard, *De ambachten en neringen van Brugge* (Bruges, 1854), pp. 166–7; Paul Trio, 'Ambacht, nering or neringilde? De identiteit van het corporatieve karakter van het Brugse librariërsgilde in de vijftiende eeuw', in *Boeken uit Brugge: Studies over Brugse boekgeschiedenis*, ed. Ludo Vandamme (Bruges, 2021), pp. 38–45.

21 Désiré van de Casteele, ed., *Documents divers de la Société S. Luc à Bruges.
     Deuxième partie: Livre d'admission des confrères de la société* (Bruges, 1866),
     pp. 7–11, 28–30; Arthur Van de Velde, *Het schildersgild te Brugge: Of de
     unie der ambachten van de beeldemakers, huusscrivers, cleerscrivers, zadelaars,
     gareelmakers, boomhauwers, glazemakers en spiegelmakers, van de XIVe tot de XIXe
     eeuw* (Bruges, 1905), pp. 32–6.
22 Gailliard, *De ambachten*, pp. 79, 108; Maximiliaan P. J. Martens et al.,
     'Texts, Images and Sounds in the Urban Environment, *c.* 1100–
     c. 1500', in *Medieval Bruges, c. 850–1550*, ed. Andrew Brown and
     Jan Dumolyn (Cambridge and New York, 2018), p. 403.
23 Cornelius, 'De Kunstenaar (I)', pp. 99, 99 n. 12.
24 Blockmans, 'Creative Environment', p. II.
25 Peter Stabel, Jerome Puttevils and Jan Dumolyn, 'Production:
     Markets and Socio-Economic Structures I: *c.* 1100–*c.* 1300', in
     Medieval Bruges, ed. Brown and Dumolyn, pp. 95–6; Murray, *Cradle*,
     pp. 16–17.
26 Marc Ryckaert, *Brugge: Historische Stedenatlas van België*, ed. Adriaan
     Verhust and Jean-Marie Duvosquel (Brussels, 1991), p. 72.
27 Désiré van de Casteele, ed., *Documents divers de la Société S. Luc à Bruges.
     Première partie: Keuren* (Bruges, 1866), pp. 18–20, 56, 61–224.
28 Van de Velde, *Schildersgild*, p. 12.
29 William Henry James Weale, 'Inventaire des chartes et documents
     appartenant aux archives de la Corporation de Saint Luc et Saint Eloi
     à Bruges (I)', *Le Beffroi: Art et littérature modernes*, I (1863), pp. 205–6;
     Van de Velde, *Schildersgild*, pp. 12–13.
30 Martens, 'Petrus Christus', p. 15; Martens, 'Artistic Patronage', p. 29.
31 Peter Stabel, 'Selling Paintings in Late Medieval Bruges: Marketing
     Customs and Guild Regulations Compared', in *Mapping Markets for
     Paintings in Europe, 1450–1750*, ed. Neil De Marchi and Hans J. Van
     Miegroet (Turnhout, 2006), pp. 89–103.
32 Van de Casteele, *Keuren*, p. 20; Stabel, 'Selling Paintings', p. 95; Rachel
     Billinge et al., 'Methods and Materials of Northern European
     Painting in the National Gallery, 1400–1500', *National Gallery
     Technical Bulletin*, XVIII (1997), p. 10.
33 Van de Casteele, *Keuren*, pp. 28–33; Billinge et al., 'Methods and
     Materials', pp. 8–10, on the more elaborate regulations in Cologne,
     Tournai and Antwerp. For Cologne statutes, see Brigitte Corley,
     Painting and Patronage in Cologne, 1300–1500 (London, 2000), pp. 38–41,
     298–302.
34 Van de Casteele, *Keuren*, pp. 23–4.

35 Blockmans, 'Creative Environment', p. 16.

36 This was on the north side of the Lange Zilverstraat. Gailliard, *De ambachten*, pp. 160–61; Van de Casteele, *Keuren*, pp. 14, 29–30; Van de Velde, *Schildersgild*, pp. 105–6.

37 Gailliard, *De ambachten*, pp. 160–61; Van de Casteele, *Keuren*, p. 15.

38 Van de Casteele, *Keuren*, p. 16; Van de Velde, *Schildersgild*, p. 106.

39 Gailliard, *De ambachten*, p. 161; Paul van Calster, 'Of Beardless Painters and Red Chaperons: A Fifteenth-Century Whodunit', *Zeitschrift für Kunstgeschichte*, LXVI/4 (2003), p. 480.

40 Van de Casteele, *Keuren*, pp. 26, 35; Van de Velde, *Schildersgild*, pp. 103–4.

41 Stabel, 'Selling Paintings', pp. 90–93; Jean C. Wilson, *Painting in Bruges at the Close of the Middle Ages: Studies in Society and Visual Culture* (University Park, PA, 1998), pp. 168, 174–87.

42 Schouteet, *De vlaamse primitieven te Brugge*, vol. I, p. 54. For the selling of works at markets in Ghent, see Cornelius, 'De Kunstenaar (I)', pp. 120–22.

43 Paula Nuttall, *From Flanders to Florence: The Impact of Netherlandish Painting, 1400–1500* (New Haven, CT, and London, 2004), pp. 78–9.

44 Lane, *Hans Memling*, pp. 121–2.

45 Maryan W. Ainsworth and Keith Christiansen, eds, *From Van Eyck to Bruegel: Early Netherlandish Painting in the Metropolitan Museum of Art* (New York, 1998), p. 116.

46 Maryan W. Ainsworth, 'Workshop Practice in Early Netherlandish Painting: An Inside View', in *From Van Eyck to Bruegel*, ed. Ainsworth and Christiansen, p. 211; Lane, *Hans Memling*, p. 116; Borchert, 'Life and Work', p. 34; Lorne Campbell, 'Memlinc's Creative Processes as Seen in His Paintings in the National Gallery, London', in *Le dessin sous-jacent dans la peinture*, ed. Hélène Verougstraete and Roger van Schoute (Louvain-la-Neuve, 1995), p. 149.

47 Ainsworth, *Petrus Christus: Renaissance Master*, p. 12 n. 46.

48 Billinge et al., 'Methods and Materials', p. 11; Ainsworth, *Petrus Christus: Renaissance Master*, pp. 9–10, 12 n. 45.

49 Maximiliaan P. J. Martens, 'Het onderzoek naar de opdrachtgevers', in *'Om iets te weten van de oude meesters': De Vlaamse primitieven– herontdekking, waardering en onderzoek*, ed. Bernhard Ridderbos and Henk van Veen (Worcester, MA, 1995), pp. 367–71. Similar slivers of evidence are discussed in Cornelius, 'De Kunstenaar (I)', pp. 116–20.

50 Maryan W. Ainsworth, 'The Business of Art: Patrons, Clients, and Art Markets', in *From Van Eyck to Bruegel*, ed. Ainsworth and Christiansen, pp. 29–30; Lorne Campbell, 'Approaches to Petrus Christus', in *Petrus Christus in Renaissance Bruges*, ed. Ainsworth, p. 6. In a legal case in Bruges between Albrecht Cornelis and the guild of the fullers and textile-shearers in 1520, the plaintiffs held that he had subcontracted much of the work, while the artist argued that the contract mandated his hand only in the painting of figures' faces, and that the patrons had missed payment dates. Lisbeth M. Helmus, 'Journeymen and Servants', in *Making and Marketing: Studies of the Painting Process in Fifteenth- and Sixteenth-Century Netherlandish Workshops*, ed. Molly Faries (Turnhout, 2006), pp. 206–7.

51 Martens, 'Artistic Patronage', p. 332.

52 Marc Ryckaert, 'Het huis van Memling in Brugge', in *Hans Memling: Essays*, ed. Dirk De Vos and Maryan W. Ainsworth (Ghent, 1994), p. 104.

53 'Ex fundo domus magne lapidee'. Till-Holger Borchert, 'Memling's Workshop', in *Harmony in Bright Colours*, ed. Klaassen and Lampens, p. 168; Janssens, 'Schilder', pp. 76–7; Ryckaert, 'Huis van Memling', p. 105; Weale, 'Documents', pp. 28, 46.

54 Borchert, 'Memling's Workshop', p. 168.

55 Ryckaert, 'Huis van Memling', p. 104.

56 Ainsworth, *Gerard David*, p. 279; Ryckaert, 'Huis van Memling', p. 104; Borchert, 'Life and Work', p. 14.

57 Jean-Pierre Sosson, 'Une approche des structures économiques d'un métier d'art: La corporation des Peintres et Selliers de Bruges (xve–xvie siècles)', *Revue des archeoloques et historiens d'art de Louvain*, III (1970), p. 99.

58 Maximiliaan P. J. Martens, 'Discussion', in *Petrus Christus in Renaissance Bruges*, ed. Ainsworth, p. 43.

59 Lane, *Hans Memling*, p. 95.

60 Charles Vanden Haute, *La corporation des peintres de Bruges* (Kortrijk, 1913), p. 28; Borchert, 'Memling's Workshop', p. 168.

61 Van de Casteele, *Keuren*, p. 117; Vanden Haute, *Corporation*, p. 35.

62 Albert Schouteet, *De vlaamse primitieven te Brugge: Bronnen voor de schilderkunst te Brugge tot de dood van Gerard David*, vol. II: (L–Z) (Brussels, 1989), p. 42.

63 Schouteet, *De vlaamse primitieven te Brugge*, vol. I, p. 17.

64 Borchert, 'Memling's Workshop', p. 168.

65 Ibid.; Paul Lambotte, *Memling Tentoonstelling ingericht door het Stadsbestuur in het Stedelijk Museum te Brugge (22 Juni–1 October 1939) Catalogus* (Bruges, 1939), p. 26; Weale, 'Documents', p. 46.

66 'Clais Hendricx zuene van Keersbach, ghebooren van Cuelne' paid his citizenship fee in August 1473. He does not seem to have remained in Bruges until his death, since he does not appear in the guild's *obituarium*. Schouteet, *De vlaamse primitieven te Brugge*, vol. I, p. 288.

67 Borchert, 'Memling's Workshop', p. 168; for documentation of Boels's career in Bruges, see Schouteet, *De vlaamse primitieven te Brugge*, vol. I, pp. 53–5.

68 Schouteet, *De vlaamse primitieven te Brugge*, vol. I, p. 54; Weale, 'Documents', p. 28.

69 Lane, *Hans Memling*, pp. 98–111.

70 Arguments found in: Lane, *Hans Memling*, pp. 102–3; Matthias Weniger, 'Bynnen Brugge in Flandern: The Apprenticeships of Michel Sittow and Juan de Flandes', in *Memling Studies: Proceedings of the International Colloquium (Bruges, 10–12 November 1994)*, ed. Roger van Schoute, Maurits Smeyers and Hélène Verougstraete (Leuven, 1997), pp. 115–18; John Oliver Hand et al., eds, *Michael Sittow: Estonian Painter at the Courts of Renaissance Europe* (New Haven, CT, and London, 2017), pp. 40–43, 60–62, 78–82; and De Vos, *Complete Works*, p. 46.

71 A number of statements regarding his training were recorded in connection with an inheritance lawsuit against his stepfather. Weniger suggests that he may already have been in Castile by 1489. Weniger, 'Bynnen Brugge in Flandern', p. 115; Matthias Weniger, 'Michael Sittow: An Artist's Career between the Hanseatic City of Tallin and the Princely Courts of Europe', in *Michael Sittow*, ed. Hand et al., pp. 27–8, 35; De Vos, *Complete Works*, pp. 46–7.

72 Lane, *Hans Memling*, p. 103. It is possible that Sittow was one of several hands who collaborated on the Luna Chapel altarpiece in Toledo, or that he accompanied the Nájera work to Spain, where he remained and established his own career. Weniger, 'Michael Sittow', p. 34.

73 Weniger, 'Bynnen Brugge in Flandern', pp. 118–31; Lane, *Hans Memling*, p. 98. For an overview of his works, see Maryan W. Ainsworth, 'Juan de Flandes, Chameleon Painter', in *Invention: Northern Renaissance Studies in Honor of Molly Faries*, ed. Julien Chapuis (Turnhout, 2008), pp. 104–23.

74 Ainsworth, 'Workshop Practice', pp. 205–6.

75 Ibid., p. 207.

76 Borchert, 'Memling's Workshop', pp. 169–82.

77 Maryan W. Ainsworth, 'Memling's Preliminary Working Stages: The
    Nájera Panels in Context', in *Harmony in Bright Colours*, ed. Klaassen
    and Lampens, pp. 158–9; Borchert, 'Memling's Workshop', p. 189.

78 For a brief but solid overview of materials in painting of the period
    (not limited to Flanders), see Susie Nash, *Northern Renaissance Art*,
    Oxford History of Art (New York, 2008), pp. 197–209.

79 Peter Klein, 'Dendrochronological Analyses of Panels of Hans
    Memling and His Contemporaries', in *Memling Studies*, ed. Van
    Schoute, Smeyers and Verougstraete, pp. 287–95; Lizet Klaassen et
    al., 'Materials and Painting Technique of Memling's Nájera Panels',
    in *Harmony in Bright Colours*, ed. Klaassen and Lampens, p. 87; Billinge
    et al., 'Methods and Materials', pp. 16–18.

80 Martens and Miegroet note that this wood was sought after owing
    to its density, hardness, low moisture content and resistance to
    wood parasites. Maximiliaan P. J. Martens and Hans J. van
    Miegroet, 'Nieuwe inzichten omtrent de omstreden du Cellier-
    diptiek, toegeschreven aan Hans Memling', *Gentse bijdragen tot de
    kunstgeschiedenis en oudheidkunde*, XXVI (1984), pp. 66–7; Micheline
    Comblen-Sonkes and Philippe Lorentz, *Le Musée du Louvre, Paris: II,
    Corpus de la peinture des Anciens Pays-Bas méridionaux et de la
    Principaut é de Liège au quinzième siècle*, 17 (Brussels, 1995),
    p. 277.

81 Hélène Verougstraete, 'Cadres et supports chez Memling', in *Memling
    Studies*, ed. Van Schoute, Smeyers and Verougstraete, pp. 269–86.

82 Carmen Garrido, 'Hans Memling: Le *Triptyque de l'Adoration des Mages
    du Musée de Prado*: Quelques considérations techniques', in *Memling
    Studies*, ed. Van Schoute, Smeyers and Verougstraete, pp. 229–31;
    Klaassen et al., 'Materials', pp. 91–7; Geert Van der Snickt et al.,
    'Material Analyses of "Christ with Singing and Music-Making
    Angels", a Late 15th-C Panel Painting Attributed to Hans Memling
    and Assistants: Part I. Non-Invasive in Situ Investigations', *Journal
    of Analytical Atomic Spectrometry*, XXVI (2011), p. 2222; Billinge et al.,
    'Methods and Materials', p. 23; Iwona Szmelter et al., 'Multi-Criterial
    Studies of the Masterpiece *The Last Judgement*, Attributed to Hans
    Memling, at the National Museum of Gdańsk (2010–2013)',
    in *Science and Art: The Painted Surface*, ed. Antonio Sgamellotti,
    Brunetto Giovanni Brunetti and Costanza Miliani (Cambridge,
    2014), pp. 234, 242.

83 Marika Spring, 'The Technique and Materials of the Paintings Attributed to Memling in the National Gallery, London', in *Memling Studies*, ed. Van Schoute, Smeyers and Verougstraete, p. 213; Klaassen et al., 'Materials', p. 106; Billinge et al., 'Methods and Materials', pp. 22–3; 'The Materials and Techniques of Five Paintings by Rogier van der Weyden and his Workshop', *National Gallery Technical Bulletin*, XVIII (1997), p. 72.

84 Molly Faries, 'The Underdrawing of Memling's *Last Judgment Altarpiece* in Gdansk', in *Memling Studies*, ed. Van Schoute, Smeyers and Verougstraete, pp. 248–50; Klaassen et al., 'Materials', pp. 99–103. These determinations are based on visual characteristics rather than chemical analyses.

85 Klaassen et al., 'Materials', p. 122 n. 53; Maryan W. Ainsworth, 'The Evolution of Jan Crabbe's Triptych', in *Hans Memling: Portraiture, Piety, and a Reunited Altarpiece*, ed. John Marciari (London, 2016), p. 78; Gianluca Poldi and Giovanni C. F. Villa, 'A New Technical Study of the Vicenza Crucifixion', in *Hans Memling*, ed. Marciari, p. 88; Szmelter et al., 'Multi-Criterial', p. 247.

86 Maryan W. Ainsworth, 'Minimal Means, Remarkable Results', in *Memling's Portraits*, ed. Borchert et al., p. 97.

87 Campbell, 'Memlinc's Creative Processes', pp. 149–50; Lorne Campbell, *The Fifteenth Century Netherlandish Schools*, National Gallery Catalogues (London, 1998), pp. 26–7, 374, 384; Billinge et al., 'Methods and Materials', p. 26; Lorne Campbell, 'The *Donne Triptych*', in *Memling Studies*, ed. Van Schoute, Smeyers and Verougstraete, p. 71. Faries notes that pouncing has not been documented earlier than 1500 in Flanders. Molly Faries, 'Making and Marketing: Studies of the Painting Process', in *Making and Marketing*, ed. Faries, p. 2.

88 Klaassen et al., 'Materials', pp. 99, 118; Ainsworth, 'Memling's Preliminary Working Stages', pp. 158–9.

89 Campbell, *Fifteenth Century*, pp. 354, 374; Klaassen et al., 'Materials', pp. 103–6.

90 Susie Nash, '"Pour couleurs et autres choses prise de lui . . .": The Supply, Acquisition, Cost and Employment of Painters' Materials at the Burgundian Court, *c.* 1375–1419', in *Trade in Artists' Materials: Markets and Commerce in Europe to 1700*, ed. Jo Kirby, Susie Nash and Joanna Cannon (London, 2010), pp. 133–7.

91 This base contains quartz, goethite clay and lead siccative. Klaassen et al., 'Materials', pp. 107–8, 123 n. 84; Van der Snickt et al., 'Material Analyses', pp. 2227–8.

92 Klaassen et al., 'Materials', pp. 107–8; Nash, 'Pour couleurs', p. 133.

93 Szmelter et al., 'Multi-Criterial', p. 242; Cyriel Stroo, Pascale Syfer-d'Olne and Anne Dubois, *The Flemish Primitives*, vol. II: *The Dirk Bouts, Petrus Christus, Hans Memling and Hugo Van der Goes Groups Catalogue of Early Netherlandish Painting in the Royal Museums of Fine Arts of Belgium* (Brussels, 1999), pp. 204–5.

94 Linseed oil has been detected in several of Memling's works, while both oils have been detected in the works of Gerard David, also working in Bruges. Campbell, *Fifteenth Century*, pp. 354, 359, 362, 374. For Gerard David, see Billinge et al., 'Methods and Materials', pp. 40–41, 53–5.

95 Billinge et al., 'Methods and Materials', pp. 34–40; Klaassen et al., 'Materials', pp. 108–19.

96 J. A. Van Houtte, *De Geschiedenis van Brugge* (Tielt and Bussum, 1982), p. 82; Wendy R. Childs, 'Painters' Materials and Northern International Trade Routes of Late Medieval Europe', in *Trade in Artists' Materials*, ed. Kirby, Nash and Cannon, p. 34. On the trade of woad from Arezzo into Flanders, see Laura Galoppini, *Mercanti Toscani e Bruges nel Tardo Medievo* (Pisa, 2014), pp. 269–86.

97 Klaassen et al., 'Materials', p. 123 n. 109; An order from 1399 to Jean Malouel, for example, specifies 'Bourre de fine escarlate vermeille de Bruxelles pour faire cynopple' (fluff sheared off fine scarlet cloth from Brussels, dyed 'in grain' to make red lake [Nash's translation]). Nash, 'Pour couleurs', pp. 121, 143.

98 Van Houtte, *Geschiedenis*, p. 82; Julia A. DeLancey, 'Shipping Colour: *Valute*, Pigments, Trade and Francesco di Marco Datini', in *Trade in Artists' Materials*, ed. Kirby, Nash and Cannon, pp. 78–80.

99 'Materials and Techniques', pp. 74–80; Lorne Campbell, 'Suppliers of Artists' Materials to the Burgundian Court', in *Trade in Artists' Materials*, ed. Kirby, Nash and Cannon, p. 183.

100 De Vos, *Complete Works*, pp. 382–3, 385 n. 31; Klaassen et al., 'Materials', p. 109; Van der Snickt et al., 'Material Analyses', p. 2222; Rutherford J. Gettens, Herman Kühn and W. T. Chase, 'Lead White', in *Artists' Pigments: A Handbook of Their History and Characteristics*, ed. Ashok Roy (Washington, DC, and London, 1992; reprinted 2012), vol. II, p. 67.

101 Van der Snickt et al., 'Material Analyses', p. 2222; Klaassen et al., 'Materials', p. 109.

102 No manganese has been detected in the samples studied, so Memling does not appear to have used the pigments commonly

known as 'umber' or 'sienna'. Jo Kirby, 'The Price of Quality:
Factors Influencing the Cost of Pigments during the Renaissance',
in *Revaluing Renaissance Art*, ed. Gabriele Neher and Rupert Kirby
Shepherd (Aldershot, 2000), p. 29; Van der Snickt et al., 'Material
Analyses', p. 2227; Klaassen et al., 'Materials', pp. 109–11; Szmelter
et al., 'Multi-Criterial', p. 243.

103 Spring, 'Technique', pp. 217–18; Poldi and Villa, 'New Technical',
p. 89; Van der Snickt et al., 'Material Analyses', p. 2224; De Vos,
Complete Works, pp. 382–3, 385 n. 31; Klaassen et al., 'Materials',
pp. 109–12; Garrido, '*Triptyque*', pp. 231–3; Nicole Goetghebeur,
'Étude technique de trois tableaux de Memling', in *Memling Studies*,
ed. Van Schoute, Smeyers and Verougstraete, p. 261; Szmelter et al.,
'Multi-Criterial', pp. 243–4.

104 Herman Kühn, 'Verdigris and Copper Resinate', in *Artists' Pigments II*,
ed. Roy, pp. 131–2.

105 Hermann Kühn, 'Lead-Tin Yellow', in *Artists' Pigments II*, ed. Roy,
pp. 83–4; Spring, 'Technique', p. 217; Van der Snickt et al., 'Material
Analyses', p. 2222; Klaassen et al., 'Materials', p. 109; Szmelter et al.,
'Multi-Criterial', p. 243; Goetghebeur, 'Étude technique', p. 261;
Campbell, *Fifteenth Century*, pp. 362, 370. On relative prices for many
of these pigments earlier in the late fourteenth and early fifteenth
century, see Nash, 'Pour couleurs', pp. 141–6.

106 Nash, 'Pour couleurs', pp. 141–6.

107 De Vos, *Complete Works*, pp. 382–3, 385 n. 31; Van der Snickt et al.,
'Material Analyses', p. 2222; Campbell, *Fifteenth Century*, pp. 357, 362,
374.

108 Rutherford J. Gettens, Robert L. Feller and W. T. Chase,
'Vermilion and Cinnabar', in *Artists' Pigments II*, ed. Roy, pp. 159–62;
Childs, 'Painters' Materials', p. 34; Both vermilion and cinnabar,
specifically, were noted by Szmelter et al., 'Multi-Criterial',
pp. 243–4.

109 Van der Snickt et al., 'Material Analyses', p. 2227.

110 Elisabeth West Fitzhugh, 'Red Lead and Minium', in *Artists' Pigments:
A Handbook of Their History and Characteristics*, ed. Robert L. Feller
(Washington, DC, and London, 1986; reprinted 2012), vol. I,
pp. 109–13; Nash, 'Pour couleurs', pp. 146–7.

111 Van der Snickt et al., 'Material Analyses', p. 2222; Klaassen et al.,
'Materials', p. 109; De Vos, *Complete Works*, pp. 382–3, 385 n. 31;
Szmelter et al., 'Multi-Criterial', p. 243; Campbell, *Fifteenth
Century*, p. 362; Helmut Schweppe and John Winter, 'Madder

and Alizarin', in *Artists' Pigments II*, ed. Roy, pp. 109–15; Kirby, 'Price', pp. 26–7.

112 Several species of kermes are found in different areas of Europe and further east; the 'Polish kermes' was harvested from the roots of the knawel shrub, which grew in sandy soils in an area stretching from Saxony to Lithuania. Red lake particles found in some of Memling's paintings are rich in protein, an indication that the pigment was prepared from the recycled, dyed shearings of woollen textiles. This indicates that it was derived from the madder plant rather than the kermes insect, attained via a similar process from the silk shearings for which that more expensive dye was reserved. With either red lake pigment, alum was required as a mordant to 'fix' the colour, and also removed oily residue from the production process. Peter Spufford, *Power and Profit: The Merchant in Medieval Europe* (New York, 2003), pp. 246–7; Nash, 'Pour couleurs', p. 142; Kirby, 'Price', pp. 22, 27; Helmut Schweppe and Heitz Roosen-Runge, 'Carmine – Cochineal Carmine and Kermes Carmine', in *Artists' Pigments I*, ed. Feller, pp. 255–61; Klaassen et al., 'Materials', p. 123 n. 109. One study has indicated that Rogier van der Weyden, however, used lakes derived from both plant and insect sources, and the same may be true of Memling's workshop. 'Materials and Techniques', pp. 75–8;
Poldi and Villa, 'New Technical', p. 89.

113 Rutherford J. Gettens and Elisabeth West Fitzhugh, 'Azurite and Blue Verditer', in *Artists' Pigments II*, ed. Roy, pp. 24–5; Kirby, 'Price', pp. 24–5; De Vos, *Complete Works*, pp. 382–3, 385 n. 31. It is found alongside the more abundant malachite, which, however, has not been detected in Flemish paint samples of the period, and Nash notes that no mention of malachite is found in pre-sixteenth-century documents or recipe books; reported samples from earlier decades were probably misidentifications. Nash, 'Pour couleurs', p. 150; Rutherford J. Gettens and Elisabeth West Fitzhugh, 'Malachite and Green Verditer', in *Artists' Pigments II*, ed Roy, pp. 183–5.

114 Campbell, 'Suppliers of Artists' Materials', p. 184.

115 Klaassen et al., 'Materials', pp. 109–12; Szmelter et al., 'Multi-Criterial', p. 242; Campbell, *Fifteenth Century*, pp. 354, 362.

116 DeLancey, 'Shipping', p. 79; Peter Spufford, 'Lapis, Indigo, Woad: Artists' Materials in the Context of International Trade

before 1700', in *Trade in Artists' Materials*, ed. Kirby, Nash and Cannon, p. 13.

117 Spufford, 'Lapis', pp. 11–12.

118 Van der Snickt et al., 'Material Analyses', p. 2223; Nash, 'Pour couleurs', pp. 125–6; Spufford, 'Lapis', pp. 11–13.

119 Nicholas Hilliard, the sixteenth-century English painter, noted this Venetian connection. Joyce Plesters, 'Ultramarine Blue, Natural and Artificial', in *Artists' Pigments II*, ed. Roy, pp. 37–8.

120 Nash, 'Pour couleurs', pp. 127–9, 130–31.

121 Spring, 'Technique', p. 214; Klaassen et al., 'Materials', pp. 109–11; De Vos, *Complete Works*, pp. 382–3, 385 n. 31; Szmelter et al., 'Multi-Criterial', p. 242; Campbell, *Fifteenth Century*, pp. 354, 362, 374.

122 Klaassen et al., 'Materials', p. 111; Van der Snickt et al., 'Material Analyses', p. 2222.

123 Spring, 'Technique', p. 217. While used in other contexts, we do not find in Memling work smalt, indigo, woad-based blue lake, orpiment or realgar.

124 Poldi and Villa, 'New Technical', p. 89; Klaassen et al., 'Materials', pp. 111–14.

125 Nash, 'Pour couleurs', pp. 119–23, 161–5.

126 Billinge et al., 'Methods and Materials', pp. 9, 13. For the Tournai statutes, particularly Article 44 on materials, see Alphonse Goovaerts, 'Les Ordonnances doneés en 1480, à Tournai, aux métiers des peintres et des verriers', *Compte-rendu des séances de la Commission royale d'histoire*, VI (1896), pp. 141–2, 178–80.

4 Memling and His Clientele

1 Maryan W. Ainsworth, 'Intentional Alterations of Early Netherlandish Paintings', *Metropolitan Museum Journal. Essays in Memory of John M. Brealey*, XL (2005), p. 58; Dirk De Vos, *Hans Memling: The Complete Works*, trans. Ted Alkins (Antwerp, Ghent and New York, 1994), p. 241.

2 Shirley Neilsen Blum, *Early Netherlandish Triptychs: A Study in Patronage* (Berkeley and Los Angeles, CA, 1969), p. 100; Barbara G. Lane, *Hans Memling: Master Painter in Fifteenth-Century Bruges* (London and Turnhout, 2009), pp. 138–9; De Vos, *Complete Works*, p. 241.

3 Blum, *Early Netherlandish Triptychs*, pp. 97–8, 156 n. 2. On Willem and his eighteen children, as well as early theories about Memling's works for the family, see William Henry James Weale, 'Genealogie

de la famille Moreel', *Le Beffroi: Art et littérature modernes*, II (1864–5), pp. 181–93.

4 Jelle Haemers, *For the Common Good: State Power and Urban Revolts in the Reign of Mary of Burgundy (1477–1482)* (Turnhout, 2009), pp. 81–2. His brother Lievin seems to have likewise dealt with finances for the Despars company and Italian clients. Albert Janssens, 'Willem Moreel en Hans Memling: Bijdrage tot het onderzoek naar de schilderijen van Memling in opdracht van de familie Moreel', *Handelingen van het Genootschap voor Geschiedenis 'Société d'Émulation' te Brugge*, CXL/1–2 (2003), p. 69.

5 Haemers, *Common Good*, p. 81.

6 Maximiliaan P. J. Martens, 'Artistic Patronage in Bruges Institutions, ca. 1440–1482', PhD diss., University of California, Santa Barbara, 1992, p. 296.

7 Haemers, *Common Good*, p. 80.

8 Ibid., pp. 82–6, 145. The others arrested were Maarten Lem and Jan van Nieuwenhove. This Jan van Nieuwenhove, son of Klaas, would in 1486 be banished for his support of the emperor, a fate preferable to that of his cousin, also named Jan but son of Michiel van Nieuwenhove (and brother of Maarten van Nieuwenhove, Memling's patron), who in 1488 would be executed.

9 Banished again by Maximilian and his supporters in late 1490, he was pardoned and returned to Bruges in 1493. Moreel remained financially well-off; in late 1490 he remained one of the forty wealthiest citizens from whom a loan was extracted to finance Bruges's reparations to Maximilian, and later Moreel would receive an additional income from Philip the Handsome. Haemers, *Common Good*, p. 81; Jelle Haemers, 'Factionalism and State Power in the Flemish Revolt (1482–1492)', *Journal of Social History*, XLII/4 (Summer 2009), pp. 1014–15; Janssens, 'Willem Moreel', p. 71; Blum, *Early Netherlandish Triptychs*, p. 98.

10 It is not known whether the inscription records the date of the commission or the installation of the work. De Vos, *Complete Works*, p. 131; Till-Holger Borchert et al., eds, *Memling's Portraits* (Ghent and Amsterdam, 2005), p. 168; Maximiliaan P. J. Martens, 'Het onderzoek naar de opdrachtgevers', in *'Om iets te weten van de oude meesters': De Vlaamse primitieven—herontdekking, waardering en onderzoek*, ed. Bernhard Ridderbos and Henk van Veen (Worcester, MA, 1995), p. 362.

11 Martens, 'Artistic Patronage', pp. 292–3. The year is 1485 by modern reckoning; this date in March would then have been understood as

1484, since it falls before Easter, and is consistent with the date on the frame of 1484 – probably indicating the date of commission.

12 Blum, *Early Netherlandish Triptychs*, p. 98.

13 Maximiliaan P. J. Martens, 'Hans Memling and His Patrons: A Cliometrical Approach', in *Memling Studies: Proceedings of the International Colloquium (Bruges, 10–12 November 1997)*, ed. Roger van Schoute, Maurits Smeyers and Hélène Verougstraete (Leuven, 1997), pp. 35–6. Dirk De Vos accepts 95 works from Memling's hand, while Barbara Lane culls the selection to 75. De Vos, *Complete Works*, pp. 74–338; Lane, *Hans Memling*, p. 115; Wim Blockmans, 'The Burgundian Court and the Urban Milieu as Patrons in 15th-Century Bruges', in *Economic History and the Arts*, ed. Michael North (Cologne and Vienna, 1996), pp. 23–4.

14 Lane, *Hans Memling*, p. 115.

15 Till-Holger Borchert, 'Memling – Life and Work', in *Memling's Portraits*, ed. Borchert et al., p. 34; Lane, *Hans Memling*, p. 117.

16 Possible copies of lost Memling originals are images depicting Antoine the Grand Bâtard of Burgundy; Jacques of Savoy, Count of Romont; and King Edward IV of England and his wife, Elizabeth Woodville. Lorne Campbell, 'Memling and the Netherlandish Portrait Tradition', in *Memling's Portraits*, ed. Borchert et al., pp. 55–6; Lorne Campbell, 'The *Donne Triptych*', in *Memling Studies*, ed. Schoute, Smeyers and Verougstraete, p. 71; Fedja Anzelewsky, 'An Unidentified Portrait of King Edward IV', *Burlington Magazine*, CIX/777 (December 1967), pp. 702–5; Blanche Bauchau, 'Jacques de Savoie: Historie d'un portrait et portrait historique', *Handelingen van de Koninklijke Kring voor Oudheidkunde, Letteren an Kunst van Mechelen*, XCV/2 (1991), pp. 117–46.

17 Jean C. Wilson, *Painting in Bruges at the Close of the Middle Ages: Studies in Society and Visual Culture* (University Park, PA, 1998), pp. 74, 83.

18 Ibid., pp. 43–61, 75–80.

19 Ibid., p. 61.

20 Martens, 'Artistic Patronage', pp. 240–45; Blockmans, 'Burgundian Court', p. 24.

21 Blockmans, 'Burgundian Court', p. 24. Maximiliaan Martens has ventured an analysis in terms of painted surface area: by square metreage, more than 31 per cent of his production was destined for the identifiably local market; 22 per cent for Spain (this number would need revision in light of recently discovered works in Soria); the Italian states 17 per cent; and other nationals almost 18 per cent

of known commissions. Less than 12 per cent of surface area of works remains for the half of his clients that remain impossible to place. Martens, 'Hans Memling', pp. 36–7; Borchert, 'Life and Work', p. 42.

22 Lane, *Hans Memling*, p. 118.

23 Lynn F. Jacobs, 'Strategies of Intimacy: Memling's *Triptych of Adriaan Reins*', in *The Primacy of the Image in Northern European Art, 1400–1700: Essays in Honor of Larry Silver*, ed. Debra Cashion, Henry Luttikhuizen and Ashley West (Boston, MA, and Leiden, 2017), pp. 3–15; Beth Williamson, 'Altarpieces, Liturgy, and Devotion', *Speculum*, LXXIX/2 (April 2004), pp. 377, 380–81.

24 Borchert et al., *Memling's Portraits*, pp. 36, 168; Cyriel Stroo, Pascale Syfer-d'Olne and Anne Dubois, *The Flemish Primitives*, vol. II: *The Dirk Bouts, Petrus Christus, Hans Memling and Hugo Van der Goes Groups Catalogue of Early Netherlandish Painting in the Royal Museums of Fine Arts of Belgium* (Brussels, 1999), pp. 210–11. See also Maximiliaan P. J. Martens, 'Some Reflections on the Social Function of Diptychs', in *Essays in Context: Unfolding the Netherlandish Diptych*, ed. John Oliver Hand and Ron Spronk (New Haven, CT, 2006), p. 87.

25 Douglas Brine, *Pious Memories: The Wall-Mounted Memorial in the Burgundian Netherlands* (Leiden and Boston, MA, 2015), p. 48.

26 Maryan W. Ainsworth and Keith Christiansen, eds, *From Van Eyck to Bruegel: Early Netherlandish Painting in the Metropolitan Museum of Art* (New York, 1998), p. 238.

27 Ibid., p. 162; Borchert et al., *Memling's Portraits*, p. 168; Lane, *Hans Memling*, pp. 295–6.

28 De Vos, *Complete Works*, pp. 312–14. Barbara Lane sees this as a piece by a workshop assistant. Lane, *Hans Memling*, pp. 327–8.

29 Recent arguments that the costume is Spanish rather than Italian are supported by Barbara Lane. Lane, *Hans Memling*, pp. 289–90, 290 n. 1; on the format of the work and the sitter's possible Spanish identity, see Colin T. Eisler, ed., *The Thyssen-Bornemisza Collection: Early Netherlandish Painting* (London, 1989), pp. 110–12.

30 A coat of arms on the reverse of the panel has been identified by some authors as that of the L'Espinette family of Franche-Comté, related to the Vautravers family, who were active at the court of Burgundy. Lorne Campbell has noted elsewhere that the L'Espinette family arms is nearly identical to that of the de Visen family, also stemming from Franche-Comté; he thus identifies this sitter as the courtier Charles de Visen (d. 1486) of Dijon, a *valet de chambre* and *sommelier de corps* to Charles the Bold (his father was also prominently

the Receiver General of Burgundy during Philip the Good's reign).
De Vos, *Complete Works*, p. 184; Lorne Campbell, '*Hans Memling, The Complete Works* by Dirk De Vos', *Burlington Magazine*, CXXXVII/1105 (April 1995), p. 254; Campbell, 'Netherlandish Portrait', p. 54; Borchert et al., *Memling's Portraits*, p. 171.

31 De Vos, *Complete Works*, p. 196; Lane, *Hans Memling*, p. 286.

32 De Vos, *Complete Works*, p. 200; Lane, *Hans Memling*, pp. 297–8.

33 Ainsworth and Christiansen, *From Van Eyck to Bruegel*, p. 69; Lane, *Hans Memling*, pp. 261–2, 296–7; Berthold Hinz, 'Studien zur Geschichte des Ehepaarbildnisses', *Marburger Jahrbuch für Kunstwissenschaft*, XIX (1974), pp. 142–67. On the latter pair, see De Vos, *Complete Works*, pp. 56, 115, 230. Bauman dates this pair to rather early in Memling's career. Guy Bauman, 'Early Flemish Portraits 1425–1525', *Metropolitan Museum of Art Bulletin* (Spring 1986), p. 34; Micheline Comblen-Sonkes and Philippe Lorentz, *Le Musée du Louvre, Paris: II*, Corpus de la peinture des Anciens Pays-Bas méridionaux et de la Principauté de Liège au quinzième siècle, 17 (Brussels, 1995), pp. 284, 286, 290.

34 Douglas Brine, 'Evidence for the Forms and Usage of Early Netherlandish Memorial Paintings', *Journal of the Warburg and Courtauld Institutes*, LXXI (2008), pp. 139, 145.

35 De Vos, *Complete Works*, pp. 124–5.

36 Argued by, among others, Bernhard Ridderbos and Molly Faries, 'Hans Memling's Last Judgement in Gdańsk', *Oud Holland*, CXXX/3–4 (2017), pp. 64–5.

37 Raymond de Roover, *The Rise and Decline of the Medici Bank, 1397–1494* (Cambridge, MA, and London, 1963), pp. 325, 338–9; Paula Nuttall, *From Flanders to Florence: The Impact of Netherlandish Painting, 1400–1500* (New Haven, CT, and London, 2004), p. 43.

38 Wilson, *Painting in Bruges*, pp. 75–7.

39 Borchert, 'Life and Work', pp. 22, 24–6; Nuttall, *From Flanders*, pp. 54–5; De Roover, *Rise and Decline*, pp. 338–9; De Vos, *Complete Works*, p. 88 n. 10.

40 Lane, *Hans Memling*, p. 132.

41 Nuttall, *From Flanders*, p. 57.

42 Barbara Lane, 'The Patron and the Pirate: The Mystery of Memling's Gdansk Last Judgment', *Art Bulletin*, LXXIII/4 (1991), pp. 633–8; Ridderbos and Faries, 'Last Judgement', p. 75.

43 Barbara Lane holds that the inclusion was made without Tani's approval. Lane, *Hans Memling*, pp. 278–9. Nuttall suggests that it was intended earlier but, not knowing when Tommaso would again be in

the city, Memling completed it in advance to add at a later moment in the process. Paula Nuttall, 'Memlinc's Last Judgement, Angelo Tani and the Florentine Colony at Bruges', in *Polish and English Responses to French Art and Architecture: Contrasts and Similarities*, ed. Francis Ames-Lewis (London, 1995), pp. 161–2; Nuttall, *From Flanders*, p. 59; Margaret L. Koster, 'New Documentation for the Portinari Altar-Piece', *Burlington Magazine*, CXLV/1200 (March 2003), pp. 169–70.

44 R. J. Walsh, *Charles the Bold and Italy, 1467–1477: Politics and Personnel* (Liverpool, 2005), p. 138; Nuttall, *From Flanders*, p. 45.

45 De Roover, *Rise and Decline*, pp. 319–20; Nuttall, *From Flanders*, p. 43. In the 1330s Andrea di Andrea Portinari had been present in Bruges as a representative of the Peruzzi and Bardi families. Marc Boone, 'Apologie d'un banquier médiéval: Tommaso Portinari et l'état Bourguignon', *Le Moyen âge*, CV/1 (1999), pp. 32–3.

46 De Roover, *Rise and Decline*, pp. 321–5, 340; Nuttall, *From Flanders*, pp. 70–71.

47 Boone, 'Apologie', p. 33; De Roover, *Rise and Decline*, pp. 319–21, 340; Susanne Franke, 'Between Status and Spiritual Salvation: The Portinari Triptych and Tommaso Portinari's Concern for His Memoria', *Simiolus: Netherlands Quarterly for the History of Art*, XXXIII/3 (2007), p. 123 n. 2; Walsh, *Charles the Bold*, p. 121.

48 Nuttall, *From Flanders*, p. 44; Walsh, *Charles the Bold*, pp. 121–2; Boone, 'Apologie', p. 33; Franke, 'Between Status', pp. 133–4; Campbell, 'Netherlandish Portrait', p. 49.

49 Walsh, *Charles the Bold*, pp. 120–53. On the Gravelines toll and papal alum monopoly efforts, see Boone, 'Apologie', pp. 38–47. Ainsworth and Christiansen, *From Van Eyck to Bruegel*, p. 162.

50 Peter Stabel, 'De gewenste vreemdeling: Italiaanse kooplieden en stedelijke maatschappij in het laat-middeleeuws Brugge', *Jaarboek voor middeleeuwse Geschiedenis*, IV (2001), p. 209.

51 Boone, 'Apologie', p. 52; De Roover, *Rise and Decline*, p. 357; Koster, 'New Documentation', p. 178.

52 Franke, 'Between Status', pp. 126–8; Nuttall, *From Flanders*, p. 51.

53 Franke, 'Between Status', pp. 123–5; Nuttall, *From Flanders*, pp. 45–7; De Roover, *Rise and Decline*, p. 355.

54 Franke, 'Between Status', pp. 124–30. By the time Portinari had Hugo's work shipped to Florence in 1483 he had run into financial trouble and had to borrow cash for its transport. Franke, 'Between Status', p. 141.

55 Blum, *Early Netherlandish Triptychs*, pp. 128–9.

56 Portinari and Baroncelli's identities are based on the sitters'
    resemblance to those in Hugo van der Goes's better-documented
    commission. De Vos, *Complete Works*, pp. 100–101.

57 Louis Alexander Waldman, 'New Documents for Memling's
    Portinari Portraits in the Metropolitan Museum of Art', *Apollo*,
    CLIII/468 (2001), p. 29.

58 With the later endowment at Sint-Jakobskerk in 1474 he may have
    intended to replace it with the *Altarpiece of the Nativity* by Hugo van
    der Goes, now in the Uffizi. Their portraits seem to Franke to be
    inflected with a sort of claim to Burgundian courtliness that would
    have been received closer to intention in Bruges than in Florence.
    Franke, 'Between Status', pp. 138–40; Nuttall, *From Flanders*, p. 69.
    Barbara Lane in 1991 suggested that Portinari intended the *Last
    Judgement* for the Sant'Egidio site, but following its piracy ordered
    the *Adoration* from Hugo van der Goes as a replacement. Lane,
    'Patron and the Pirate', p. 638.

59 Waldman, 'New Documents', pp. 29–30.

60 The small portraits of Tommaso and Maria appear to be based on
    the other portraits, which reveal a more complicated preparatory
    stage via infrared reflectography. De Vos, *Complete Works*, p. 108;
    Bauman, 'Early Flemish', p. 53.

61 De Vos, *Complete Works*, p. 109.

62 Nuttall, *From Flanders*, p. 64; De Vos, *Complete Works*, p. 109. Waldman
    suggests that it was retrieved by Francesco di Tommaso, Tommaso's
    son, and donated to Santa Maria Nuova. Waldman, 'New
    Documents', p. 30.

63 Elements reflected in Master of the Bruges Passion scenes around
    1515. If it were at the Franciscans, the relocation of the friars in 1518
    would have been an occasion for redecoration and the forwarding of
    the work to Florence. Franke, 'Between Status', pp. 137 n. 85, 138;
    Nuttall, *From Flanders*, p. 64.

64 Vida Hull, 'Spiritual Pilgrimage in the Paintings of Hans Memling',
    in *Art and Architecture of Late Medieval Pilgrimage in Northern Europe and the
    British Isles*, ed. Sarah Blick and Rita Tekippe, 2 vols (Leiden and
    Boston, MA, 2005), vol. I, pp. 32, 34; Lane, *Hans Memling*, p. 154.

65 Folco and Benedetto initially operated for the Medici branch in
    Milan under another uncle, Accerito. Borchert et al., *Memling's
    Portraits*, p. 174. Lodovico ordered a devotional portrait from the
    Bruges Master of the Legend of St Ursula in the same years. Nuttall,
    From Flanders, pp. 70–71.

66   Borchert et al., *Memling's Portraits*, p. 174. On the reverse of the lost
     portrait panel identified as Benedetto, Aby Warburg reported traces
     of an emblem of an oak tree with the motto *de bien en mieuls*, a device
     and variant of the motto found on the devotional triptych connected
     to Benedetto. De Vos, *Complete Works*, pp. 222–4.

67   The image of Folco is held in the Uffizi (Inv. 1101). Nuttall offers
     the possibility of Tommaso's cousins, the brothers Giovanni and
     Folco di Adoardo Portinari, also active in Bruges. Nuttall, *From
     Flanders*, p. 70; De Vos, *Complete Works*, pp. 284, 222–5; Borchert et al.,
     Memling's Portraits, p. 174.

68   Borchert et al., *Memling's Portraits*, p. 174; Nuttall, *From Flanders*, p. 71;
     De Vos, *Complete Works*, pp. 284–6.

69   Susanne Kress, 'Memlings Triptychon des Benedetto Portinari und
     Leonardos Mona Lisa: Zur Entwicklung des weiblichen
     Dreiviertelporträts im Florentiner Quattrocento', in *Porträt-
     Landschaft-Interieur: Jan van Eycks Rolin-Madonna im ästhetischen Kontext*, ed.
     Christiane Kruse and Felix Thürlemann (Tübingen, 1999), p. 226.
     Barbara Lane notes in support that Leonardo would have known
     the portrait panel of Benedetto's triptych and had personal
     correspondence with Benedetto. Lane, *Hans Memling*, p. 249.

70   Lorne Campbell, *The Fifteenth Century Netherlandish Schools*, National
     Gallery Catalogues (London, 1998), p. 367; Michael Rohlmann,
     'Memling's "Pagagnotti Triptych"', *Burlington Magazine*, CXXXVII/1108
     (July 1995), p. 444. On the reconstitution of the original triptych,
     see Didier Martens, 'Une Triptyque mutilé de Hans Memling',
     Gazette des beaux-arts Ser. 6, CXXIII (1994), pp. 5–9.

71   Rohlmann, 'Memling's "Pagagnotti Triptych"', p. 441; Paula Nuttall,
     'Memling and the European Renaissance Portrait', in *Memling's
     Portraits*, ed. Borchert et al., p. 70; Campbell, *Fifteenth Century*,
     pp. 367–8; Borchert, 'Life and Work', p. 34; Till-Holger Borchert,
     ed., *Memling: Rinascimiento Fiammingo* (Milan, 2014), p. 162;
     Paula Nuttall, 'Memling's Pagagnotti *Virgin and Child*: Italian
     Renaissance Sculpture Reimagined', *Sculpture Journal*, XXVI/1 (2017),
     p. 25.

72   Borchert, 'Life and Work', p. 34.

73   Campbell, *Fifteenth Century*, p. 366; Rohlmann, 'Memling's
     "Pagagnotti Triptych"', p. 441.

74   Rohlmann, 'Memling's "Pagagnotti Triptych"', p. 443; Campbell,
     Fifteenth Century, pp. 362, 369 n. 7; Ainsworth and Christiansen,
     From Van Eyck to Bruegel, p. 174.

75 Martens, 'Triptyque', pp. 1–2; Nuttall, 'Pagagnotti Virgin', esp.
    pp. 25–6, 29–32.

76 Martens, 'Triptyque', p. 4; Campbell, *Fifteenth Century*, p. 366; Michael
    Rohlmann, 'Zitate flämischer Landschaftsmotive in Florentiner
    Quattrocentromalerei', in *Italienische Frührenaissance und nordeuropäisches
    Spätmittelalter: Kunst der frühen Neuzeit im europaïschen Zusammenhang*,
    ed. Joachim Poeschke (Munich, 1993), pp. 244–5; Borchert,
    Rinascimiento, p. 162; Lane, *Hans Memling*, p. 203.

77 Mary Sprinson de Jesús, 'Hans Memling', in *From Van Eyck to Bruegel*,
    ed. Ainsworth and Christiansen, p. 166; Lorne Campbell, 'Memlinc
    and the Followers of Verrocchio', *Burlington Magazine*, CXXV/968
    (November 1983), pp. 675–6; Borchert et al., *Memling's Portraits*,
    pp. 161, 165; Ainsworth and Christiansen, *From Van Eyck to Bruegel*,
    p. 166; Ainsworth, 'Intentional Alterations', pp. 51, 54; Nuttall,
    From Flanders, pp. 69–70; De Vos, *Complete Works*, pp. 192, 194.

78 Barbara G. Lane, 'Memling and the Workshop of Verrocchio', in
    La peinture dans les Pays-Bas au 16e siècle, ed. Hélène Verougstraete, Roger
    van Schoute and Anne Dubois (Leuven, 1999), p. 245. His influence
    on Italian painters and artistic trends has been well considered by
    scholars in recent years. Among the broader surveys: Nuttall, *From
    Flanders*, pp. 133–252; Paula Nuttall, 'Memling e la pittura italiana', in
    Rinascimiento, ed. Borchert, pp. 38–51; Michael Rohlmann, 'Memling
    und Italien: Flämische malerei für die Bologneser Familie Loiani',
    in *Memling Studies*, ed. Van Schoute, Smeyers and Verougstraete,
    pp. 91–104.

79 See, for example, Lane, 'Workshop of Verrocchio', pp. 243–50;
    Rohlmann, 'Zitate flämischer Landschaftsmotive', esp. pp. 244–5;
    Nuttall, *From Flanders*, pp. 133–252; Keith Christiansen, 'The View
    from Italy', in *From Van Eyck to Bruegel*, ed. Ainsworth and
    Christiansen, p. 55; Lane, *Hans Memling*, pp. 226–342.

80 Margaret L. Koster, 'Reconsidering "St Catherine of Bologna
    with Three Donors" by the Baroncelli Master of Bruges', *Simiolus:
    Netherlands Quarterly for the History of Art*, XXVI/1–2 (1998), p. 8 n. 23;
    Federica Veratelli, 'I tratti del potere: I clienti italiani di Hans
    Memling', in *Rinascimiento*, ed. Borchert, p. 65 n. 84; Rohlmann,
    'Memling und Italien', pp. 95–9. In addition to this work and the
    Baroncelli Master's work discussed by Koster, a third Netherlandish
    work is tied to the family, a Deposition triptych preserved at the
    Palazzo Durazzo Pallavacini in Genoa. Koster, 'Catherine', pp. 5–17,
    esp. 7–9.

81 Lane, *Hans Memling*, pp. 249, 331–2; De Vos, *Complete Works*, pp. 245–7;
    Rohlmann, 'Memling und Italien', pp. 95–9; Borchert, *Rinascimiento*,
    p. 158. Neither Lorne Campbell nor Barbara Lane favour this
    assignment to Memling. Campbell, '*Hans Memling, The Complete Works*',
    p. 253.

82 The palm and laurel as emblems of Bernardo Bembo were noted
    by Dirk De Vos, drawing attention to Fletcher's work. De Vos,
    Complete Works, p. 190 n. 2; Jennifer Fletcher, 'Bernardo Bembo
    and Leonardo's Portrait of Ginevra de' Benci', *Burlington Magazine*,
    CXXXI/1041 (December 1989), p. 811.

83 Fletcher, 'Bembo', pp. 814–15; Borchert et al., *Memling's Portraits*,
    p. 160; Peter Eikemeier, ed., *Hans Memling: Johannes und Veronika:
    Meditationsbilder aus dem späten Mittelalter* (Munich, 1995), p. 6.

84 Lorne Campbell, 'Notes on Netherlandish Pictures in the Veneto
    in the Fifteenth and Sixteenth Centuries', *Burlington Magazine*,
    CXXIII/941 (August 1981), p. 471; John Oliver Hand, Catherine
    A. Metzger and Ron Spronk, eds, *Prayers and Portraits: Unfolding the
    Netherlandish Diptych* (New Haven, CT, and London, 2006), p. 175;
    De Vos, *Complete Works*, p. 205; Borchert et al., *Memling's Portraits*,
    p. 160; Eikemeier, *Johannes und Veronika*, p. 6 n. 9.

85 Nuttall, 'European Renaissance Portrait', p. 73; Nuttall, 'Pittura
    italiana', p. 42; De Vos, *Complete Works*, p. 190; Kenneth Bruce
    McFarlane, *Hans Memling* (Oxford, 1971), pp. 14–15.

86 Borchert et al., *Memling's Portraits*, p. 160; for a discussion of Bembo's
    emblems in the context of Leonardo's portrait of Ginevra de' Benci,
    see Fletcher, 'Bembo', pp. 811–12, 816.

87 Fletcher, 'Bembo', pp. 816, 816 n. 50.

88 Anna Muntada Torrellas, 'Unas ignotas tablas de Hans Memling
    en Almazán: A propósito de la investigación para "Pajsaje interior"',
    in *Jornadas de Estudio y Difusión del Patrimonio*, ed. Bango Torviso and
    Isidro Gonzalo (Soria, 2010), pp. 235–62; Borchert, *Rinascimiento*,
    p. 170.

89 Alicia Yela Yela, 'La Casa de Almazán', in *Damas de la Casa de Mendoza:
    Historias, leyendas y olvidos*, ed. Esther Alegre Carvajal (Madrid, 2014),
    p. 712; Muntada Torrellas, 'Ignotas tablas', p. 261.

90 Additionally, in 1496 the city would become the stable court of Prince
    Juan when he reached eighteen and preparations for his marriage to
    Margaret commenced (a wedding diplomatically engineered in part
    by Francisco de Rojas). Muntada Torrellas, 'Ignotas tablas', p. 258;
    Yela Yela, 'Casa de Almazán', pp. 707–8, 710–11.

91 De Vos, *Complete Works*, pp. 56–7.

92 Bart Fransen and Louise Longneaux, 'Hans Memling's Altarpiece of the Benedictine Abbey Church of Nájera', in *Harmony in Bright Colours: Memling's God the Father with Singing and Music-Making Angels Restored*, ed. Lizet Klaassen and Dieter Lampens (Brussels, 2021), pp. 39, 51 n. 48; Lane, *Hans Memling*, pp. 102–3; Marie Postec and Lizet Klaassen, 'The Frames and Framing of Memling's Nájera Panels', in *Harmony in Bright Colours*, ed. Klaassen and Lampens, pp. 134–5.

93 Bart Fransen, 'Hans Memling's Nájera Altarpiece: New Documentary Evidence', *Burlington Magazine*, CLX/1379 (February 2018), pp. 101–5; Fransen and Longneaux, 'Hans Memling's Altarpiece', pp. 35–7; Martens, 'Hans Memling', p. 38 n. 11; De Vos, *Complete Works*, p. 56.

94 A connection to Memling's workshop of this panel is very tentative: some overpainting has recently been removed and technical examination in the future is likely to reveal much about this work. Dirk De Vos's catalogue includes a fragment that may have belonged to the same larger work; Barbara Lane finds the smaller fragment in particular too problematic to attribute safely to Memling. Rojas commissioned at least one Flemish-produced manuscript. De Vos, *Complete Works*, p. 78; Lane, *Hans Memling*, p. 323; Muntada Torrellas, 'Ignotas tablas', pp. 259–60.

95 A preliminary alliance was engineered in Antwerp in 1495; Rojas had his arms included in the manuscript marriage agreements, and he would serve as the representative of Prince Juan at the proxy wedding in Mechelen in 1497. Muntada Torrellas, 'Ignotas tablas', pp. 259–60; Yela Yela, 'Casa de Almazán', p. 708.

96 De Vos, *Complete Works*, p. 54; Blum, *Early Netherlandish Triptychs*, p. 103.

97 To St Mary in Lübeck they donated a *Mass of Saint Gregory* attributed to Berndt Notke and a Passion diptych by Herman Rode (both destroyed in 1942). Peter G. Bietenholz and Thomas Brian Deutscher, *Contemporaries of Erasmus: A Biographical Register of the Renaissance and Reformation* (Toronto, 2003), vol. II, p. 128.

98 The Master of the Lucy Legend or the workshop of Memling itself produced a large altarpiece of uneven quality with the same polyptych format for a Baltic, Livonian destination in Reval/Tallinn. Max Hasse, 'Der Lübecker Passionsaltar Hans Memlings', *Der Wagen: Ein Lübecksches Jahrbuch* (1958), pp. 38–40; De Vos, *Complete Works*, pp. 54–5; Anu Mänd, 'The Altarpiece of the Virgin Mary of the

Confraternity of the Black Heads in Tallinn: Dating, Donors, and
the Double Intercession', *Acta Historiae Artium Balticae*, II (2007),
pp. 35–53. The altarpiece has been attributed directly to Memling's
workshop (with the Master of the Lucy Legend as a possible
assistant, as well as the hand of Michael Sittow) by Maiste, who
draws attention to early attributions to Memling. Juhan Maiste,
'Artistic Genius Versus the Hanse Canon from the Late Middle
Ages to the Early Modern Age in Tallinn', *Baltic Journal of Art History*,
xx (2020), pp. 59–80.

99 Campbell, *Fifteenth Century*, pp. 381–91; Campbell, 'The *Donne
Triptych*', pp. 77–80; McFarlane, *Hans Memling*, pp. 1–10; Borchert,
'Life and Work', p. 32; De Vos, *Complete Works*, p. 182.

100 Ingrid Falque, *Devotional Portraiture and Spiritual Experience in Early
Netherlandish Painting: Catalog* (Leiden and Boston, MA, 2019), p. 1477;
Campbell, 'The *Donne Triptych*', p. 73.

101 Campbell, *Fifteenth Century*, p. 382. The year 1483 would be the latest
possible date for the work, since both sitters wear the Yorkist collar
badge of Edward IV. Campbell notes that Donne's parents were
permitted to use a portable altar, and John Donne himself probably
had chapels at his properties; the work may indeed have been
intended for private use. Campbell, *Fifteenth Century*, pp. 384–7;
Campbell, 'The *Donne Triptych*', pp. 71–3, 75–6; Borchert, 'Life and
Work', p. 25; McFarlane, *Hans Memling*, pp. 9–11.

102 De Vos, *Complete Works*, p. 131; Lane, *Hans Memling*, p. 271. A half-
length Virgin and Child in London matches the requisite
dimensions, but may simply suggest that Memling used standard
panel sizes. Stroo, Syfer-d'Olne and Dubois, *Flemish Primitives*,
pp. 209–10; Campbell, *Fifteenth Century*, p. 360.

103 Willem's arms are found on the reverse of the panel depicting
Barbara, and vice versa. Dirk De Vos, D. Marechal and Willy Le
Loup, *Hans Memling: Catalogue* (Brussels, 1994), p. 57; Borchert et al.,
Memling's Portraits, p. 168. If all three panels were the same size, the
wings might have been closed over one another successively so that
Willem's arms would be visible in the closed state (accounting for
the worn condition of that panel). Lane, *Hans Memling*, p. 271.

104 The identification of du Cellier as the donor is not universally
accepted. Discussed in Comblen-Sonkes and Lorentz, *Le Musée du
Louvre, Paris: II*, pp. 267–8.

105 De Vos, *Complete Works*, pp. 234–7; Lane, *Hans Memling*, p. 308;
Comblen-Sonkes and Lorentz, *Le Musée du Louvre, Paris: II*, p. 265.

106 Albert Janssens, 'Jan du Chelier (1446/47–1492), opdrachtgever van Hans Memling?', *Handelingen Genootschap 'Société d'Émulation' Brugge*, CXXXVIII (2001), pp. 212–13; Maximiliaan P. J. Martens and Hans J. van Miegroet, 'Nieuwe inzichten omtrent de omstreden du Cellier-diptiek, toegeschreven aan Hans Memling', *Gentse bijdragen tot de kunstgeschiedenis en oudheidkunde*, XXVI (1984), p. 66. Lane suggests that the arms, painted later, may have been copied from a lost frame. Lane, *Hans Memling*, p. 308.

107 Falque, *Devotional*, p. 456. The quartered arms on Jan du Cellier's cape in Memling's diptych indicate the du Cellier, Woestijne, Gruuthuse and Van der Aa families. Martens and Miegroet, 'Nieuwe inzichten', p. 66.

108 Du Cellier rented a plot in the spice hall in 1473–89 (next to that of Willem Moreel until 1484). Martens and Miegroet, 'Nieuwe inzichten', pp. 70–71; Janssens, 'Jan du Chelier', pp. 201, 208.

109 Janssens, 'Jan du Chelier', pp. 200–204. He figures among the comfortably off citizens in the forced-loan lists. Du Cellier's income seems to have remained relatively high, since he appears in the 1487, 1488 and 1490 lists. In the 1480/81 loan the spice merchants collectively paid a disproportionately large sum, among some of the more prosperous merchants; he, however, appears in the lower middle of this pack.

110 Martens and Miegroet, 'Nieuwe inzichten', pp. 70, 86; Janssens, 'Jan du Chelier', pp. 209–10. In that Anne does not appear in the triptych, De Vos suggests that it was commissioned after her death, although Comblen-Sonkes and Lorenz do not see Jan's solo appearance as evidence of her death. De Vos, *Complete Works*, p. 44; Comblen-Sonkes and Lorentz, *Le Musée du Louvre, Paris:* II, p. 278.

111 Lane, *Hans Memling*, pp. 302–3; Philippe Lorentz, 'La localisation originelle de la *Vierge dite de Jacques Floreins*, par Hans Memling, Paris, Louvre', in *Memling Studies*, ed. Van Schoute, Smeyers and Verougstraete, pp. 81–2; Stadarchief Brugge, *Poortersboeken* (130) 1454–78, f. 69.

112 Francisco de Quintanadueñas was installed at Bruges, perhaps representing the Burgos company operated by his brothers, and married a local woman there; the union between Floreins and his spouse may have been similarly strategic. Lorentz, 'Localisation', pp. 86–8; Comblen-Sonkes and Lorentz, *Le Musée du Louvre, Paris:* II, pp. 250–51.

113 Lorentz, 'Localisation', pp. 81–2; Lane, *Hans Memling*, pp. 302–3, 303 n. 5; Comblen-Sonkes and Lorentz, *Le Musée du Louvre, Paris: II*, p. 250.

114 Lorentz, 'Localisation', p. 88; Comblen-Sonkes and Lorentz, *Le Musée du Louvre, Paris: II*, pp. 252–5.

115 De Vos, *Complete Works*, pp. 279–80; Lane, *Hans Memling*, p. 267.

116 Wilson, *Painting in Bruges*, p. 83.

117 Martens, 'Artistic Patronage', p. 309; Frederik Buylaert, 'Lordship, Urbanization and Social Change in Late Medieval Flanders', *Past and Present*, CXXVII (May 2015), p. 60.

118 Buylaert, 'Lordship, Urbanization', pp. 63–4.

119 Wilson, *Painting in Bruges*, pp. 51–2.

120 Jelle Haemers, *De strijd om het regentschap over Filips de Schone: Opstand, facties en geweld in Brugge, Gent en Ieper (1482–1488)* (Ghent, 2014), pp. 224–5, 224 n. 854.

121 After two failed attempts by the executioner, Jan, seated in a chair on account of fatigue, was decapitated. Nicolaas Despars, *Cronijcke van den Lande ende Graefscepe van Vlaenderen*, 2nd edn, ed. J. de Jonghe (Bruges and Rotterdam, 1840), vol. IV, p. 364; Charles Louis Carton, ed., *Het boeck van al 't gene datter gheschiedt is binnen Brugghe, sichtent jaer 1477, 14 februarii, tot 1491* (Ghent, 1859), p. 197.

122 De Vos, *Complete Works*, pp. 279, 282 n. 4; Haemers, *De strijd*, p. 224 n. 854. His son and his grandson (both named Jan) would serve as heads of the Sint-Juliaansgasthuis, whose guardians were appointed by the city.

123 Martens, 'Artistic Patronage', pp. 226–7; Bauman, 'Early Flemish', pp. 24–5; Wilson, *Painting in Bruges*, p. 83. The diptych appears to have belonged to his family for a long time, so Bauman has suggested that it was not destined originally for a church setting but for private domestic use; it is possible that Jan's son's widow donated it to the Sint-Juliaansgasthuis. Bauman, 'Early Flemish', p. 49; Vida Hull, *Hans Memlinc's Paintings for the Hospital of St John in Bruges* (New York and London, 1981), p. 227.

124 De Vos, *Complete Works*, pp. 42–3.

125 William Henry James Weale, 'Inventaire du Mobilier de la Corporation des Tanneurs', *Le Beffroi: Art et littérature modernes*, II (1864–5), p. 265; Martens, 'Onderzoek', p. 353. An inventory compiled in 1480 notes a panel on the topic of Mary donated in the year 1479 'before Easter' by Pieter Bultinc, with the same stipulation that masses include a *Misere mei Deus* and *De profundis*. De Vos, *Complete Works*, pp. 42–3, 178–9, 409.

126 Haemers, *Common Good*, pp. 87, 141–2, 174–5, 185 n. 232.

127 De Vos, *Complete Works*, p. 36.

128 Van Buren has suggested that Marie Vrelant may be associated
with the provisional name of the Master of the Vraie Cronicque
Descoce, one of Vrelant's assistants. Anne Hagopian van Buren,
'Willem Vrelant: Questions and Issues', *Belgisch Tijdscrift voor
Oudheidkunde en Kunstgeschiedenis*, LXVIII (1999), pp. 24–6.

129 William Henry James Weale, 'Documents authentiques concernant
la vie, la famille et la position sociale de Jean Memlinc découverts
à Bruges', *Journal des Beaux-Arts et de la littérature*, III/7 (April 1861),
pp. 53–4; Martens, 'Artistic Patronage', pp. 330–33; M. Goetinck
and Marc Ryckaert, 'Hans Memling (°ca. 1433–†1494): Brugse
archivalia betreffende Hans Memling', in *Sint-Janshospitaal Brugge
1188/1976* (Bruges, 1976), p. 495; Albert Schouteet, 'Inventaris
van het archief van het voormalige gild van de librariers en van
de verening van schoolmeesters te Brugge', *Handelingen van het
Genootschap voor Geschiedenis 'Société d'Émulation' te Brugge*, C/1–3 (1963),
p. 244; transcribed in De Vos, *Complete Works*, p. 408.

130 Borchert, 'Life and Work', p. 20; Noël Geirnaert, 'Johannes Crabbe,
Abbot of Ter Duinen, 1457–88', in *Hans Memling: Portraiture, Piety,
and a Reunited Altarpiece*, ed. John Marciari (London, 2016), p. 63;
Noël Geirnaert, 'Le *Triptyque de la Crucifixion* de Hans Memling
pour Jean Crabbe, abbé de l'abbaye des Dunes, 1457–1488:
témoignage des documents contemporains', in *Memling Studies*, ed.
Van Schoute, Smeyers and Verougstraete, p. 29; Willem de Winter
served as an alderman in Hulst for several terms. Maximiliaan
Martens suggests that as an abbey altarpiece these identifications
are difficult to justify. Martens, 'Artistic Patronage', p. 355.

131 Geirnaert, 'Johannes Crabbe', pp. 63–7.

132 Perhaps commissioned on the occasion of the fifteenth anniversary
of Crabbe's position in 1472, a date that is argued by Dirk De Vos
on stylistic grounds. De Vos, *Complete Works*, pp. 90–92.

133 Geirnaert, 'Johannes Crabbe', p. 67; De Vos, *Complete Works*, p. 90.

134 Maximiliaan P. J. Martens, 'Patronage and Politics: Hans Memling's
St John Altarpiece and the Process of Burgundization', in *Le dessin
sous-jacent dans le processus de création*, ed. Hélène Verougstraete and
Roger van Schoute (Louvain-la-Neuve, 1995), pp. 170–71; Hull,
Hans Memlinc's Paintings, pp. 37–40.

135 Blum, *Early Netherlandish Triptychs*, pp. 87–8; Hull, *Hans Memlinc's
Paintings*, pp. 53–6.

136 De Vos, *Complete Works*, p. 156; Blum, *Early Netherlandish Triptychs*, p. 89; Hull, *Hans Memlinc's Paintings*, p. 58.

137 Hull, *Hans Memlinc's Paintings*, pp. 29–31. Hull describes the fraught career of Floreins as master (ibid., pp. 55, 93–7).

138 James Weale posited that the figure behind Jan was his brother Jacob, but offered no reasoning. Lane, *Hans Memling*, pp. 186–90; De Vos, *Complete Works*, pp. 158–61.

139 The inscription on his small triptych reads *Dit Werck dede maker Broeder Ian Floreins alias Vander Rijst*. Similarly, in letters to the burgomaster of Bruges (part of a campaign in which he pled for city assistance with the troubled community), Floreins is described as an 'homme de bonne famille, isu du sang et de la parente de Monsieur de Cambray'. De Vos, *Complete Works*, p. 160; Borchert, 'Life and Work', p. 33; Hull, *Hans Memlinc's Paintings*, pp. 93–5.

140 Adriaan Reins, another brother of this hospital, commissioned a small triptych; both triptychs may have been installed on side altars in the church of the hospital. De Vos, *Complete Works*, pp. 170, 172; Lane, *Hans Memling*, pp. 172, 187–90; Hull, *Hans Memlinc's Paintings*, pp. 43, 115, 143–2; Jacobs, 'Strategies', pp. 6–7.

Conclusion

1 The following description combines details found in a number of accounts: Auguste Dufour and Françoise Rabout, 'Description inédite des fêtes célébrées à Bruges en 1468 à l'occasion du mariage du duc Charles-le-Téméraire avec Marguerite d'York', *Mémoires de la Commission des Antiquités du Département de la Côte-d'Or*, IX (1877), pp. 311–52; Nicolaas Despars, *Cronijcke van den Lande ende Graefscepe van Vlaenderen*, 2nd edn, ed. J. de Jonghe (Bruges and Rotterdam, 1840), vol. IV, pp. 23–31; *Dits die Excellente Chronijcke van Vlaenderen* (Antwerp, 1531), ff. C.xxxvij.r–C.xxxviij.v.

2 Despars, *Cronijcke*, pp. 26–9.

3 Ibid., pp. 23–31; *Excellente Chronijcke*, ff. C.xxxvij.r–C.xxxviij.v; Dufour and Rabout, 'Description', pp. 322–3.

4 Charles Louis Carton, ed., *Het boeck van al 't gene datter gheschiedt is binnen Brugghe, sichtent jaer 1477, 14 februarii, tot 1491* (Ghent, 1859), p. 170.

5 Jelle Haemers, *De strijd om het regentschap over Filips de Schone: Opstand, facties en geweld in Brugge, Gent en Ieper (1482–1488)* (Ghent, 2014), p. 258.

6 Ibid., pp. 259–61.

7 Albert Janssens, 'De schilder Hans Memling: Als Brugs poorter financieel, sociaal en politiek doorgelicht', *Handelingen van het Genootschap voor Geschiedenis 'Société d'Émulation' te Brugge*, CXXXIV/1 (1997), pp. 86–9.

8 Haemers, *De strijd*, pp. 259–60.

9 Ibid., pp. 177–8, 252–3; Despars, *Cronijcke*, pp. 324–5.

10 Haemers, *De strijd*, p. 254; Carton, *Het boeck*, pp. 180–81.

11 Joseph Marechal, 'Le départ de Bruges des marchands étrangers', *Handelingen van het Genootschap voor Geschiedenis*, LXXXVIII (1951), pp. 27–8; Raymond van Uytven, 'Stages of Economic Decline: Late Medieval Bruges', in *Peasants and Townsmen in Medieval Europe: Studia in honorem Adriaan Verhulst*, ed. Jean-Marie Duvosquel and Erik Thoen (Ghent, 1995), p. 262.

12 Van Uytven, 'Stages', p. 260.

13 Wim Blockmans, 'Bruges and France', in *Bruges and Europe*, ed. Valentin Vermeersch (Antwerp, 1992), pp. 220–21; Van Uytven, 'Stages', p. 262.

14 Hugo Soly, *Capital at Work in Antwerp's Golden Age* (Turnhout, 2021), p. 29; J. T. Bolton and Francesco Guido Bruscoli, 'When Did Antwerp Replace Bruges as the Commercial and Financial Centre of North-Western Europe? The Evidence of the Borromei Ledger for 1438', *Economic History Review*, LXI/2 (May 2008), pp. 360–79.

15 Oscar Gelderblom, 'The Decline of Fairs and Merchant Guilds in the Low Countries, 1250–1650', *Jaarboek voor middeleeuwse Geschiedenis*, VII (2004), pp. 21–3.

16 Marc Ryckaert, *Brugge: Historische Stedenatlas van België*, ed. Adriaan Verhust and Jean-Marie Duvosquel (Brussels, 1991), p. 107; Joseph Marechal, 'Le colonie espagnole de Bruges, du XIVe au XVIe siècle', in *Europese aanwezigheid te Brugge: De vreemde kolonies (XIVde–XIXde eeuw)* (Bruges, 1985), pp. 93, 104–5, 115; J. A. Van Houtte, 'The Rise and Decline of the Market of Bruges', *Economic History Review*, XIX/1 (1966), pp. 45–6; John H. A. Munro, 'Bruges and the Abortive Staple in English Cloth', in *Textiles, Towns and Trade: Essays in the Economic History of Late-Medieval England and the Low Countries* (Aldershot and Brookfield, 1994), pp. 1149–59.

17 Van Houtte, 'Rise and Decline', pp. 45–6.

18 Van Uytven, 'Stages', p. 262.

19 Joey De Keyser, 'De visie van vreemdelingen op de verschuiving van het commerciële zwaartepunt van Brugge naar Antwerpen

(14de–16de eeuw)', *Handelingen van het Genootschap voor Geschiedenis*, CXLVI/2 (2009), pp. 279–83; Van Uytven, 'Stages', pp. 262–3.

20 Maximilian P. J. Martens, 'The Dialogue between Artistic Tradition and Renewal', in *Bruges and the Renaissance: Memling to Pourbus*, ed. Maximiliaan P. J. Martens, Paul Huvenne and Maryan Wynn Ainsworth (Brussels, 1998), p. 45.

21 Till-Holger Borchert, 'Adriaen Isenbrant', in *Bruges and the Renaissance*, ed. Martens, Huvenne and Ainsworth, p. 120.

22 Dominique Marechal, 'The Disapora of the Bruges Renaissance', in *Bruges and the Renaissance*, ed. Martens, Huvenne and Ainsworth, p. 64.

SELECT BIBLIOGRAPHY

Ainsworth, Maryan W., and Keith Christiansen, eds, *From Van Eyck to Bruegel: Early Netherlandish Painting in the Metropolitan Museum of Art* (New York, 1998), especially 'The Business of Art: Patrons, Clients, and the Art Markets', pp. 23–37

Battenberg, Friedrich, 'Zeit und Umwelt des Malers Hans Memling aus Seligenstadt. Zur Situation des Reichs und Flanderns im Spätmittelalter', *Archiv für hessische Geschichte und Altertumskunde* NF, XLVI (1988), pp. 11–72

Blockmans, Wim, 'The Creative Environment: Incentives to and Functions of Bruges Art Production', in *Petrus Christus in Renaissance Bruges: An Interdisciplinary Approach*, ed. Maryan W. Ainsworth (New York and Turnhout, 1995), pp. 11–20

—, and Walter Prevenier, *The Promised Lands: The Low Countries under Burgundian Rule, 1369–1530*, trans. Elizabeth Fackelman and Edward Peters (Philadelphia, PA, 1999)

Blum, Shirley Neilsen, *Early Netherlandish Triptychs: A Study in Patronage* (Berkeley and Los Angeles, CA, 1969)

Borchert, Till-Holger, ed., *Memling: Rinascimiento Fiammingo* (Milan, 2014)

—, et al., eds, *Memling's Portraits* (Ghent and Amsterdam, 2005)

Brown, Andrew, and Jan Dumolyn, eds, *Medieval Bruges, c. 850–1550* (Cambridge and New York, 2018)

Brulez, Wilfred, 'Bruges and Antwerp in the 15th and 16th Centuries: An Antithesis?', in *Acta Historiae Neerlandicae/Studies on the History of the Netherlands* VI, ed. Wilfred Brulez et al. (Dordrecht, 1973), pp. 1–26

Campbell, Lorne, *Renaissance Portraits: European Portrait Painting in the 14th, 15th and 16th Centuries* (New Haven, CT, and London, 1990)

De Roover, Raymond, *Money, Banking and Credit in Medieval Bruges:
    Italian Merchant-Bankers, Lombards, and Money-Changers: A Study in the
    Origins of Banking* (London and New York, 1999)
De Vos, Dirk, *Hans Memling: The Complete Works*, trans. Ted Alkins
    (Antwerp, Ghent and New York, 1994)
—, and Maryan W. Ainsworth, eds, *Hans Memling: Essays* (Ghent, 1994)
Geirnaert, Noël, 'Hans Memling, lid van het schildersambacht en
    poorter van Brugge, 1465', in *Bedenkingen vanuit het Stadsarchief van Brugge*
    (Bruges, 2017), pp. 9–17
Haemers, Jelle, *For the Common Good: State Power and Urban Revolts in the Reign
    of Mary of Burgundy (1477–1482)* (Turnhout, 2009)
Hand, John Oliver, Catherine A. Metzger and Ron Spronk, eds, *Prayers
    and Portraits: Unfolding the Netherlandish Diptych* (New Haven, CT, and
    London, 2006)
Hull, Vida, *Hans Memlinc's Paintings for the Hospital of St John in Bruges*
    (New York and London, 1981)
Janssens, Albert, 'De schilder Hans Memling: Als Brugs poorter
    financieel, sociaal en politiek doorgelicht', *Handelingen van het
    Genootschap voor Geschiedenis 'Société d'Émulation' te Brugge*, CXXXIV (1997),
    pp. 65–89
—, 'Jan du Chelier (1446/47–1492), opdrachtgever van Hans Memling?',
    Handelingen Genootschap 'Société d'Émulation' Brugge, CXXXVIII (2001),
    pp. 197–234
—, 'Willem Moreel en Hans Memling: Bijdrage tot het onderzoek naar
    de schilderijen van Memling in opdracht van de familie Moreel',
    *Handelingen van het Genootschap voor Geschiedenis 'Société d'Émulation' te
    Brugge*, CXL (2003), pp. 66–110
Kirby, Jo, Susie Nash and Joanna Cannon, eds, *Trade in Artists' Materials:
    Markets and Commerce in Europe to 1700* (London, 2010)
Klaassen, Lizet, and Dieter Lampens, eds, *Harmony in Bright Colours:
    Memling's God the Father with Singing and Music-Making Angels Restored*
    (Brussels, 2021)
Lane, Barbara G., 'The Patron and the Pirate: The Mystery of Memling's
    Gdansk Last Judgment', *Art Bulletin*, LXXIII/4 (1991), pp. 623–40
—, *Hans Memling: Master Painter in Fifteenth-Century Bruges* (London and
    Turnhout, 2009)
Lobelle-Caluwé, Hilde, 'Hans Memling, het succes van een kunstenaar',
    Openbaar Kunstbezit in Vlaanderen, II (1994), pp. 43–80
Loersch, Hugo, 'Hans Memling's Heimath und Todestag', *Zeitschrift für
    christliche Kunst*, II (1889), pp. 299–304

Martens, Maximiliaan P. J., 'Artistic Patronage in Bruges Institutions,
    ca. 1440–1482', PhD diss., University of California, Santa Barbara,
    1992
—, 'Patronage and Politics: Hans Memling's St John Altarpiece and
    the Process of Burgundization', in *Le dessin sous-jacent dans le processus
    de création,* ed. Hélène Verougstraete and Roger van Schoute
    (Louvain-la-Neuve, 1995), pp. 169–76
—, Paul Huvenne and Maryan Wynn Ainsworth, *Bruges and the Renaissance:
    Memling to Pourbus* (Brussels, 1998)
Murray, James M., *Bruges, Cradle of Capitalism, 1280–1390* (Cambridge, 2005)
Nuttall, Paula, 'Memlinc's Last Judgement, Angelo Tani and the
    Florentine Colony at Bruges', in *Polish and English Responses to French
    Art and Architecture: Contrasts and Similarities,* ed. Francis Ames-Lewis
    (London, 1995), pp. 155–65
—, *From Flanders to Florence: The Impact of Netherlandish Painting, 1400–1500*
    (New Haven, CT, and London, 2004)
Prevenier, Walter, Willem Pieter Blockmans and An Blockmans-Delva,
    The Burgundian Netherlands (Cambridge and New York, 1986)
Rohlmann, Michael, 'Memling's "Pagagnotti Triptych"', *Burlington
    Magazine,* CXXXVII/1108 (July 1995), pp. 438–5
Ryckaert, Marc, et al., *Brugge: De geschiedenis van een Europese stad* (Tielt,
    1999)
Van Houtte, J. A., 'The Rise and Decline of the Market of Bruges',
    Economic History Review, XIX/1 (1966), pp. 29–47
Van Schoute, Roger, Maurits Smeyers and Hélène Verougstraete,
    eds, *Memling Studies: Proceedings of the International Colloquium (Bruges,
    10–12 November 1994)* (Leuven, 1997)
Van Uytven, Raymond, 'Stages of Economic Decline: Late Medieval
    Bruges', in *Peasants and Townsmen in Medieval Europe: Studia in honorem
    Adriaan Verhulst,* ed. Jean-Marie Duvosquel and Erik Thoen (Ghent,
    1995), pp. 259–69
Vermeersch, Valentin, ed., *Bruges and Europe* (Antwerp, 1992)
Wilson, Jean C., *Painting in Bruges at the Close of the Middle Ages: Studies in Society
    and Visual Culture* (University Park, PA, 1998)

PHOTO ACKNOWLEDGEMENTS

The author and publishers wish to express their thanks to the sources listed below for illustrative material and/or permission to reproduce it. Some locations of artworks are also given below, in the interest of brevity:

Alte Pinakothek, Munich (CC BY-SA 4.0): 36 (Inv.-Nr. 680 and Inv.-Nr. 5), 51 (*left*; Inv.-Nr. 652), 61 (Inv.-Nr. WAF 668); Ayuntamiento de Almazán: 53, 54; Bayerische Staatsbibliothek, Munich (Clm 23638, fol. 11v): 25; Begijnhof, Bruges (0000.GRO0023.I, photo Dominique Provost): 21; Bibliothèque municipale, Rouen (MS I 2 (927), fol. 145r): 29; The Clark Art Institute, Williamstown, MA (1955.943): 43; Galleria Sabauda, Turin (Inv. 8): 9; Gallerie degli Uffizi, Florence: 13 (Inv. 9970), 45 (Inv. 1101), 46 (Inv. 1123, confiscated in 1944, whereabouts unknown), 47 (*left*; Inv. 1100, photo Scala, Florence/Ministero per i Beni e le Attività culturali/Art Resource, NY), 47 (*right*; Inv. 1090), 48 (*centre*; Inv. 1890); Gemäldegalerie, Staatliche Museen zu Berlin: 6 (Ident. Nr. 529, photo Christoph Schmidt), 47 (*centre*; Ident. nr. 528B, photo Jörg P. Anders); Getty Research Institute, Los Angeles: 64; Groeningemuseum, Bruges: 3 (0000.GRO1283.I), 14 and 15 (0000.GRO1393.I), 18, 19 and 20 (0000.GRO1382.I, photos Hugo Maertens), 23, 24 and 34 (0000.GRO1283.I), 35 (0000.GRO0091.10095.I, photo Hugo Maertens), 63 (0000.GRO1254.11255.I, photo Hugo Maertens), 65 (0000.GRO0108.I and 0000.GRO0109.I, photos Cedric Verhelst); Kaiser Friedrich Museumsverein, Staatliche Museen zu Berlin (Inv.-Nr. 529C), photo Jörg P. Anders: 42 (*left*); Koninklijk Museum voor Schone Kunsten (KMSKA), Antwerp: 30 (Inv. 778–780), 52 (Inv. 5); Koninklijke Musea voor Schone Kunsten van België, Brussels (Inv. 1451 and Inv. 1452): 57; Mauritshuis, The Hague (Inv. 595): 39; The Metropolitan Museum of Art, New York: 7 (Acc. no. 17.190.7), 12 (Acc no. 14.40.634), 31 (Acc. no. 32.100.59), 41 (Acc. no. 1975.1.112), 44 (Acc no. 14.40.626–27); The

Morgan Library & Museum, New York (AZO12.1 and AZO12.2): 62 (*left* and *right*); Musée des Beaux-Arts, Strasbourg (Inv. 185): 50; Musée du Louvre, Paris: 42 (*right*; Inv. RF 1723), 58 (RF 309 and RF 886), 59 (RF 215); Museo civico di Palazzo Chiericati, Vicenza (A 297): 62 (*centre*); Museo Nacional Thyssen-Bornemisza, Madrid: 37 (Inv. 1938.1a), 38 (Inv. 1938.1b); Museum Sint-Janshospitaal, Bruges: 4 and 5 (O.SJO173.1), 10 and 11 (O.SJO175.1), 55 (2020.GROOO12.1), 60 (O.SJO178.1); Muzeum Narodowe, Gdansk (SD/413/M): 1, 2; The National Gallery, London: 40 (NG2594), 48 (*left* and *right*; NG747.1 and NG747.2), 49 (NG747.1 and NG747.2), 56 (NG6275.1); National Gallery of Art, Washington, DC: 33 (Acc. no. 1937.1.41), 51 (*right*; Acc. no. 1952.5.46.a); The Nelson-Atkins Museum of Art, Kansas City, MO (Purchase: William Rockhill Nelson Trust, 44-43), photo courtesy Nelson-Atkins Media Services/Melville McLean: 8; private collection: 32; Sächsische Landesbibliothek – Staats- und Universitätsbibliothek Dresden (SLUB): 22; © St Annen-Museum/Fotoarchiv der Hansestadt Lübeck (Inv.-Nr. 1948/138): 16, 17; Universiteitsbibliotheek Gent (BIB.G.005840): 26, 27, 28.

INDEX

Illustration numbers are indicated by *italics*

accounting 29, 64–5
Adornes, Agnes 45
Adornes, Anselm 58, 152
Africans, presence in Bruges 19
Almazán, Spain 166–8
alum 64, 67–9, 80–81, 124, 198
Antwerp, Belgium 78, 82, 86,
 91–2, 102, 105, 198–200
apprentices, studio 24–5, 30, 96,
 103, 112–15
Aragon 73–5, 83–4, 168, 195,
 198–9
Arnolfini, Giovanni 79, 81
Arras, France 13, 63
Arras, Treaty of 198–9
art markets 70, 105
artisanal class 30–31, 48, 89, 197
artisanal guilds *see* guilds
assistants, studio 24–5, 27, 45,
 96–7, 102, 105, 110–17, 119
Augsburg, Germany 78
Augustinians 74, 83, 190
Austin Friars 74, 76, 79–81, 85, 111

Baldwin V, count of Flanders 59
banking 66–9, 73, 79, 81, 86–7,
 186
Baroncelli, Maria 36, 138, 153

Bartolommeo, Fra 161
Basques *see* Biscay
Bembo, Bernardo 164
Bembo, Carlo 164
Benedictines *see* Cistercian; Cluniac
Bening, Simon, *October 25*
Benson, Ambrosius 100, 116, 199
Bergen op Zoom, Netherlands 78
bill of exchange *see* banking
Biscay 74, 83–5, 75
Bladelin, Pieter 73, 81, 151
blockades *see* embargoes
Blondeel, Lancelot 100, 104, 112,
 199
Boels, Lodewijk 105, 110, 114–15
Bologna, Italy 79–80, 163
bookkeeping *see* accounting
Bossche, Aert van den 110
Botticelli, Sandro 164
Bouts, Dieric 27, 108
Brito, Johannes 99
Broederlam, Melchior 14, 125
brokers and brokerage, brokers
 guild 75, 79, 86–7, 104, 177
Bruges, Belgium
 administration, governance,
 and regulations 62, 88–90,
 102–3, 187

demographics 76
holidays and festivities 70,
    75–6, 89–90, 92, 105, 192–5
infrastructure and geography
    59–63, 69–74
international presence 74–86
Brugse Vrije *see* Franc
Brussels, Belgium 26–7, 59, 63,
    199
Bultinc, Pieter 182–5
Burgos, Spain 84, 179
Burgundy, duchy of 11, 58–9, 91,
    134, 152, 193–4, 198–9

Cabredo, Gonzalo 168
Cadzand, Peace of 44
Campin, Robert 106
Carmelites 58, 73–4, 78, 83, 187
Casembroodt, Agnes 188
Casinbroodt, Pieter 48
Castile 44, 73–4, 83–5, 95, 115,
    121, 166–8, 199
Catalonia 84, 193, 195, 198
Caxton, William 83, 99
Cellier, Jan du 118, 176–8
Ceunic, Jacob de 188
Champagne fairs 59, 66
Charles the Bold, duke of
    Burgundy 31, 48, 83, 91, 152–3,
    164, 173, 195, 198
    marriage to Margaret of York
    77, 173, 192–5
chequing *see* banking
Christus, Petrus 21, 27, 48, 98, 101,
    136, 152, 195
Cistercian Benedictines 186
citizenship, in Bruges 29
Claeissens, Pieter 48
    *Cityscape of Bruges (The Seven
    Wonders of Bruges)* 64

Claessens, Antoon 112
cloth, textiles, and wool
    dying and dyes 64, 121–3
    manufacture 31, 63, 89, 99
    trade 23, 63, 65, 67, 69,
    80–84, 86, 90, 95, 151–2,
    166, 177, 198
Clugny, Ferry de 26–7
Cluniac Benedictines 95, 168
Cologne, Germany 18, 23, 25–6,
    29, 67, 76, 114, 118
commercial revolution 62–3
commissions and contracts, for
    artwork 105–12, 114, 116
compagnons see assistants
confraternities in Bruges
    Crossbowmen's Guild of
    St George 82, 110, 178
    Our Lady of Roosbeke 82
    Our Lady of the Dry Tree
    49, 82, 98, 152
    Our Lady of the Snow 48,
    50, 78, 98, 132, 178
Cornelis, Albrecht 48
Costa, Andrea della 45, 79
courier services 67
Coustain, Pieter 48, 98, 103, 124
Crabbe, Jan 186–7, *63, 64*
Cranich, Hans 23

Damme, Belgium 50, 62, 197, *19*
Danzig *see* Gdansk
David, Gerard 48, 98–101,
    112, 115, 199
Dendermonde, Belgium 63
Descamps, Jean-Baptiste 50
Despars, Jacob 178
Despars, Nicolaas 22, 75
Dombild Master *see* Lochner,
    Stephan

Dominicans 74, 85, 160, 178
Donne, John 171–3
Doppere, Rombout de 22,
    49–50
dyers 31, 83
dyes, textile 63, 70, 85, 121–6

Edward IV, king of England 173
embargoes 63, 78, 82, 90–91,
    127, 197
Encomium of Queen Emma 59
England 59, 63, 74–5, 82–3, 152,
    173, 192, 200
    English merchants in Bruges
    65, 76, 78, 82–3
    English wool trade 69, 82,
    90, 198
Este, Isabella d' 164
Estonia 76, 115
exchange, currency *see* banking
Eyck, Jan van 14, 51, 79, 98, 104,
    136, 148, 199

Fabian, Jan 48
fairs 59, 66, 104–5, 198
Ferdinand, king of Aragon
    168, 199
financing 66–8, 74, 80–81,
    86, 102, 132–3, 151–2,
    186–7
    see also banking
Flandes, Juan de 115, 168
Floreins, Jacob 19, 178–9, *60*
Floreins, Jan 17–20, 178, 186,
    190, *4, 5*
Florence, Italy 9, 11, 67, 200
    Badia Fiesolana 8, 150
    Flemish art for Florentine
    patrons 11–12, 29, 33, 53–4,
    121, 136, 150–56, 160–61, 164

Florentine merchants in
    Bruges 8, 69, 72–5, 79–80
    Santa Maria Nuova 153–4, 160
Franc of Bruges 19, 29, 70
France 59, 92, 123, 136, 142, 171
Franciscans 74, 76, 82, 85, 152,
    154, 166–7
Frankfurt am Main, Germany
    22–3, 25
Frederick III, Holy Roman
    Emperor 78, 152

Gdansk, Poland 8, 11, 33, 67, 76,
    121
Genoa, Italy 45, 58, 68, 72–5,
    79–81, 124, 127, 148, 194
George Legend, Master of the 25
Gheeraerts, Marcus 70, 200
    Map of Bruges 3, 23, 24, 34
Gheere, Dieric vander 31
Ghent, Belgium 59, 63, 92, 102,
    173, 197
Goes, Hugo van der 115, 136
    Portinari Triptych 53–4, 151–2,
    160
Grand Privilege 91–2
Greverade, Heinrich and Adolf
    44, 53, 57–8, 76, 171
Grünewald, Matthias 23
Gruuthuse, Lodewijk van 48, 173,
    177–8
Guicciardini, Lodovico 21, 50, 63
guild regulations 15
guilds, in Bruges 89, 91, 101–4,
    133, 137, 182–4, 193, 195–6
    apothecaries, grocers and
    spice merchants 132, 178–9
    brokers and hoteliers 86–7
    librarians and illuminators
    99–101, 110, 118, 185–6

painters' guild of Sint-Lucas en Sint-Eloi (St Luke and Eligius) 22, 30–31, 47–9, 92, 96–8, 101–15, 112–16, 127
sculptors 102, 104, 196
tanners 182–3

Hansa *see* Hanseatic League
Hanseatic League 11–12, 57–8, 62, 69, 74, 76–8, 83, 95, 127, 152, 171, 193
Hastings, Elizabeth 173
Hertsvelde, Barbara van 121, 130, 132
Hervy, Jan de, *Map of the Zwin Delta* *18, 19, 20*
Hoeke, Belgium 62, *20*
hotels and inns 72–3, 75–6, 78, 86–7
Hulsen, Clara van 188

insurance 67–8
Intercusus Magnus, treaty 152
Isabella, queen of Castile 115, 168, 199
Isabella of Bourbon, duchess of Burgundy 85–6
Isenbrant, Adriaen 48, 199
Italy
    and art 43, 116, 123, 137, 161
    art patronage 41, 43, 108, 136, 142–3, 148, 161, 163
    merchants and trade 66, 79–80, 83, 91, 132
    see also individual cities and states

journeymen *see* assistants, studio
Joye, Gilles 147, *43*

Keersbach, Nikolaas van 114
Kortrijk, Belgium 63

Lanchals, Pieter 181
lending *see* banking, financing
Leonardo da Vinci 163–4
Lespinette family 142
Leuven, Belgium 27, 59, 108, 178
Liberty of Bruges *see* Franc
Life of Mary, Master of the 25
Lille, Belgium 63
Lippi, Filippino 161
Lochner, Stephan 25
Loiani family 163
lombards *see* pawnbrokers
Lübeck, Germany 44, 53, 57–8, 76, 78, 136, 171, 198
Lucca, Italy 63, 73–5, 79–81, 148, 195
Lyversberg Passion, Master of the 25

mail *see* courier services
Mainz, Germany 25, 49
Mander, Carel van 50
Mansion, Colard 83, 99
Margaret of Austria 171
Margaret of York, duchess of Burgundy 11, 75, 173, 192–3, *65*
Marke, Collard de 64
Mary, duchess of Burgundy 37, 91, 132–3, 173, 198
Maximilian, of Hapsburg, archduke, Holy Roman Emperor 43–5, 57, 91–2, 133, 171, 178, 181–2, 195–8
Medici family and bank 33, 66–8, 73–4, 80–81, 150–53, 160, 173, 186

Cosimo (di Giovanni) de' Medici, the Elder 150
Cosimo de' Medici, grand duke of Tuscany 154
Francesco de' Medici, grand duke of Tuscany 200
Lorenzo de' Medici 151–2
Piero de' Medici 81, 105, 150–51
Meersch, Passchier van der 113–14, 116
Memling, Hans
  birth and origins 22–3
  citizenship 29–30
  death 49–50, 101, 110
  financial status 100–101, 110
  marriage and children 30–31, 49, 100, 113
  professional reputation 47–9, 100–101
  training 23–7
  workshop and assistants 101, 110–16
Memling, Hans, works by
  Advent and Triumph of Christ 182–4, *62*
  Almazán triptych 166–8, *54*, *55*
  Altarpiece of ss John the Baptist and John the Evangelist 38–9, 187–8, *10*, *11*
  Annunciation 26–7, *7*
  Benedetto Portinari 155–6, *46*
  Descent from the Cross 45, *14*, *15*
  Diptych of Jan du Cellier 176–8, *59*
  Diptych of Maarten van Nieuwenhove 179–82, *61*
  Diptych with an Elderly Couple 143–7, *42*
  Diptych with the Virgin and Child with Angels and St George with Donor 138–9, *36*
  Folco Portinari 155–6, *45*
  Francisco de Rojas (?) 168, 171, *56*
  Gilles Joye 147–8, *43*
  God the Father with Singing and Music-Making Angels 94–7, 168, *30*
  illuminators and librarians guild altarpiece (lost) 100, 110, 118, 185–6
  John Donne triptych 106, 171–3, *57*
  Madonna and Child Enthroned (Berlin) 24, *6*
  Madonna and Child Enthroned (Kansas City) 31–3, *8*
  Madonna and Child with Angels (Washington, DC) 107–8, *33*
  Man at a Loggia (New York) 143, 161, *41*
  Man at Prayer before a Landscape 142, *39*
  Man with a Roman Coin 164, *53*
  Moreel Triptych 129–34, *35*
  Pagagnotti triptych 107–8, 160–61, *48*, *49*
  Passion (Greverade) altarpiece 44, 53–8, 171, *16*, *17*
  Passion of Christ (Turin) 33–7, 154–5, *9*
  Polyptych of Earthly Vanity and Divine Salvation 163, *50*
  Portrait of a Man with a Letter (Florence) 40–43, 161, *13*
  Portrait of a Young Man (Madrid) 142–3, *37*, *38*
  St John and Veronica diptych (Bembo diptych) 163–4, *51*, *52*
  St Ursula Shrine 21, 25, *44*

*Tommaso Portinari and Maria
Baroncelli* 138, 153, *44*
Tondo with the Virgin and Child
(New York) 106–7, *31*
Tondo with the Virgin and Child
(private collection) 106–7,
32
Triptych of Benedetto Portinari
156–60, *47*
Triptych of Jan Crabbe 186–7, *63*
Triptych of Jan Floreins 17–20,
190, *4, 5*
Triptych of the Last Judgement
7–12, 33, 38, 69, 121, 124, 150,
1, 2
*Virgin and Child Enthroned with
ss Catherine of Alexandria and
Barbara* 40, 106, *12*
*Virgin and Child with ss James and
Dominic* 178–9, *60*
*Willem Moreel and Barbara van
Hertsvelde (Vlaenderberch)* 137,
174–5, *58*
Young Man at Prayer (London)
143, *40*
merchant class 63–4
Meyere, Jacobus de 22, 49
Milan, Italy 74–5, 79, 152
monastic orders in Bruges 74,
90
see also specific orders
money-changing *see* exchange
currency
Moreel, Willem 48, 100, 121,
129–34, 136–7, 174–5, *35, 58*

Nachtegale, Pieter 48
Nájera, Spain 120, 168
Navarre, kingdom of 83, 85, 168
Nieuwenhove, Jan van 152, 181

Nieuwenhove, Maarten van
179–82, *61*
noble class, nobility 89–90
Nuremberg, Germany 23, 78–9,
198

oak *see* wood
Orsini, Clara 151
Osterlingen see Hanseatic League

Pagagnotti, Benedetto 107–8,
160–61, *48, 49*
painting, materials and techniques
117–27
panden *see* art markets
patrician class 89–90
pawnbrokers and pawnshops 87
Pazzi family 81, 153
Pedro IV Hurtado de Mendoza,
count 166–7
Perugino, Pietro 163
Philip of Alsace, count of Flanders
62
Philip the Good, duke of
Burgundy 29, 65, 68, 85–6, 91,
98, 104, 151, 197
Philip the Handsome, duke of
Burgundy 37, 91–2, 171, 197,
199
pigments, painting 96, 108,
121–6
pilgrimage, virtual 37, 154–5
piracy 12, 68, 82, 197
Pisa, Italy 11, 67, 69, 73, 79, 152
Plantagenet, Richard *see* Richard,
duke of York
Portinari, Benedetto 142, 155–60,
47
Portinari, Bernardo 150
Portinari, Folco 155

Portinari, Ludovico 155
Portinari, Pigello 150, 155
Portinari, Tommaso 11, 33–6,
    54, 74, 79, 82, 105, 136, 138,
    150–55, 194, *44*
portraiture 40–43, 130–31,
    136–9, 143–8, 153–6, 168–82
Portugal 73, 83, 85–6, 136, 195
Pourbus, Frans I 200
Pourbus, Pieter 48, 112, 199–200
    *Jan van Eyewerve and Jacquemyne
    Buuck 66*
privateers *see* piracy
Provost, Jan 48, 112, 199

Quintanadueñas family 179

Raphael *see* Sanzio, Raphael
Ravensburg, Germany 23, 78
Reie canal, Bruges 62, 71
Reval, Estonia *see* Tallinn
Richard, duke of York 173, 193
Ries, Adam, *Rechnung auff der Linihen
    und Federn 22*
Rogier *see* Weyden, Rogier van
    der
Rojas, Francisco de 168, 171, *56*
Rybeke family 183–4

Sanderus, Antonius, *Flandria
    illustrata 26, 27, 28*
Sanzio, Raphael 163
Schlegel, Friedrich 50–51
Schongauer, Martin 177
Scotland 58, 74, 82–3, 187
Seghers, Antheunis 188–9
Seligenstadt, Germany 22–5,
    50
shipping 23, 67–8, 79, 117, 124,
    182, 198

Sint-Janshospitaal, Bruges 18–21,
    44, 50, 74, 135, 168, 187–90
Sittow, Michael 115
Sluis, Belgium 11, 62, 80, 90–92,
    198, *20*
Sluter, Claus 14
spice
    merchants 19, 67, 86, 96, 100,
    118, 125, 127, 132, 174, 176,
    178–81, 190
    trade 13, 64, 67, 70, 79, 80,
    85–6, 120, 151, 181
Spinola family 80
staples 63, 75–6, 82–3, 85, 152,
    198

Tafur, Pero 12–13
Tallinn, Estonia 76, 115
Tanagli, Caterina di Francesco 10,
    150, *1*
Tani, Agnolo 8–12, 13, 29, 33, 38,
    136, 150–52, 195, *1*
Ter Duinen abbey, Belgium 186–7
timber *see* wood
tokens, counting 65
Tournai, Belgium 127
trade guilds *see* guilds

Valkenaere, Lodewijk de 30–31
Vasari, Giorgio 21, 50, 154, 200
Venice, Italy 63, 73–6, 79–80,
    124–5, 127, 132, 151, 163–4,
    26
Verhanneman, Hannekin 113,
    116
Verrocchio, Andrea del 163
Visen de, family 142
Vrelant, Willem 48, 74, 99–100,
    111–12, 185–6
Vrije *see* Franc

Weale, James 51, 177
Weyden, Rogier van der 21,
25–7, 33, 53, 108, 122
Beaune altarpiece 53
Columba altarpiece 18,
25, 27
Miraflores altarpiece
33
Wilhelm v, duke of
Bavaria 200
Willems, Josse 188

wood
as painting support 95–6,
103–4, 110, 117–18
trade 58, 67, 80, 85, 122
wool *see* cloth, textiles, and
wool

Ypres, Belgium 63

Zwin river delta 11, 62, 90, 197,
18, 19, 20